THE
WORKING
WOMAN'S
WEDDING
PLANNER

D0131642

THE
WORKING WOMAN'S
WEDDING PLANNER

THIRD EDITION

SUSAN TATSUI-D'ARCY

"Congratulations on your recent
engagement. This wedding planner is a
free gift to you compliments of your Good
Neighbor State Farm Agent.
Best Wishes."

STATE FARM

Auto *Life* *Fire*

INSURANCE ®

Library of Congress Cataloging-in-Publication Data
Tatsui-D'Arcy, Susan.
    The working woman's wedding planner / Susan Tatsui-D'Arcy. — 3rd ed.
        p.   cm.
    Includes index.
    ISBN 0-7352-0107-2 (pbk.)   ISBN 0-13-087572-4
    1. Weddings United States—Planning—Handbooks, manuals, etc.   I. Title.
HQ745.T28   2000
395.2'2—dc21   99-10318
                                                                        CIP

©2000 by Prentice Hall, Inc.

All rights reserved. No part of this book may be reproduced in any form or by any
means, without permission in writing from the publisher.

ISBN 0-13-087572-4 (State Farm Edition)

Printed in the United States of America
10 9 8 7 6 5 4 3

Originally published as *The Working Woman's Wedding Planner*
ISBN 0-7352-0107-2

This publication is designed to provide accurate and authoritative information in regard
to the subject matter covered. It is sold with the understanding that the publisher is not
engaged in rendering legal, accounting, or other professional service. If legal advice or
other expert assistance is required, the services of a competent professional person
should be sought.

     . . . From the Declaration of Principles jointly adopted by a Committee of the
    American Bar Association and a Committee of Publishers and Associations.

Prentice Hall
Paramus, NJ 07652
On the World Wide Web at http://www.phdirect.com

This Book is lovingly dedicated to my husband, Rob D'Arcy,
whose love and support inspires me to create,
and to our two precious daughters,
Nicole Tatsui D'Arcy and Jaclyn Tatsui D'Arcy.

It is respectfully dedicated to the memories of my grandfather,
Kunio Tatsui, and my grandmother, Kume Kawana.

Special thanks to Raihan Kadri for compiling and editing
new information for this third edition.

CONTENTS

15 The Wedding Ceremony   196

16 The Wedding Reception   236

17 Destination Weddings   257

INTRODUCTION

Congratulations, Bride-to-be! You are probably feeling the excited, nervous, and altogether tumultuous emotions that brides have felt for centuries. However, unlike most of the women who have stepped up to the altar before you, you don't have weeks of uninterrupted time to plan your wedding leisurely. Like most working brides-to-be, you may be overwhelmed by demands placed on you by your job, your family, your children (if this is a second wedding), and your fiancé. *The Working Woman's Wedding Planner* is designed to keep you in control of your wedding. This newly revised edition is your all-in-one resource book. You will find timely and practical information on virtually every topic that concerns your wedding, including such special issues as etiquette, second marriages, divorced parents, how much liquor to serve, on-line resources, whom to invite, types of ceremonies, honeymoon tips, and prenuptial agreements.

The Working Woman's Wedding Planner can be used whether you are planning an elaborate formal wedding for 300 guests, or an intimate, at-home affair for only 25. In each chapter you'll find helpful notes on etiquette (both traditional and contemporary views) and ready-to-use checklists to help organize every facet of your wedding. Here are some of the invaluable planning tools you'll find:

Six-month Wedding Countdown Calendar— this pre-wedding "To-Do" list for the six months prior to the big day gives you the long overview of what to do when, while the fill-in calendars help keep you on target for short-term tasks.

Wedding Budget Planning List— keeps track of actual and estimated costs for everything from the ceremony to the honeymoon and which parties are paying for each expense.

Wedding Attire Checklists— for use when shopping not only for your own gown but also for the gowns of your attendants. Bring this checklist with you so you can record vital information and make the most informed decisions.

Ceremony and Reception Time Lines— will help you organize events down to the minute. Make copies of the time lines for your attendants and helpers to ensure a successful ceremony.

Individual Responsibility Planner— to help you delegate those little wedding-day tasks to friends or family so you can relax and enjoy your wedding and guests.

Dozens of Checklists— dealing with all the outside services you'll be depending upon, including caterers, photographers, florists, musicians, limousine services, and parking attendants. The checklists will also help you keep track of vital information regarding expenses, addresses, phone numbers, and personal responsibilities.

The Working Woman's Wedding Planner is the one book you'll need for all your wedding plans. It's your checklist, appointment book, telephone and address book, and etiquette guide. Just pick and choose what you need to make your wedding exactly the way you and your fiancé want it to be.

Budgeting

You must know how your wedding will be financed *before* you can start planning. Once you know how much money is available you can then begin to set the arrangements for your wedding. There is no sense in planning an elaborate formal wedding for 200 guests before you know if and how it would be funded.

WHO PAYS FOR WHAT?

This has become such a hot subject among brides, grooms, and their families that it often creates unnecessary feuds. Your wedding is supposed to be a public announcement and celebration of your new married life. It is not meant to impose a financial strain on you *or* your family.

Traditionally, the bride and her family pay for most of the wedding costs. However, relationships and roles in marriage have changed considerably in recent years. As a result, having the financial burden on the bride's family is no longer standard in today's world.

Different family incomes, long distance weddings, divorced parents, second weddings, destination weddings, and uneven guest lists make each wedding situation unique. All three parties—bride, groom, and parents—should talk about the wedding plans ahead of time so that everyone's concerns can be taken into consideration.

You will probably have an inclination about whether or not your parents will help finance the wedding. Parents usually drop hints or make comments about your wedding day long before you're engaged. For instance, you may know their general financial status; whether they would be able to support an extravagant wedding. If your parents don't approve of your husband-to-be, they may be less inclined to help pay for any wedding expenses. Diplomatically ask each side of the family if they will be able to help with the cost of the wedding. Tell the families some of the plans you're considering and ask them if there is anything special they would like during the ceremony or reception. They may have a traditional family ceremony they would like you to include or a special poem they would like to have read. Be careful not to promise anything until you are sure you can follow through with their request. This is also a good time to get an approximate number of guests each of the parents would like to invite. Let them know that you are getting as many ideas as possible and will make decisions based on all the input you receive. Remember that this is *your* wedding.

Bride and Her Family

Traditionally the bride's family pays for:

- Wedding dress, veil, accessories
- Invitations, announcements, enclosures, and personal stationery
- Trousseau and lingerie
- Bouquets/corsages for attendants
- Flowers for the ceremony and reception site
- Rental fee for church or chapel
- Engagement and wedding photographs
- Fees for the sexton, organists, and soloist
- Rental fees for aisle carpet and other equipment
- Transportation for the bridal party to the ceremony and reception sites
- Complete reception: all food, beverages, music, decorations, gratuities, and other services
- Groom's ring
- Wedding gift for the groom
- Gifts for the bride's attendants
- Hotel lodging for any attendants and friends from out-of-town
- Gratuities to police directing traffic and/or parking

- Bridesmaids' luncheon
- Rehearsal dinner (optional)
- Corsages for mothers, grandparents, and special guests (optional)

GROOM AND HIS FAMILY

Traditionally the groom's family pays for:

- Bride's engagement and wedding ring
- Marriage license
- Ceremony official's fee
- Bride's flowers (bouquet and going away flowers)
- Wedding gift for the bride
- Gifts for the best man and ushers
- Hotel lodging for out-of-town ushers
- Wedding night suite
- Rehearsal dinner (optional)
- Honeymoon
- Blood tests
- Gloves, ties, and ascots for men in the wedding party

ATTENDANTS

Traditionally attendants pay for:

- Personal wedding attire (except flowers)
- Personal travelling expenses (except hotel)

BRIDE AND GROOM

Today many brides and grooms opt to pay for the entire wedding themselves. Couples who choose to live together before they tie the knot often pay for the wedding expenses themselves since their parents aren't giving them away or helping them get a start in life. Those who are marrying for the second or more times usually pay for the wedding themselves. If parents are living on fixed incomes and don't have the financial means to pay for the type of wedding their children are planning, the bride and groom fund the wedding.

THE SPLIT

With the cost of formal weddings going as high as $50,000 or more, a three-way split with your family, the groom's family, and you and the groom may be the solution. All three parties would then be able to contribute funds towards the total wedding budget.

Each party can pay for their own guests. This is a fair way to distribute the major cost and to minimize awkward feelings about the guest list. One party may want to invite the whole extended family and all of their friends and business associates while another party may feel it necessary to invite only the immediate family. This allows for each party to have a little control over how much money they will spend.

HIRING A WEDDING CONSULTANT OR COORDINATOR

For those couples who are unsure of how to plan all the extensive details of their wedding or who simply don't have the time and energy to do everything that is needed, hiring a bridal consultant or wedding coordinator may prove useful. Consultants can help guide you through all the intricacies of contracting vendors, staging rehearsals, seeing that proper wedding etiquette is followed, and basically ensuring that no loose ends are left unattended. A consultant can be used just for the beginning or ending arrangements of your wedding or throughout all the planning stages. It's up to you to decide what you want from your wedding and how much you will be able to do yourself.

TYPES OF BRIDAL CONSULTANTS

There are several kinds of professional wedding consultants. Here are some of the more prominent ones:

Bridal Consultant: A bridal consultant is a person who works for a particular vendor to assist brides and grooms with their wedding arrangements. For instance, certain florists or photography studios may have bridal consultants on hand to deal specifically with their clients' weddings.

Independent Bridal Consultant: These consultants do not work for a vendor but rather work directly with their clients on all aspects of the wedding.

Wedding Coordinator: A wedding coordinator is hired to actually conduct wedding activities on-site, staging rehearsals and ceremony procedure.

Church Wedding Coordinator: These coordinators work with the staff of a church or religious site to make sure that church rules are followed.

Wedding Day Coordinator: The wedding day coordinator conducts rehearsals and wedding-day activities but does not coordinate initial planning.

INTERVIEW PROSPECTIVE CONSULTANTS

Before hiring a consultant or coordinator, set up interviews to discuss their costs, references, contacts with vendors, and theories about weddings. You could find that a particular bridal consultant's aesthetic sensibility is far different from yours. You may want a traditional wedding with the bridal party all in white; but the coordinator may be ordering red gowns for everyone. Make sure that you can work together with your bridal consultant and that you keep control of your wedding.

COSTS

While the bridal consultant's fee may not be inexpensive, using a consultant can save you money nonetheless. Good consultants and coordinators have contacts and, in some cases, special agreements with vendors to get discounted prices on services. Also, consultants keep up with the latest prices and trends within the wedding industry to get you the best deals.

PREPARING YOUR BUDGET

After you decide who is paying for the wedding and agree upon a comfortable figure that all parties can live with, it is time to start charting your budget. Go to the Wedding Budget Planning List on pages 6–7. The expenses are listed with columns for estimated costs, actual costs, your family's expense, the groom's family's expense, your expense, and other expenses.

As you read through this planner and start filling in the information you retrieve, enter the figures in the estimated costs column on the Budget Planning List. This will help you control your spending and mediate between different costs. For example, if you decide to go all out for flowers, you may need to use prerecorded music instead of hiring a five-piece band. The Budget Planning List will help you stay within your budget and give you an exact total cost of your wedding for those who are financing your big day.

WEDDING BUDGET PLANNING LIST

| DESCRIPTION | ESTIMATED COSTS | ACTUAL COSTS | FAMILY EXPENSES | | BRIDE AND GROOM'S EXPENSES | OTHERS' EXPENSES |
			BRIDE	GROOM		
CEREMONY						
Site Fees						
Clergymember						
Marriage License						
Other:						
RECEPTION						
Caterer						
Equipment						
Liquor/Bar						
Cake						
Site Fees						
Accessories						
Other:						
ATTIRE						
Brides' Gown/Accessories						
Bride's Hair/Nails						
Bride's Attendants						
Groom's Formal Wear						
Groom's Attendants						
Flower Girl						

WEDDING BUDGET PLANNING LIST (continued)

| DESCRIPTION | ESTIMATED COSTS | ACTUAL COSTS | FAMILY EXPENSES | | BRIDE AND GROOM'S EXPENSES | OTHERS' EXPENSES |
			BRIDE	GROOM		
Ring Bearer						
FLOWERS						
PHOTOGRAPHY						
VIDEOGRAPHY						
MUSIC						
RINGS						
STATIONERY						
GIFTS						
TRANSPORTATION						
PARTIES						
Engagement						
Showers						
Bridesmaids'						
Bachelor's						
Rehearsal						
Other:						
HONEYMOON						
PRENUPTIAL AGREEMENTS						
INSURANCE						

HOW TO AVOID OVERPAYING

Weddings have come to support a multi-billion dollar industry and they are back in vogue. Here are some tips to help you get the best value and pay the least amount for your own wedding.

INSURE YOUR WEDDING

Most service companies will require a nonrefundable deposit. If there is a possibility that your wedding may be canceled or postponed, you may consider the Catered Affair Cancellation Insurance coverage. This may be good protection if a close family member is terminally ill or if you're having second thoughts about marrying your fiancé.

This insurance policy will protect you from losing your deposits and possible liability for loss of revenues to service companies. The policy will pay up to the total amount for the service you schedule for a relatively low premium. Read through the fine print to make sure you're getting the right coverage.

KNOW THE MARKET

Research various wedding options to select the style of your wedding and to learn the correct terminology used around the industry. You will want retailers to know they are talking to a woman who knows the market and can't be fooled into buying more than she needs or paying for more than what's necessary.

CALL AROUND

Use your phone book's yellow pages or the World Wide Web to find businesses under each budget item, such as floristry, catering, and photography. Ask about their policies and get a list of references to compare prices for specific items. Make sure you ask the same questions of each vendor to ensure that you are really comparing the same prices. For instance, you don't want to ask one florist about the cost of a bridal bouquet of roses and then ask the next florist about the cost of a bridal bouquet with 20 baby white roses and 10 stephanotis.

By calling around you'll get a good idea of the general price ranges and policies used within the industry. Call for references or get recommendations from friends for specific services. Ask about vendors' availability for your particular wedding dates and time frames.

VISIT SHOPS

Make an appointment with the manager before you visit, even if you plan to just look. You will get better service and you'll be using your time wisely. While you meet with the manager, make mental notes about their organization, cleanliness, and customer service.

Ask to see the exact rental equipment they will use for your wedding so you can see the condition of the merchandise you are discussing. You are watching day-to-day operations which can give you some insight as to how well the company is managed. You wouldn't want your order to get lost or mixed up with another bride's!

Look through their portfolio and take literature. Ask for a sample contract and list of policies that you can review at home.

ASK FOR DISCOUNTS

Before you make your final decision, ask the retailer about quantity discounts. Don't be embarrassed—this is a business transaction. When you order large quantities, why should you pay the same price as someone who orders only one? It costs less per unit to process larger orders and the retailers get quantity discounts that lower their costs. Sometimes retailers offer "extras" at no cost.

READ THE CONTRACTS

Once you've decided on the retailer, it's time to sit down and sign contracts. If there isn't a contract, be wary! Contracts protect you and the retailer from miscommunication and responsibilities. If you're working with a friend or a friend of the family, write up a contract yourself listing all the details about the goods and services you expect. Look for:

- Dates and times
- Details about the items you're ordering
- Itemized lists of all goods and services to be provided
- Delivery time schedules
- Names of people in charge of your wedding
- Backup services available
- Cancellation policies
- Payment schedules
- Last dates to make changes

USE CREDIT CARDS

Credit card purchases are the best method of payment to protect consumers. If your bakery drops the cake or the band shows up an hour late, you have recourse with your credit card company. First you will have to negotiate terms with the retailer yourself (do it in writing and keep copies). If you can't settle between yourselves, send a letter of explanation with copies of contracts and receipts to the credit card company. They will contact the retailer and let you know your rights. In most cases, if the retailer didn't follow his or her obligations according to the contract, your credit card company will not release funds from your account to the retailer. This gives you the upper hand. The retailer will have to file a claim against you for payment. If you pay in cash or check, the retailer has your money and you have to file a claim against him or her to get a refund.

CHECK REFERENCES

Ask for a list of references. Reputable companies have lists readily available. By checking with the Better Business Bureau, Consumer Affairs, and/or the Federal Trade Commission you will know if other consumers have filed complaints against the company you are considering. It is worth the few extra minutes it takes to check these companies so you aren't left helplessly standing at the altar.

TIPS OR GRATUITIES

CATERERS

The contracted fees for catering usually include 15 percent gratuities, which are paid under terms of the contract. Special services beyond the contract should be tipped at the end of the reception.

CHAUFFEURS

The chauffeur's tips are usually included in the total bill. If they aren't, 10 to 15 percent of the total bill is standard.

COAT ROOM/RESTROOM ATTENDANT

The host usually pays the coat room fees ahead of time. There is either a flat fee or a per-guest fee. A sign should be posted at the coatroom so guests know that gratuities have been taken care of.

OFFICIANT

Talk to the clergymember or other officiant who will be conducting your ceremony. Many clergymembers depend on this honorarium as a necessary supplement to their comparatively small incomes. In some religions it is not appropriate to pay the officiant. They may request that you donate the fees to the church in the officiant's name. It's best to be direct and ask the officiant how he would like to handle the honorarium. Ask how the check should be written. Although the host pays for the fees, the best man is responsible for giving the officiant the fees after the ceremony.

SPECIAL SERVICES

Most services include gratuities in their fees or gratuities are not expected. If you receive extra services that deserve attention, give a special tip after the reception in cash (1 to 15 percent).

2

The Bridal Party

HOW TO CHOOSE YOUR BRIDAL PARTY

You're thrilled about your engagement, and now it's time to start thinking about your choices for attendants and ushers. If you have one best friend or one sister, it makes the maid of honor decision easy. But what if you have two best friends, or your fiancé wants his sister to be part of the bridal party when you've already selected your limit? What if your best friend is pregnant and doesn't want to appear "fat" in your wedding photographs? What if your fiancé has children from a previous marriage that you would like to include? What if you've been part of seven wedding parties and feel obligated to invite those friends to be part of your wedding party but really you just wanted a small ceremony? The "what-ifs" can go on forever.

A good general guideline is to go with what your heart says and be honest with everyone involved. If you have two special people, have two maids/matrons of honor. If it is important to have your fiancé's sister or sister-in-law in the wedding party, consider making the wedding party larger to accommodate them. He may also ask them to be one of his attendants. It is becoming more common to see mixed sexes in the wedding party. Men and women have friends and relatives of the opposite sex; why not have them be part of their wedding party too?

If your best friend is pregnant and embarrassed about appearing fat at the wedding, respect her feelings and choose another attendant. If one of your

attendants becomes sick just before the wedding, choose another friend/relative to join the wedding party.

If you've been part of many wedding parties and prefer to have a small wedding with just a few attendants, choose your attendants carefully. Truly good friends will understand. Ask them to be involved by giving them special tasks like reading a poem or prayer at the ceremony or offering a special toast.

The number of bridesmaids and ushers can vary from one to twelve or more. It is customary to have one usher per fifty guests to keep the seating flow going before the ceremony. Formal weddings tend to have larger wedding parties than informal affairs. The number of attendants is a personal choice. Junior bridesmaids' ages range from nine to twelve.

The flower girl or ring bearer can either add the perfect touch to your wedding or create anxiety for you just before you make your entrance down the processional. The perfect age depends largely on the child you are considering. As a rule of thumb, the best ages for children attendants are five to nine years old. If the child handles directions well and is reasonably poised, he or she will do well.

Your bridal party can consist of men or women who are married or divorced, tall or short, old or young. Use your good judgment and the preferences of those involved to do what is best for your wedding.

TRADITIONAL RESPONSIBILITIES OF THE BRIDAL PARTY

Once you have selected your wedding party, these are the traditional responsibilities.

MAID/MATRON OF HONOR

If your maid of honor has good penmanship, she can help you address the wedding invitation envelopes. She is also the witness by law and signs the marriage certificate.

The maid of honor is responsible for her attire whether the dress is store bought or sewn. She makes sure that the other attendants are dressed perfectly to the last detail before the ceremony and reception. She precedes you and your father down the aisle. During the ceremony she arranges your veil and train and holds your bouquet. She is responsible for passing the groom's ring when the officiant orders her to.

At the reception, the maid of honor stands next to the groom in the receiving line and sits next to the groom at the bridal table. She reminds you of the reception timetable at the appropriate times.

At the end of the reception, the maid of honor helps you change into your going away clothes. At the gift opening, she helps you record all of the gifts.

BEST MAN

The best man is chief of staff at the wedding. He is responsible for carrying your wedding ring before the ceremony. He signs the wedding certificate and gives the officiant the honorarium. He also makes sure that the ushers are properly dressed and briefed about the ceremony procedures and their responsibilities.

The best man proposes the first toast to you and the groom and often announces the family members. He reads telegrams and letters at the reception. He sits to your right at the bridal table. He is responsible for making sure that the reception goes as planned unless there is a wedding coordinator. To keep the party moving on schedule, the best man reminds the groom of the reception timetable.

The best man helps locate the groom's going-away clothes and locks the new-lywed's luggage in the trunk of their car for their departure. He escorts the couple to depart for their honeymoon. He also deposits money gifts into the appropriate accounts and makes sure that all rental items are returned.

BRIDESMAIDS

The bridesmaids traditionally don't have any responsibilities other than taking care of their attire (buying or sewing) and standing in line at the ceremony and receiving line. They are escorted by ushers during the processional and recessional. They also sit next to the ushers during the reception. If there is a traditional first dance, the bridesmaids usually dance with their usher partners. During the bouquet ceremony, the bridesmaids encourage single women to participate. The bridesmaids are also invited to all pre-wedding parties.

USHERS

The ushers seat guests at the ceremony and act as escorts for the bridesmaids. There is usually an usher for every fifty guests to avoid seating delays. They should arrive at the ceremony site forty-five minutes early. One usher is selected as head usher and is the supervisor of any special seating arrangements. He should have a pew-seating chart. As the ushers are seating guests, the ushers offer female guests their right arm. Men follow the escort down the aisle unless they are elderly or handicapped. Traditionally, the bride's guests are seated on the left side. When the bride or groom has substantially more guests than the other, seat

all guests together. The eldest woman should be escorted first should a group of guests arrive at the same time.

The mother of the groom is seated about five minutes before the mother of the bride. When the mother of the bride is seated it is a signal that the processional is about to begin. No guests are seated after the bride's mother is in place.

Ushers traditionally walk down the processional in pairs and escort the bridesmaids down the aisle during the recessional. In some ceremonies, the ushers escort the bridesmaids up the aisle. The attendants usually prefer being escorted rather than walking themselves down the aisle.

After the ceremony, the ushers roll up the aisle carpet and loosen the pew ribbons one row at a time. They face the pew and signal to the guests to file out row by row from the front to the back. These ushers need to return to the church quickly after the recessional. Other ushers should escort elderly and handicapped guests.

The ushers should be prepared to direct guests to parking and restroom facilities as well as the reception site. They should check for lost or forgotten items and be the last to leave the ceremony site. They are not expected to be in the receiving line because of these responsibilities.

The ushers should be available for pictures before or after the ceremony. They are responsible for encouraging single men to participate in the garter ceremony after the reception.

FLOWER GIRL

The flower girl's parents are responsible for making sure that she gets a good night's sleep before the ceremony. They take care of her attire except for the basket of flowers.

Traditionally the flower girl carried a basket full of rose petals and strewed them along the bride's path. This has proven dangerous both for the bride and the guests and is rarely done today.

The flower girl carries a basket of flowers, a tiny nosegay, or a flower-covered muff. The flowers should look the same all the way around so it doesn't matter how she holds them.

The flower girl always walks immediately before you and your father in the processional. Depending on her age and maturity she may stand next to the maid of honor during the ceremony and follow you and the groom during the recessional. If there is a doubt about whether or not she will be able to stand during the ceremony, have her stand in line until the bride meets with the groom and the ceremony begins. Then she can quietly sit in the first pew with her parents.

During the reception the flower girl sits with her family. If they announce the wedding party at the reception, the flower girl participates in the lineup.

RING BEARER

The ring bearer's parents also make sure that he gets a good night's sleep. They are responsible for his entire attire except for the ring cushion.

The ring bearer carries a cushion with two fake rings tied to it. The real rings are held by the best man. The ring bearer walks down the aisle either before the flower girl or next to her. If he is mature enough he can stand throughout the wedding. Otherwise he can stand until the ceremony begins and then sit down in the first pew with his parents.

During the recessional, he walks next to the flower girl if there is one or alone behind the bride and groom if he stood during the ceremony. He carries the cushion upside down so the rings don't appear on the cushion. If he took a seat during the ceremony he should not participate in the recessional.

During the reception the ring bearer sits with his family. If the master of ceremonies announces the wedding party at the reception, the ring bearer participates in the lineup.

PAGE OR TRAINBEARERS

Pages always come in pairs and are needed only if you wear a cathedral train. They carry your train during the processional and recessional. They are usually little boys but they can also be girls. They are responsible for their own attire and like other children in the wedding party, a good night's sleep.

BRIDE'S MOTHER

Traditionally, your mother is responsible for the guest list on your side of the family providing that both parents are still married. She helps plan the details of the ceremony and reception. She also helps select a wedding gown and trousseau. She keeps track of gifts if they are sent to her house and displays them in an attractive, safe location. The bride's mother selects her dress and then informs the groom's mother of her choice so both dresses will be the same length and accessorized the same way. However, this is an old custom and often is not followed by contemporary families. Mothers of the bride and groom are entitled to follow their own styles and may prefer to choose a dress based on their own preferences rather than to fit into the general color scheme of the wedding.

In a traditional wedding, the bride's mother is the official hostess. If the parents are divorced, the party who is financing the wedding generally hosts the reception. The bride's mother is the last person to be seated at the wedding and the first person to be escorted out after the recessional. She greets the guests at the head of the receiving line and sits in a place of honor at the parents' table.

BRIDE'S FATHER

Your father is also the official host. He rides with you to the ceremony. He escorts you down the aisle and sits in the first pew next to your mother. If they are divorced and friendly, he sits next to your mother. If they are unfriendly or one or both have remarried, your mother sits in the first pew and your father sits in the second or third pew. If your parents are divorced, your father would typically be responsible for his guest list.

GROOM'S PARENTS

In the past, the groom's parents received less attention than yours due to your family's financial input in the affair. Nowadays, the groom's parents often contribute to the total wedding cost and are becoming active hosts in the wedding celebration. They are responsible for their own guest list.

The groom's family traditionally hosts the rehearsal dinner. They make accommodations for the groom's out-of-town guests. They should arrive at the ceremony site at least fifteen minutes early. The head usher escorts the parents down the aisle and seats them in the front pew.

At the reception, the groom's parents share the role of host with your parents. In the receiving line, the groom's parents stand between you and your mother. The groom's mother stands next to your mother and the father stands next to you. They encourage single guests to participate in the bouquet and garter ceremonies.

DIVORCED PARENTS

When parents are divorced, a wedding can become a heated battleground. It can stir up emotions that may have settled over the years. The anticipation of seeing ex-spouses can be uncomfortable for your parents and you should try to understand their feelings.

On the other hand, your parents should try to control their feelings and not play tug of war with you during the wedding preparation. That could be the best gift your divorced parents could give you: a peaceful wedding celebration. Parents

should accept the arrangements that you set for the ceremony and reception procedures; after all, this is *your* day.

If your parents are still in the battlefields, you may find it necessary to separate them physically as much as possible. During the ceremony don't include procedures that will make both parents stand next to each other or share in dialogue together. At the reception, place each parent at a separate table so they can be with their own relatives and close friends. Don't include your father in the receiving line since it isn't traditional that he be there. Good planning can help make all parties feel more comfortable.

STEPPARENTS

Stepparents have become an integral part of the modern-day family structure. Handling stepparents during a wedding celebration can be difficult if there is animosity between an ex-spouse and stepparent. Each family is unique and there are no set guidelines for proper etiquette.

If you or the groom dislike one of the stepparents and if there is considerable tension between the ex-spouse and the stepparent, it might be best if the stepparent excuse himself or herself from the wedding celebration. Talk this over with both of your natural parents and make a decision based on your situation. If you would be uncomfortable or fearful that there may be an unpleasant confrontation because the stepparent is unreasonable and unpredictable in emotional situations, write a note explaining that you think it would be in everyone's best interest if that stepparent did not attend the wedding. Suggest that you have a special dinner another time to celebrate your wedding with the stepparent and your natural parent. If the stepparent contributes financially towards the wedding budget then he or she will be hosting the wedding with the other contributors.

CHECKLISTS FOR ALL YOUR HELPERS

You'll want to spend your wedding day enjoying your guests and all the festivities you spent months organizing. Your friends and family will often offer to help. Consider their history of handling responsibility before you accept their offers. Don't be caught waiting for flowers to be transferred from the ceremony site to the reception site because an irresponsible volunteer ends up at the bar and forgets. Designate responsibilities to people who are not in the wedding party or in your, or the groom's, family. Your attendants and family will have enough on their minds

and will want to enjoy the guests themselves. Some guests often like to be involved and helpful at weddings.

Fill in the Wedding Coordinator's Checklist on pages 20–21. If you have hired a professional, you will need to provide this information to the coordinator.

Fill in a checklist for each member of the wedding party and family members. This will keep them aware of fitting dates, parties, photography sessions, and other schedules. If they have several responsibilities, this is the place to document them.

Each of your helpers should have a checklist. Decide who will be in charge of each detail and enter it on the Bridal Party's Checklist on page 23 for the appropriate person along with the Individual Responsibilities Checklist on page 22 so you'll remember who has been assigned to each task.

Make copies of these checklists and send them to the helpers, wedding party, and family. Keep the original so you can access the information easily. Give these to the appropriate people as soon as you have all the information ready. Seven to ten days before the wedding is usually the best time. Review the checklist with each individual at the rehearsal dinner or on the phone a few days before the wedding. Go over the details even if they say they understand everything. Verbally repeating details may bring up other questions or help clarify the circumstances.

WEDDING COORDINATOR'S CHECKLIST

	HOME PHONE	WORK PHONE
Wedding Coordinator:		
FAMILY	HOME PHONE	WORK PHONE
Bride:		
Groom:		
Bride's Mother:		
Bride's Father:		
Groom's Mother:		
Groom's Father:		
WEDDING PARTY	HOME PHONE	WORK PHONE
Maid of Honor:		
Bridesmaid:		
Bridesmaid:		
Bridesmaid:		
Bridesmaid:		
Bridesmaid:		
Junior Bridesmaid:		
Junior Bridesmaid:		
Flower Girl:		
Best Man:		
Usher:		
Usher:		
Usher:		
Usher:		
Usher:		
Other:		
Other:		

Ring Bearer:		
Page/Trainbearer:		
SERVICES FOR THE CEREMONY	HOME PHONE	WORK PHONE
Clergymember:		
Organist:		
Soloist:		
Other Musician:		
Manager:		
Photographer:		
Videographer:		
Other:		
Other:		
SERVICES FOR THE RECEPTION	HOME PHONE	WORK PHONE
Reception Manager:		
Florist:		
Bakery:		
Photographer:		
Videographer:		
Musicians:		
Video Operator:		
Audio Operator:		
Caterer:		
Bartender:		
Other:		
Other:		

INDIVIDUAL RESPONSIBILITIES CHECKLIST

AT CEREMONY	HELPER	AT RECEPTION	HELPER
Coordinate with Manager		Help Florist Set Up	
Organize Wedding Party		Help Set Up Gift Table	
Help Set Up Tent/Equipment		Help Band Set Up	
Help Florist Set Up		Help Caterer Set Up	
Put Vows in Book at Altar		Set Up Prerecorded Music	
Help Videographer Set Up		Set Up Place Cards and Accessories	
Help Photographer Set Up		Place Centerpieces on Tables	
Give Attendants/Guests Flowers		Help Set Up Cake	
In Charge of Guest Book		Help Set Up Bar	
Manage Seating Chart for Pews		Take Liquor to Reception	
Escort Guests Down Aisle		Help Photographer Set Up	
Pass Out Wedding Programs		Help Videographer Set Up	
Remind Guests of Photo Sessions		Help Set Up Audio System	
Have Extra Maps to Reception for Guests		Help Set Up Video System	
Bring/Keep Marriage License		Carry Stain Removers — Bride	
Bring/Keep Ring Cushion		Carry Bride's Make-up	
Give Fees to Clergymember		Announce Bride and Groom	
Pass Rice to Guests		Give Wedding Toast	
Move Ceremony Flowers to Reception		Announce Family Members	
Move Gifts to Reception Site		Announce Cake Cutting Ceremony	
Lock up Ceremony Site and Meet with Janitor		Announce Bouquet Ceremony	
		Announce Garter Ceremony	
		Watch Gifts at the Reception	
AFTER RECEPTION	HELPER	AFTER RECEPTION	HELPER
Move Gifts to Safe Place		Return Unopened Bottles of Liquor	
Move Reception Flowers to Wedding Suite		Take Remaining Liquor (Opened Bottles) to Bride and Groom's Suite	
Store Prerecorded Music		Return Rented Plants to Florist	
Give Fees to Musicians		Deposit Money in Accounts	
Give Fees for Reception		Watch House During Rehearsal	
Give Fees to:		Watch House While Honeymooning	
		Cut Announcement Out of Paper	
Save Cake Top and Accessories		Store Cake Top Layer in Freezer	
Collect Extra Favors and Accessories		Return Ceremony and Reception Equipment	
Take Bouquet to be Preserved		Lock up Reception Site and Meet with Janitor	
Clean and Store Gown		Drive Couple to Airport	
Return Cake Stand to Bakery		Check Luggage	
Return Tuxedos/Men's Attire			
Develop Film			

BRIDAL PARTY'S CHECKLIST

Dear _____

Thank you for all the support and help you've given us during this exciting, yet hectic time. We have enclosed a copy of the ceremony and reception agendas so you know what to expect on the big day.

We've listed all the details and your responsibilities below.

Parties

Date: _____ Time: _____ Host: _____

Location: _____

Date: _____ Time: _____ Host: _____

Location: _____

Date: _____ Time: _____ Host: _____

Location: _____

Rehearsal at Ceremony Site

Date: _____ Time: _____ Phone: _____

Rehearsal Dinner Party

Date: _____ Time: _____ Phone: _____

Location: _____

Fitting Dates

First Fitting Date: _____ Final Fitting Date: _____ Time: _____

Location(s): _____ Phone: _____

Get Your Attire Ready

Men:			Women:		
_____ Coat	_____ Cummerbund	_____ Suspenders	_____ Gown	_____ Jewelry	_____ Change of Clothes
_____ Trousers	_____ Shoes	_____ Cuff Links	_____ Slip/bra	_____ Make-up	_____ Comfortable Shoes
_____ Shirt	_____ Socks	_____ Studs	_____ Hose	_____ Brush/Comb	
_____ Vest	_____ Gloves	_____ Tie or Ascot	_____ Hair	_____ Spray	_____ Purse
			_____ Shoes	_____ Perfume	_____ Gloves

Ceremony

Arrival Time: _____ Where to Dress: _____

Transportation: _____

Photo Session

Location: _____ Time: _____

Photos to Be Included In: _____

Reception

Location: _____ Phone: _____

Receiving Line: _____ Time: _____

Transportation: _____

Individual Responsibilities

Important Phone Numbers

Bride: _____ Bride's Parents: _____

Groom: _____ Groom's Parents: _____

Other: _____ Other: _____

If you have any questions, please call me. Thanks for all your help,

_____

The Countdown Calendar

SETTING THE DATE

Setting the date for your wedding can become complicated when you consider your work and/or school schedules, holidays, and seasons. Start by selecting the type of wedding you plan to have: formal indoor, informal outdoor, destination, or theme. For instance, if you plan to have a garden wedding and you live in Maine, you'll need to plan a late spring or summer wedding. Or, you may have your heart set on a winter wedding with the attendants all dressed in red velvet. After deciding on the type of wedding, choose the best season to accommodate it.

HONEYMOON

If you plan to honeymoon immediately after the wedding, consider your vacation time at work or school. Discuss with the groom what amount of time you can take off together and speak to your employers as soon as possible. If you select a holiday season, arrange to get the time off early. See Chapter 19 for the best time of year to travel to your honeymoon destination.

HOLIDAYS

Guests may find it difficult to attend weddings that take place around big holidays like Christmas/Hanukkah and Thanksgiving because of other family and religious

24

commitments. Three-day weekends are convenient since everybody gets an extra day to recuperate. Out-of-town guests may appreciate the extra day too. Although some guests appreciate the three-day weekend weddings, others who live in your home town may resent having to stay home on a three-day weekend when they may have made plans for a mini-vacation. Check to make sure that your wedding date doesn't land on a religious holiday. Christian clergymembers usually won't perform ceremonies during Lent or other religious holidays.

Menstrual Cycle

In some societies, the bride considers her menstrual cycle when planning the wedding date. In this ancient tradition, sexual consummation of the marriage takes place on the wedding night so careful planning of the wedding date is important. Menstrual cycles may be difficult to predict when planning your wedding six to nine months ahead. Setting your wedding date so you won't have your period, will make your big day that much better.

Special Occasions

Before finalizing your wedding date, make sure that it doesn't conflict with a birthday, anniversary, graduation, or some other special date for close family members or friends. This would make it difficult for mutual guests to decide which event to attend. Once you decide on your date, let those special people know the date right away so they can plan their own special occasions around yours. Don't wait until invitations go out.

Day of the Week

Saturdays are more popular than Sundays because it is convenient for the guests. They can stay out all night and have the next day to recover. Christians usually don't choose Sundays and Jews don't choose the Sabbath (Friday sundown to Saturday sundown). Weddings officiated by a judge have to be held during the week. Many guests will not be able to attend a wedding held during the week, especially if it is held during the day.

Time of Day

The time of day is usually dictated by your budget. Allow five hours for the ceremony and reception when planning the time of day. It is traditional for afternoon

weddings to be less formal and less expensive than evening ones. Garden weddings are best in the early afternoon. If you want a candlelight ceremony, it will have to take place in the evening. If you would like an afternoon wedding to be held during daylight hours, start at 1:00 p.m. Consider daylight savings; when will the sun go down?

SIX-MONTH COUNTDOWN CALENDAR

The Six-Month Countdown Calendar on the following pages is designed to help you prioritize the many responsibilities for the six months prior to your wedding. Start by filling in the six calendar months with the months and dates. The first calendar month should be the sixth month before your wedding date. For example, if your wedding is in August, the first Six-Month Countdown Calendar month will be March. The fifth month will be April, and so on. Consult a conventional calendar to fill in the exact dates. Below each Calendar is a list of items that should be taken care of during that month. Use the Monthly Countdown Calendar as an appointment book. When you've completed each task, just check it off under the "done" column. As the countdown progresses, you'll be able to see all of your accomplishments "checked-off"!

SUNDAY	MONDAY	TUESDAY	WEDNESDAY	THURSDAY	FRIDAY	SATURDAY

SIX-MONTH COUNTDOWN	Done
Prepare Guest List: Bride's, Groom's, Bride's Family, Groom's Family	
Decide Type of Wedding	
Set Wedding Date	
Plan Wedding Budget	
Choose Wedding Location	
Choose Reception Location	
Plan Reception Luncheon/Dinner	
Select Bride's Attendants and Groom's Ushers	
Consult Clergymember	
Choose Wedding Dress, Headpiece, Shoes	
Choose Attendants' Dresses, Headpieces, Shoes	
Select Groom's Tuxedo and Attire	
Select Ushers' and Men's Tuxedos and Attire	
Reserve Wedding Night Suite	
Select Flower Girl and Ring Bearer	
Choose Flower Girl's Dress and Ring Bearer's Attire	

SUNDAY	MONDAY	TUESDAY	WEDNESDAY	THURSDAY	FRIDAY	SATURDAY

FIVE-MONTH COUNTDOWN	Done
Select Florist	
Select Band/Musician/Disc Jockey	
Make Honeymoon Plans	
Select Photographer and Discuss Plans	
Look for New Home Together	

		29				

SUNDAY	MONDAY	TUESDAY	WEDNESDAY	THURSDAY	FRIDAY	SATURDAY

FOUR-MONTH COUNTDOWN	Done
Design/Select Wedding Invitations and Order	
Design/Select Wedding Announcements and Order	
Design/Select Wedding Accessories and Order	
Design Maps to be Inserted in Invitations (Wedding/Reception)	
Design Transportation Inserts for Out-of-Town Guests	
Select/Make Ring Cushion	
Tape Prerecorded Music	
Write or Review Wedding Vows	
Select Special Readings	
Write Ceremony	
Register Gifts with Department Store	
Select Videotaper and Discuss Plans	

SUNDAY	MONDAY	TUESDAY	WEDNESDAY	THURSDAY	FRIDAY	SATURDAY

THREE-MONTH COUNTDOWN	Done
Mothers Select Gowns	
Address Invitations and Announcements..	
Schedule Attendants' Fitting	
Bride and Groom Get Physical Checkups	
Schedule Ushers' Fittings	
Make Entertainment Guide for Out-of-Town Guests	
Draw Up Pre-wedding Itinerary and Map for Out -of-Town Guests	
Order Wedding Cake and Cake Accessories	
Reserve Limousine (or other transportation) for Bridal Party	
Give Ceremony Musicians Copies of Ceremony Music Work Sheets	
Give Reception Musicians Copies of Ceremony Music Work Sheets	

SUNDAY	MONDAY	TUESDAY	WEDNESDAY	THURSDAY	FRIDAY	SATURDAY

TWO-MONTH COUNTDOWN

	Done
Set Date and Time for Ceremony Rehearsal and Dinner/Party	
Set Date for Bridesmaids' Luncheon and Bachelor Party	
Mail Invitations	
Buy Attendants' and Ushers' Gifts	
Select Wedding Rings	
Order Centerpieces for Tables, Corsages, etc.	
Arrange Parking Attendant for Wedding Ceremony and/or Reception	
Set Date for Bridal Portrait (for Newspaper)	
Buy Bride and Groom's Wedding Accessories	
Prepare Wedding Reception Agenda	
Buy Bride and Groom's Presents to Each Other	
Send Copies of Special Readings to Friends Who Will Participate in the Ceremony	

SUNDAY	MONDAY	TUESDAY	WEDNESDAY	THURSDAY	FRIDAY	SATURDAY

ONE-MONTH COUNTDOWN

	Done
Have Florist Visit Chapel and Reception Hall to Plan	
Schedule Final Fitting for Wedding Dress and Headpiece	
Apply for Marriage License	
Get Blood Tests	
Make Hotel Arrangements for Out-of-Town Guests and Send Confirmation Letters	
Arrange Transportation for Out-of-Town Guests and Send Confirmation Letters	
Send Announcement to Local Newspaper	
Change Insurance Policies	
Change Name and Address on Credit Cards, License, etc.	
Write New Will and Prenuptial Agreement	
Try Hairdo with Hair Stylist (Nails)	
Set Seating Arrangements/Write Place Cards	
Prepare Individual Responsibility Checklists for Helpers	
Have Bridesmaids' Luncheon and Bachelor Party	
Pack for Honeymoon	
Have Ceremony Rehearsal and Dinner	
Give Photographer Checklist of Wedding Photos	
Give Videographer Events to Videotape Work Sheet	
Give Caterer Final Head Count	

Engagement and Other Parties

ANNOUNCING YOUR ENGAGEMENT TO FRIENDS AND RELATIVES

PARENTS

If this is your first wedding, announce the news of your engagement to your parents first. You could both visit or call together. If you think the news may not be well received, you may want to break the news to your parents by yourself. This will give them time to think it through and adjust to the concept before they see their future son-in-law or daughter-in-law.

YOUR CHILDREN

If either of you have children from a previous marriage, announce the news of your engagement to your children first. Remember, you're excited about this news but consider how your children will respond. This is especially true if you have young children who will be living with you and their new stepparent. Tell the children about the engagement by yourself. As their natural parent, you're making changes that will affect their future as well as your own.

Some children respond well to the engagement. If their natural parent is deceased or not involved, they may look at this as an opportunity to have "a real

family." Other children may resent a new person trying to take over a parental role that, in their opinion, is already filled. This is especially true with young children who have two actively involved parents. They may secretly hope that their natural parents may get back together and this news would shatter their last hope for a reunited family. Some children may be sensitive during the transition period while they seek their new roles and experiment with new guidelines.

Before you announce the engagement to your children, decide how you would like to involve them in the wedding. Getting the children involved makes them feel that you've considered their roles in the new family structure. Discussing the wedding as a group can be like building the new foundation as a family. Offer to include all the children in the ceremony. If you get resistance, don't push. Let the children work out their anxiety and confusion without the pressure to support a marriage they're confused about.

If you both have children, tell them separately. There will be times when both sets of children will be with you as a new family unit and they'll need time to get familiar with each other. Be fair in your decisions about involvement in the wedding plans. Favoritism is one of the most common accusations you will receive from your future stepchildren, so beware.

Consider the changes yourselves. Discuss how your living situation will change along with your budget, household responsibilities, discipline, weekends, vacations, and so forth. The more prepared you are as a couple, the easier it will be for your children to adapt to the new family. Children like to know their parameters and the expectations you have of them. They will test you both until you set down the ground rules.

Ex-Spouse

If you had children with an ex-spouse, you should tell him about the engagement yourself. Don't send messages through the children. If there is tension between the two of you, try writing a note. This is a good opportunity to have a more mature relationship as parents of your mutual children. Be diplomatic. Don't write things that will start a feud. Let him know how the marriage will change the alimony and/or child support responsibilities. Not knowing what to expect while changes are taking place can be hard on your ex-spouse. Try to answer questions that you know will come up.

If you are friendly with your ex-spouse, arrange a time when you both can get together to talk. Let him know your plans about your living situation: where you will live, where the children will live, what schools the children will attend, and so forth.

Ex-In-Laws

If you are widowed, or friendly with your ex-in-laws, send them a note to inform them of your engagement. This may come as a surprise to them and a note will give them a chance to swallow the news. Initially, they will probably have mixed feelings. Let them know that you will still keep in touch with them.

Others

Once you've told the few special people that you wanted to share your good news with first, it's time to let everybody know. Many engaged couples call their friends to tell them personally.

To formally announce your engagement, you can put an announcement in the local newspaper in both of your hometowns. Check with your local newspaper about their policies and wording.

Customary Announcement

Mr. and Mrs. Robert Stevens of Kite Hill announce the engagement of their daughter, Nicole Jaclyn to Mr. Ian James, son of Mr. and Mrs. Jordan James of Florida. The wedding will take place in March.

Divorced Parents—Bride's Mother Announces

Mrs. Joanne Stevens announces the engagement of her daughter, Lauren Ashley, to Mr. Joseph Webster, son of Mr. and Mrs. Roy Webster of San Francisco. Miss Stevens is also the daughter of Mr. Alan Stevens of Santa Cruz.

Divorced Parent—Bride's Mother and Father Announce

Mr. Alan Stevens of Santa Cruz and Mrs. Joanne Stevens of Malibu announce the engagement of their daughter, Lauren Ashley to Mr. Joseph Webster, son of Mr. and Mrs. Roy Webster of San Francisco.

DIVORCED PARENTS—BRIDE'S MOTHER AND STEPFATHER ANNOUNCE

Mr. and Mrs. Robert Dressel announce the engagement of Mrs. Dressel's daughter, Heather Dodge, to Mr. Thomas Mitchell, son of Mr. and Mrs. Jacob Mitchell of Beverly Hills. Miss Dodge is also the daughter of Mr. Alan Dodge of Saratoga, California.

GROOM'S PARENTS DIVORCED—BRIDE'S PARENTS ANNOUNCE

Mr. and Mrs. Flaniken of San Jose announce the engagement of their daughter, Jaclyn Anne to Mr. Gordon Statton, son of Mr. Matthew Statton of San Francisco and Laura Statton of Carmel.

ONE PARENT HAS DIED—BRIDE'S MOTHER ANNOUNCES

The engagement of Miss Brittany Matta, daughter of Mrs. Heidi Matta and the late Mr. John Matta, to Mr. Ryan Walker, son of Mr. and Mrs. Steven Walker of New York, is announced by the bride's mother.

BOTH PARENTS HAVE DIED—UNCLE ANNOUNCES

Mr. Brian Cayton of Portland announces the engagement of his niece Rachel Allman to Mr. Bruce Baker, son of Mr. and Mrs. Peter Baker of Ashland. Miss Allman is the daughter of the late Mr. and Mrs. Frank Allman of Main Avenue.

THE ENGAGEMENT PARTY

The engagement party can he hosted by anyone. It is traditionally given by the parents. The party can be a formal dinner, buffet luncheon, or cocktail party. Invitations are necessary only when the engagement party is a formal affair. The host/s will appreciate having copies of the Engagement Party checklist on page 37.

There are many types of parties for you to enjoy before your wedding. Make sure that none of them takes place the night before the wedding. The guests who attend the party the night before may celebrate too much and end up with a hangover. This is especially good advice for you and the wedding party. You wouldn't want to miss your big day by being sick or ruin your wedding photos with pictures of you or your bridal party looking a little green.

ENGAGEMENT PARTY

Location:

Hosts: | Phone:

Date: | Time: | Reservation:

Type of Party:

Menu:

Other:

Total Costs:

INVITATIONS

Stationer: | Wording:

Address:

Hours:	Phone:
Style:	Color:
Paper:	Typestyle:
Number:	Costs:
Date Ordered:	Date Ready:

GUEST LIST

NAME	ADDRESS	PHONE	WILL ATTEND

BRIDAL SHOWERS

Showers are hosted by friends but not the immediate family. They are usually given by the attendants. If a member of your immediate family hosts the shower it appears that the family is trying to soak the guests for more gifts. Invitations can be mailed or given in person by the hostess. If it is a casual affair, a simple phone call will do.

SHOWER THEMES

The bridal shower is an informal party among women. There is usually food and beverages. Some parties have games to play but the highlight of the party tends to be the gift opening.

PARTY THEMES

- Kitchen
- Recipes
- Lingerie
- Plants
- Cocktail/Bar
- Pool
- Barbecue
- Recreation
- Bathroom
- Bedroom
- Last Night on the Town

SHOWER GAMES

- Bride's Bingo: This is similar to regular Bingo but wedding terms are used instead of letters. This can be purchased in stationery stores.
- Pin the Boutonniere: This is similar to Pin the Tail on the Donkey, but the groom's picture is used with a boutonniere to be pinned to the groom's lapel.
- Twenty Questions: The hostess asks the groom questions about his past before the party. During the party, the guests ask you questions about the groom to see how well you know him.

SHOWER GIFTS

All guests who attend a wedding shower are expected to bring a shower gift and a separate wedding gift to the wedding. Shower gifts are usually less expensive than wedding gifts.

THANK-YOU NOTES

Send thank-you notes to all the guests even if you said thank you to the gift giver at the shower. The notes should be handwritten and mention the gift in the body of the note.

GUEST LIST

As soon as you are informed that a friend will host a shower for you, start making up a guest list. Ask the hostess how many guests she would like to entertain so you don't hand her a list of twenty-five guests when she expected only ten in her small apartment. Once you finalize the guest list, give the hostess a list of names with addresses and phone numbers. Use the Shower Guest List form on page 40.

The guest list should include only people who will be invited to the wedding. If you are having two showers, divide your guest list up so that the guests attend only one shower. If friends, relatives, and office staff insist on having showers for you and the guest lists overlap, ask the hostesses if they could have a joint party.

BRIDESMAIDS' LUNCHEON (BACHELORETTE PARTY)

The bridesmaids' party is given by the bride for all of her attendants before the wedding. It can be a simple party with hors d'oeuvres or a hosted dinner at a popular restaurant. The purpose of this party is for the bride to thank all the attendants for being in her wedding party. Use the Bridesmaids' Luncheon checklist on page 41. This is a good time to give your attendants their gifts. See Gifts to the Bridal Party on pages 194–195.

BACHELOR'S PARTY

The bachelor's party can be given by the groom, the ushers, or any friends before the wedding. Women are not supposed to attend the traditional bachelor's party. The traditional purpose of the bachelor party is for the groom to celebrate his last

SHOWER GUEST LIST

NAME	ADDRESS	PHONE	WILL ATTEND

BRIDESMAIDS' LUNCHEON

Location:

Hosts: | Phone:

Date: | Time: | Reservation:

Type of Party:

Menu:

Other:

Total Costs:

INVITATIONS

Stationer: | Wording:

Address:

Hours: | Phone:

Style: | Color:

Paper: | Typestyle:

Number: | Costs:

Date Ordered: | Date Ready:

GUEST LIST

NAME	ADDRESS	PHONE	WILL ATTEND

BACHELOR'S PARTY

Location:

Hosts: Phone:

Date: Time: Reservation:

Type of Party:

Hors d'oeuvres: Liquor:

Mixers:

Toasting Glasses: Stag Party Favors:

Total Costs:

INVITATIONS

Stationer:		Wording:
Address:		
Hours:	Phone:	
Style:	Color:	
Paper:	Typestyle:	
Number:	Costs:	
Date Ordered:	Date Ready:	

GUEST LIST

NAME	ADDRESS	PHONE	WILL ATTEND

night out on the town as a single man. It is also a good time for the groom to give the ushers their gifts. The Bachelor's Party checklist on page 42 will be helpful.

The bachelor party can be hosted at a friend's house or a popular bar. Everyone traditionally toasts the bride. Some go as far as breaking the glass so that it may never be used again for a less worthy cause. The host pays for all the broken glass. If this toast takes place in a restaurant or a bar, notify the management in advance so that inexpensive glasses are used.

Some bachelor parties invite strippers for entertainment. This can be a controversial subject for the bride and groom. Talk to your fiancé about concerns you may have regarding the type of entertainment and drinking at the bachelor's party.

HIS AND HERS PRE-WEDDING PARTY

It is becoming cosmopolitan to have pre-wedding parties for both the bride and groom together instead of two separate parties. This is more common for couples who have lived together before their engagement where the traditional theme behind the wedding shower, to help prepare the bride prepare for living with her future husband, and the bachelor party, to recognize the groom's last night out, are outdated concepts.

The His and Hers Party takes the place of both the bridal shower and the bachelor party. This is a great way to have a party with all of your friends. Since when have brides had only female friends and grooms only male friends?

The party theme can be as simple as hors d'oeuvres and beverages or a wild bash with live music and dancing. Guests can help pay for the entertainment and a large gift. Theme parties based on the bride and groom's interests and/or needs are popular.

If you prefer this type of party to the individual parties, let your bridal party know before they put a lot of energy into planning the others. Ask the person who offers to give the shower and the man who offers to throw the bachelor party to work together in preparing a joint party. Let them decide how simple or elaborate the party will be. Make sure to give them the His and Hers Pre-Wedding Party Guest List on page 45.

REHEARSAL DINNER PARTY

The rehearsal dinner is traditionally hosted by the groom's family when the bride's family hosts the entire reception. It can be hosted by either family or by you and the groom. Even though it is called the "Rehearsal Dinner," it doesn't have to

include a meal. It may be difficult to have the whole bridal party together for a long period of time and the rehearsal itself holds priority over dinners and parties. It could be an elaborate dinner at a restaurant or cocktails and hors d'oeuvres at your house. Use the Rehearsal Dinner Party form on page 46 for easy planning.

The rehearsal dinner party provides a time for you to mingle with the wedding party and to introduce the individuals who haven't yet met. This is a special time to thank them for being part of your wedding.

Guests should include all members of the wedding party, your parents, the groom's parents, the clergymember and spouse, the musicians, and the coordinator. Inviting spouses of the bridal party and out-of-town guests is optional.

Toasts are traditionally offered to you by the best man. The groom can offer a toast to his future parents-in-law and you to your future parents-in-law.

WEDDING-DAY BREAKFAST/LUNCHEON

Friends of the family or relatives often host a wedding day breakfast or luncheon for your out-of-town guests. This warm welcome helps to make your guests' stay comfortable as they wait for the wedding to start. This allows you the freedom to spend the morning getting ready and relaxing before the ceremony. You are not expected to attend this affair. Make sure you give the hosts a copy of the Wedding Day Breakfast/Luncheon form on page 47.

HIS AND HERS PRE-WEDDING PARTY GUEST LIST

NAME	ADDRESS	PHONE	WILL ATTEND

REHEARSAL DINNER PARTY

Location:

Hosts: Phone:

Date: Time: Reservation:

Type of Party:

Menu:

Other:

Total Costs:

INVITATIONS

Stationer:		Wording:
Address:		
Hours:	Phone:	
Style:	Color:	
Paper:	Typestyle:	
Number:	Costs:	
Date Ordered:	Date Ready:	

GUEST LIST

NAME	ADDRESS	PHONE	WILL ATTEND

WEDDING DAY BREAKFAST/LUNCHEON

Host:	Phone:
Host's Address:	City:
Date:	Time:
Location:	
Directions:	

GUEST LIST

NAME	HOTEL/ADDRESS	PHONE	TRANSPORTATION	WILL ATTEND

Guest List and Stationery

GUEST LIST

WHO'S INVITED?

Traditionally the guest list gets divided into thirds: your family, the groom's family, and you and the groom. This can be an awkward situation if one party is financing the wedding and another party wants to invite too many guests.

Assuming that your budget and total number of guests have been set, you can start making your guest list. If your wedding is financed by all three parties, the guest list should be divided in thirds. If financing is coming from only one source, then how the guest list is divided will have to be decided by all of the parties involved. If one party has a larger guest list than the others, it may create tension between the families. A good solution is for you to decide how many guests each party will invite and then additional guests can be paid for by the party who invites them. A guest list with unlimited guests depends upon the size limit at the ceremony and reception sites and, of course, on your budget.

Once you decide on the total number of guests you can invite, start making a list of names right away. The sooner you start the list, the less likely you will be to forget someone important. Be sure to check such things as personal and business phone books, alumni directories, holiday card lists, club rosters, work personnel lists, and family trees to make sure you're not forgetting anyone.

When you ask both families to compile their guest lists, ask them to include the full names of the guests along with their address (with ZIP Codes) and telephone numbers (with area codes). You'll need the guests' names and addresses for the invitations and possibly their phone numbers if they don't respond to the invitation.

SOCIAL PRESSURES

DISTANT RELATIVES

If you were invited to a distant relative's wedding, you don't have to invite them to your wedding. Trying to limit your wedding size by inviting close friends and relatives is your choice. Once word gets out that you are having a small wedding, good friends and relatives will understand.

GUESTS' DATES

Single guests often feel uncomfortable attending a wedding without an escort or date. This is especially true if they don't know any of the other guests. When you know that a guest has a steady partner, invite the partner with a separate invitation. If you think a guest will be uncomfortable alone, write "and guest" on the invitation. This will give him or her the opportunity to invite a date.

If you are trying to minimize your guest list, ask single guests to attend the wedding alone so that you can invite more guests. Seat singles at the same table during the reception so they can meet each other and will feel more comfortable together.

CHILDREN

Children can add levity to a wedding. Guests love to watch the little ones running around and dancing with the adult guests. You may have a few special young people in your life whom you would like to have at your wedding. If your wedding is casual and the setting appropriate for children, then by all means invite the children.

On the other hand, children can have tantrums just as you say your vows, interrupting the ceremony and ruining the videotaping. Most caterers charge the full amount for children so you'll have to count each child as a guest when you give a head count. Inviting couples with children can double your guest list.

If you have just a few special children whom you would like to have at the wedding, but don't want to invite all of your friends' and family's children, ask the special children to be part of the wedding party. Then get the word out that children will not

be invited to your wedding. On the invitation, either write "adults only" or just write the adults' names. Emphasize that children are not invited or that children under a certain age are not invited.

Once parents know that children are not invited, they can make other arrangements to care for the children that day and enjoy the wedding themselves. This policy usually doesn't create problems as long as you don't invite *any* of the children. By inviting some children and not others, it may be awkward for those guests who leave their children at home only to see other children attend the wedding.

BUSINESS ASSOCIATES

Weddings can be a good way to solidify business relations with associates. If your guest list allows for you to invite business associates and fellow employers, then splurge and invite them. You may need to invite a group of people who socialize together at your office in order to avoid hard feelings. If you are trying to limit your guest list then business associates should be the first group of guests to be eliminated from the list.

UNINVITED GUESTS

What do you do when a friend asks about the wedding and incorrectly assumes that he or she is invited? It's best to tell the person the truth right away. Explain that you are having a small wedding for just the families. Most people understand that limiting guests is difficult and will not take offense. You might have a party at some later time and invite all of the people you couldn't invite to the wedding.

EX-SPOUSES AND EX-IN-LAWS

This depends solely on the relationship you have with your ex-spouse and his family, as well as your fiancé, his family, and your own interests. Consider all of the families involved in the situation. If everybody feels comfortable with each other then invite them all. Usually though, ex-spouses and ex-in-laws are not invited.

HANDICAPPED GUESTS

Don't let a guest's handicap stop you from inviting that guest to your wedding. Most facilities have ramps for wheelchairs and accommodations to make guests with special needs feel more comfortable.

SPECIAL GUESTS

You may invite guests who live far away even if you know they will not be able to attend. They will appreciate the remembrance. Guests who do not attend the wedding reception do not need to send gifts.

You may also want to invite special people such as the parents of the wedding party members. Consider inviting people like your housekeeper, personal secretary, and babysitter.

MUSICIANS, ETC.

Decide ahead of time whether or not you will be inviting the musicians, clergymember and spouse, photographers, videographers, and so on to the reception.

The clergymember and spouse traditionally are invited to the reception. They usually are assigned to sit at the parents' table.

Many musicians, photographers, and others expect to be invited to enjoy the meal also. They may get hungry while they are working and it is a nice gesture. Let them know ahead of time so they can plan their schedule around their meal.

THE GUEST LIST

Start entering the names of your guests on the Wedding Invitation and Gift List on page 52. Use a pencil since you will probably be adding and deleting information. Number the list under Invitations Sent to get a total number of invitations to order. When you actually send each invitation out, circle the number so you know that an invitation has been addressed and mailed.

Make two copies of your guest list to give to both sets of parents. This will help parents become familiar with who will be invited. You may want to make notes next to the guests' names to help the parents remember the guests. For instance, write: high school friend, college roommate, business partner. This will help the hosts feel more at ease with all the guests they will be greeting on your wedding day.

CHAPTER 5

WEDDING INVITATION AND GIFT LIST

INV. SENT	NAME STREET ADDRESS CITY, STATE ZIP CODE	RESPONSE			SHOWER GIFT	THANKS	WEDDING GIFT	THANKS	NOTES
		YES	NO	HOW MANY?					

See Recording Gifts, page 190.

WEDDING INVITATION AND GIFT LIST

INV. SENT	NAME STREET ADDRESS CITY, STATE ZIP CODE	RESPONSE			SHOWER GIFT	THANKS	WEDDING GIFT	THANKS	NOTES
		YES	NO	HOW MANY?					

See Recording Gifts, page 190.

WEDDING INVITATION AND GIFT LIST

INV. SENT	NAME STREET ADDRESS CITY, STATE ZIP CODE	RESPONSE			SHOWER GIFT	THANKS	WEDDING GIFT	THANKS	NOTES
		YES	NO	HOW MANY?					

See Recording Gifts, page 190.

WEDDING INVITATION AND GIFT LIST

INV. SENT	NAME STREET ADDRESS CITY, STATE ZIP CODE	RESPONSE			SHOWER GIFT	THANKS	WEDDING GIFT	THANKS	NOTES
		YES	NO	HOW MANY?					

See Recording Gifts, page 190.

WEDDING INVITATION AND GIFT LIST

INV. SENT	NAME STREET ADDRESS CITY, STATE ZIP CODE	RESPONSE			SHOWER GIFT	THANKS	WEDDING GIFT	THANKS	NOTES
		YES	NO	HOW MANY?					

See Recording Gifts, page 190.

WEDDING INVITATION AND GIFT LIST

INV. SENT	NAME STREET ADDRESS CITY, STATE ZIP CODE	RESPONSE			SHOWER GIFT	THANKS	WEDDING GIFT	THANKS	NOTES
		YES	NO	HOW MANY?					

See Recording Gifts, page 190.

WEDDING INVITATION AND GIFT LIST

INV. SENT	NAME STREET ADDRESS CITY, STATE ZIP CODE	RESPONSE			SHOWER GIFT	THANKS	WEDDING GIFT	THANKS	NOTES
		YES	NO	HOW MANY?					

See Recording Gifts, page 190.

WEDDING INVITATION AND GIFT LIST

INV. SENT	NAME STREET ADDRESS CITY, STATE ZIP CODE	RESPONSE			SHOWER GIFT	THANKS	WEDDING GIFT	THANKS	NOTES
		YES	NO	HOW MANY?					

See Recording Gifts, page 190.

WEDDING INVITATION AND GIFT LIST

INV. SENT	NAME STREET ADDRESS CITY, STATE ZIP CODE	RESPONSE			SHOWER GIFT	THANKS	WEDDING GIFT	THANKS	NOTES
		YES	NO	HOW MANY?					

See Recording Gifts, page 190.

WEDDING INVITATION AND GIFT LIST

INV. SENT	NAME STREET ADDRESS CITY, STATE ZIP CODE	RESPONSE			SHOWER GIFT	THANKS	WEDDING GIFT	THANKS	NOTES
		YES	NO	HOW MANY?					

See Recording Gifts, page 190.

WEDDING INVITATION AND GIFT LIST

INV. SENT	NAME STREET ADDRESS CITY, STATE ZIP CODE	RESPONSE			SHOWER GIFT	THANKS	WEDDING GIFT	THANKS	NOTES
		YES	NO	HOW MANY?					

See Recording Gifts, page 190.

WEDDING INVITATION AND GIFT LIST

INV. SENT	NAME STREET ADDRESS CITY, STATE ZIP CODE	RESPONSE			SHOWER GIFT	THANKS	WEDDING GIFT	THANKS	NOTES
		YES	NO	HOW MANY?					

See Recording Gifts, page 190.

WEDDING INVITATION AND GIFT LIST

INV. SENT	NAME STREET ADDRESS CITY, STATE ZIP CODE	RESPONSE			SHOWER GIFT	THANKS	WEDDING GIFT	THANKS	NOTES
		YES	NO	HOW MANY?					

See Recording Gifts, page 190.

WEDDING INVITATION AND GIFT LIST

INV. SENT	NAME STREET ADDRESS CITY, STATE ZIP CODE	RESPONSE			SHOWER GIFT	THANKS	WEDDING GIFT	THANKS	NOTES
		YES	NO	HOW MANY?					

See Recording Gifts, page 190.

WEDDING INVITATION AND GIFT LIST

INV. SENT	NAME STREET ADDRESS CITY, STATE ZIP CODE	RESPONSE			SHOWER GIFT	THANKS	WEDDING GIFT	THANKS	NOTES
		YES	NO	HOW MANY?					

See Recording Gifts, page 190.

WEDDING INVITATION AND GIFT LIST

INV. SENT	NAME STREET ADDRESS CITY, STATE ZIP CODE	RESPONSE			SHOWER GIFT	THANKS	WEDDING GIFT	THANKS	NOTES
		YES	NO	HOW MANY?					

See Recording Gifts, page 190.

WEDDING INVITATION AND GIFT LIST

INV. SENT	NAME STREET ADDRESS CITY, STATE ZIP CODE	RESPONSE			SHOWER GIFT	THANKS	WEDDING GIFT	THANKS	NOTES
		YES	NO	HOW MANY?					

See Recording Gifts, page 190.

WEDDING INVITATION AND GIFT LIST

INV. SENT	NAME STREET ADDRESS CITY, STATE ZIP CODE	RESPONSE			SHOWER GIFT	THANKS	WEDDING GIFT	THANKS	NOTES
		YES	NO	HOW MANY?					

See Recording Gifts, page 190.

WEDDING INVITATION AND GIFT LIST

INV. SENT	NAME STREET ADDRESS CITY, STATE ZIP CODE	RESPONSE			SHOWER GIFT	THANKS	WEDDING GIFT	THANKS	NOTES
		YES	NO	HOW MANY?					

See Recording Gifts, page 190.

WEDDING INVITATION AND GIFT LIST

INV. SENT	NAME STREET ADDRESS CITY, STATE ZIP CODE	RESPONSE			SHOWER GIFT	THANKS	WEDDING GIFT	THANKS	NOTES
		YES	NO	HOW MANY?					

See Recording Gifts, page 190.

WEDDING INVITATIONS

How to Word the Invitations

If the invitation is addressed to Mr. and Mrs. Thomas Mitchell, then only Mr. and Mrs. Thomas Mitchell are invited. Their children's names did not appear on the envelope so the children should stay home. If the invitation is addressed to Miss Nicole Stevens, only Miss Nicole Stevens is invited. If the invitation reads Mr. and Mrs. Alan Dodge, Brian Dodge and Jaclyn Dodge, then the whole family is invited.

Spread the word to the bridal party and your families if children or dates are not invited. If you do receive a response card from someone listing more guests than you invited, it is acceptable to make a polite phone call to let them know that the guest list is at its maximum capacity.

The bride's parents traditionally send the wedding invitations when they host the wedding. There are endless combinations of who hosts the wedding ceremonies and therefore who sends the invitations. Here are some guidelines:

TRADITIONAL

Bride's Parents

Mr. and Mrs. Robert Darcy
request the honour of your presence
at the wedding of their daughter
Nicole Sarah
to Mr. Douglas Crawford
Saturday, the eighth of January
Two thousand
at half past six o'clock
Wind Chime Cathedral
Santa Cruz, California

Bride's and Groom's Parents

Mr. and Mrs. Steven Robertson
request the honour of your presence
at the marriage of their daughter
Jaclyn Anne
to
Mr. Justin Gordon
son of
Mr. and Mrs. Lawrence Gordon
Sunday, the twenty-fifth of February
Two thousand and one
Queen Mary
Long Beach, California

SPECIAL

Groom's Parents

Mr. and Mrs. Gregory Matthews
request the honour of your presence
at the marriage of
Joanne Francio
to their son
Trevor Matthews
etc.

Bride's Mother and Stepfather

Mr. and Mrs. Thomas Mitchell
request the honour of your presence
at the marriage of Mrs. Mitchell's daughter
Kathryn Lynn
etc.

Bride's Father and Stepmother

Mr. and Mrs. Michael Panza
request the honour of your presence
at the marriage of Mr. Panza's daughter
Gail Lauren
etc.

Bride's Parents Divorced

Jennifer Smith Levine
and
Kenneth Levine
request the honour of your presence
at the marriage of their daughter
Carole Marcia
etc.

Bride's Parents Divorced
and Remarried

Mr. and Mrs. William Fuller
and
Mr. and Mrs. George Tanner
request the honour of your presence
at the marriage of
Brenda Patricia
etc.

Groom's Parents Divorced

Mr. and Mrs. Thomas Quinlan
request the honour of your presence
at the marriage of their daughter
Deborah Ann
to Mr. Gregory Stevens
son of
Mrs. Sharon Smith Stevens
and Mr. Frank Stevens
etc.

Bride's Stepmother

Mr. and Mrs. Michael Sudbrink
request the honour of your presence
at the marriage of Mrs. Sudbrink's stepdaughter
Jennifer Kimberly
etc.

One Living Parent

Mrs. Kevin Garth
requests the honour of your presence
at the marriage of her daughter
Rebecca Claira
etc.

No Living Parents

Mr. and Mrs. George Carpenter
request the honour of your presence
at the marriage of their niece
Miss Tamara Colette
etc.

Bride and Groom

James Edward Blort
and
Kathryn Ann Johnston
request the honour of your presence
at their marriage
etc.

Double Ceremony—
Two Sisters

Mr. and Mrs. Roy Peterson
request the honour of your presence
at the marriage of their daughters
Gail Katelyn
to Mr. James Wright
and
Adrienne Lynn
to
Stephen Wagner
etc.

CHAPTER 5

Double Ceremony—
Brides Are Not Related

Mr. and Mrs. Peter Jones
and
Mr. and Mrs. Samuel Smith
request the honour of your presence
at the marriage of their daughters
Jaclyn Jones
to
Mr. Charles Jenkins
and
Nicole Smith
to Mr. Joseph Sutter
etc.

Military Titles

The bride, groom, or bride's father may use her or his military title. An officer whose rank is equal to or higher than captain in the army or lieutenant in the navy places the title before his or her name. Those of lower ranks place their rank on the line below. Also include the branch of service on the second line.

Colonel Curtis Johnson
United States Army

Brian Schermer
Ensign, United States Navy

Jaclyn Ann Montgomery
Lieutenant, Women's Army Corps

CONTEMPORARY

Bride's Parents

Mr. and Mrs. Jeffrey Coleman
would like you to
join with their daughter
Candace Kaycee
and Victor Alexanders
in their celebration of love
etc.

Bride and Groom

Gail Sanders
and
Daren Daniels
invite you to share their joy
of the beginning of their new life together
as they exchange marriage vows
on Sunday, the fifth of September
etc.

PRINTER/STATIONERS

Most stationery stores have a complete line of wedding invitation catalogues with all of the accessories. Order the invitations at least three months before your wedding date. Ask the stationer about the approximate completion date so you can put in your order at the right time. Allow two weeks to address and mail the invitations. Invitations should be mailed out four to six weeks before the wedding. If your wedding will be held on a holiday weekend, send invitations eight weeks before.

TYPES OF INVITATIONS

TRADITIONAL

The traditional wedding invitation is white with black raised lettering. There are two techniques used to achieve the raised-letter effect: (1) stemography is the technique that requires dusting the letters to create a raised letter, and (2) copperplate engraving is made with a male and female dye to raise the letter through the paper. The copperplate engraving technique is more expensive.

The style and formality of the wedding invitations usually sets the tone for the wedding. If the invitation is white and formal, guests expect a formal wedding. The location and time of the wedding also gives the guests hints about what to expect at the wedding.

CONTEMPORARY

Contemporary invitations are as colorful and unique as the bride and groom themselves. Some include photographs or poems. Design your invitation and get estimates from printers. The use of colors can be expensive but with large quantities

the costs may be the same as traditional invitations. Use your creative flair to make the invitation unique. If you have a large budget, hire a graphic artist to design your invitations.

COMPUTER-GENERATED INVITATIONS

Stationery stores and computer software dealers carry wedding invitation packages that include elegant paper with preprinted designs and software loaded with all of the options you will need to design a beautiful invitation. Simply have the invitation you want printed and you will be ready to start addressing envelopes.

SECOND OR SMALL WEDDINGS

Second weddings and smaller (under fifty) weddings don't require formal printed invitations. You could handwrite the invitations. On the other hand, you could have elaborate formal invitations if your wedding is formal and you want to have an elegant, small wedding.

COAT OF ARMS

If your family has a coat of arms or a family crest, it can be embossed on the cover of the invitation. It should be in color. This is used only when the bride's family issues the invitations and announcements. If the groom's family or the groom and you issue the invitations, the groom's coat of arms can be used.

ORDERING INVITATIONS

When ordering your invitations from the stationer or printer, make sure you order a few extras. You may want to give invitations out at the last minute or keep some for mementos. Order a few extra envelopes in case you make mistakes addressing them. If you are running into a time crunch, ask if you can get the envelopes ahead of time so you can start addressing them while you wait for the invitations to be printed.

Order all your invitations at the same time. Placing two smaller orders is more costly than placing one large order. Most stationers charge most for the first twenty-five, regardless of how many times you've ordered. For example, if you order twenty-five at $10 and add another twenty-five a few weeks later, you will pay $20 ($10 for each twenty-five). If you order fifty the first time, you may pay as little as $15 to $17. The savings add up!

HINTS ON PROOFREADING

When you proofread all of your wedding stationery, take a friend along to help. He or she can double-check for errors. Ask the following questions as you proofread each card:

1. Are all the names spelled correctly?
2. Are the times and dates correct?
3. Are the addresses and directions correct?
4. Does the day of the week and the date correspond?
5. Are the words honour and o'clock spelled out?
6. Are all the numbers spelled out?
7. Do all the lines end at the appropriate spaces?
8. Are there periods after abbreviations?
9. Are the card size, color, typesetting, and designs correct?

RECEPTION INVITATIONS

The reception invitation is used when the guest is invited to the reception only and not to the ceremony. Some wedding ceremonies are for the immediate family only and the reception is for all of the friends and relatives. If the guests are invited to both the ceremony and the reception you could use a smaller reception card and place it in the ceremony invitation or you could invite the guests to the reception at the bottom of the ceremony invitation. Here are a few guidelines:

TRADITIONAL

Reception Only

Mr. and Mrs. Christopher Newell
request the pleasure of your company
Sunday, the thirty-first of January
at six o'clock
Serra Retreat
R.S.V.P.
thirty-three Pacific Coast Highway
Malibu, California 12345

**Reception Card Included
with Ceremony Invitation**

*Reception
immediately following the ceremony
Yellowstone Country Club
Kindly respond
Forty-four Kite Hill Road
New York, New York 12345*

**Ceremony and Reception
Invitation All in One**

*Mr. and Mrs. John Peterson
request the honour of your presence
at the marriage of their daughter
Jaclyn Nicole
to Mr. Michael Woods
Saturday, the first of January
at three o'clock
Princess Louise
San Pedro, California*

*Reception
immediately following the ceremony
Princess Louise
R.S.V.P.*

RESPONSE CARDS

Response cards are optional but convenient for guests. Most wedding invitations include them because guests tend to have a hard time remembering to call or to write a note responding to the invitation. Response cards are used only for the reception, unless the ceremony is at home. If you send response cards with your invitations the return envelope should be addressed to either the host or to you. The return envelope should include a stamp for convenience. Commemorative stamps are nice to use.

The date you select for the last day to respond should be two to four weeks before the wedding. This will allow enough time to contact those who have not responded and get a final head count to give to your caterer.

There are several ways to word a response card. If you use response cards, eliminate the R.S.V.P. on the invitation. It can be worded:

1. Please respond
2. R.S.V.P.
3. Kindly respond
4. The favour of a reply is requested
5. R.S.V.P. to bride's parent's house

Traditional Response Card

Please respond on or before
March 3, 20XX

M_____

Will/will not attend.
Number of Persons____

Guests are responsible for responding to your invitation in a timely manner. If you provided a response card, all they need to do is fill in their names and let you know how many guests will or will not be attending. If you don't enclose a response card, be prepared to make a lot of phone calls.

MAPS TO THE CEREMONY AND RECEPTION

Enclose a map to the ceremony and to the reception with the invitations as a courtesy to your guests even if the location is a famous or popular site. Out-of-town guests will especially appreciate the maps.

Check with the site coordinator for ready-made maps. Many hotels and banquet facilities have maps available to patrons. You can also check the Internet for specific maps linking the wedding site to the reception site.

Another way to draw a map is to trace over a city map. Include major highways, boulevards, and streets. If there are any landmarks, include them. Lay the map over a transparent surface like a window where light can shine through. Then lay tracing paper or regular white paper over the map. Pencil in the lines for the major roadways. Use black ink to draw in the final roads. Remember to put the direction symbol pointing north. Include both wedding and reception sites on the map.

You may also write out the directions. Some guests don't have good visual sense and need to have the directions written out. Give directions for guests

coming in various directions. Make sure your directions are complete and correct. Ask a friend to read the directions to make sure the directions can be understood.

RESERVED SECTION CARDS (PEW CARDS)

If your wedding is large and you'd like to reserve two or three pews for close family members, send pew cards with your wedding invitations. These special guests give the pew cards to ushers at the wedding ceremony before they are seated so the ushers know where to seat them. The first row is usually reserved for the parents. Often grandparents or brothers and sisters share the front row. The second and third rows can be reserved for aunts, uncles, and special friends.

Reserved-section card can be printed or handwritten.

Traditional Reserved Section Card

Nicole and Taylor
Seven Seas Cathedral
Bride's section
Pew Number____

AT-HOME CARDS

At-home cards are sometimes sent with the invitations and announcements to let friends and family know where you will live and what name you plan to take after the wedding. With so many women keeping their maiden names or hyphenating the husband's and wife's surnames, this little card helps avoid any confusion or awkward moments when being introduced.

Traditional At-Home Card

Mr. and Mrs. Curtis Honda
after the second of September
777 West Union Street
Bellingham, Washington 55555

Contemporary At-Home Card

Mr. David Hollingsworth
and
Ms. Jaclyn Stevenson
after the first of July
333 Pacific Coast Highway
Malibu, California 12345

PLACE CARDS

Place cards are used in larger weddings to let the guests know where they should be seated. They are very helpful for the caterer so they know how many tables to set. Without place cards, seven people may sit together leaving unfamiliar guests stranded. If you plan the seating chart well by seating groups together (relatives, old college friends, business associates, singles, and teenagers) guests will feel more comfortable and you will solve any seating problems.

The place cards are laid out on a table at the entrance to the reception facility. They are usually put in alphabetical order for the guests' convenience. The tables are numbered so the guests can easily find their tables.

Place cards come in two basic designs: (1) folded card and (2) folded match book. Both have the same information on them. Both of your names are listed on the first line and the wedding date is on the second line. The third line is left blank so you can handwrite the guests' names and the fourth line is for the table number.

Sample Place Card

Nicole and Russ
October 1, 2000

_____

Table Number: ___

ANNOUNCEMENTS

Send announcements to friends and family who will not be invited to the wedding. If you eloped, then send announcements to everybody. Often, announcements are sent to people who live so far away that it is not possible for them to attend. Don't send announcements to anybody who received a wedding invitation. Use the Announcement List on pages 86 and 87 to make sure you order the right amount and keep track of the mailing.

Announcements are worded and addressed in the same way as invitations. They should be mailed out immediately after the wedding, not before.

Traditional Bride's Family

Mr. and Mrs. Ryan Grant
have the honour of announcing
the marriage of their daughter
Nicole Mackenzie
to Mr. Lawrence Cartwright
on Saturday, the twenty-second of May
Nineteen hundred and ninety-nine
R.M.S. Queen Mary
Long Beach, California

Contemporary Bride and Groom

Ms. Jaclyn Collins
and Mr. William Baldwin
announce their marriage
Sunday, the twenty-sixth of September
One thousand nine hundred and ninety-nine
San Francisco, California

NEWSPAPER ANNOUNCEMENT

Most newspapers have a form that you can fill out or a standard format to announce your wedding in a newspaper. Call the newspaper to request the forms be mailed to you. If the newspaper doesn't have a standard form, use the Newspaper Announcement Worksheet on page 88. Most papers require that your photograph and wedding information be submitted at least ten days before the scheduled publication date. Put your photograph in a manila envelope with

cardboard to prevent bending. Include your announcement form. Your wedding information should include:

1. Bride's maiden name
2. Groom's name
3. Bride's name after the wedding (if she keeps her maiden name or hyphenates it)
4. Bride's parents' names
5. Groom's parents' names
6. Place and date of marriage
7. Place of reception
8. Names of the wedding party
9. Colleges of the bride and groom (if applicable)
10. Notes on parents of the bride and groom
11. Officiant's name
12. Optional: description of the bride's gown, professional backgrounds, honeymoon plans, honors, military service, and special clubs.

THANK-YOU NOTES

Send handwritten thank-you notes for each gift you receive, even if you thanked the giver at the reception. Thank-you notes are traditionally sent on white paper and written in black or blue ink. Notes can have your name or your initials printed or engraved. Your maiden name should be used on these notes before the wedding but your married name should be used afterwards for any correspondence. Any stationery is acceptable as long as it is in good taste. Don't use thank-you notes that have a pre-printed statement. Receiving a pre-printed card that says, "Thank-you for the lovely wedding gift" will not make the giver feel you are sincere in your thanks.

Gifts will start arriving soon after you send the invitations. Enter each gift received on your Wedding Invitation and Gift List on pages 52–71. Send thank-you notes within two weeks after you have received the gift and no later than two months after the wedding date. Enter the date the thank-you note was sent on your Wedding Invitation and Gift List so you will remember whom you've thanked. Don't mention broken items or returns in your thank-you notes.

Thank-you notes traditionally are sent by the bride. However, it is more meaningful for the groom's friends and relatives to receive a thank-you note from him. The bride may wish to send thank-you notes to her friends and family and the groom may send thank-you notes to his guests. If one of you is better at writing than the other, then let the author of the family do the honors.

ANNOUNCEMENT LIST

NUMBER	NAME STREET ADDRESS CITY, STATE ZIP CODE	COMMENTS	NUMBER	NAME STREET ADDRESS CITY, STATE ZIP CODE	COMMENTS

ANNOUNCEMENT LIST

NUMBER	NAME STREET ADDRESS CITY, STATE ZIP CODE	COMMENTS	NUMBER	NAME STREET ADDRESS CITY, STATE ZIP CODE	COMMENTS

NEWSPAPER ANNOUNCEMENT WORKSHEET

Your name: ———————————————————— Date to appear: ————————————————

Your address: ——

Your phone: ———————————————— Your work phone: ————————————————

Friend available for questions if you are out-of-town: ——————————————————————

Friend's phone: ——

(Your name) ———————————————— , daughter of (your parents' names) ————————————

of (your parents' hometown) ———————————————————— , was married this (morning, afternoon,

evening) ———————————— to (your fiancé's name) ———————————— ,

son of (his parents' names) ———————————— of (his parents' home town) ———————— .

(Clergyman) ———————————— of (town or state) ————————————————

performed the ceremony at (wedding site) ———————————— in (city or state) ————————

———————————————— .

The bride, was attended by her maid/matron of honor (name) ———————————— . Bridesmaids were

(names) ———————————— , ———————————— ,

and ———————————— .

(Name of best man) ———————————— was best man.

Ushers were (names) ———————————— , ———————————— ,

and ———————————— .

The bride, who will keep her name, is a (profession) ———————————— with (company) ————————

———————————————— .

The groom is a (profession) ———————————— with (company) ————————————

———————————————— .

After a trip to (honeymoon site) ———————————— , the couple (Mr. and Mrs.) will reside in (town) ————————

———————————————— .

ADDRESSING INVITATIONS AND ANNOUNCEMENTS

Address invitations by hand, not by typewriter or computer. Use black or blue ink. Ask a friend, bridesmaid, or calligrapher to help with the addressing. Common titles can be abbreviated (Mr., Mrs., Ms.). Formal titles should be written out: Doctor, Captain, and Reverend. Teenagers should also have a title before their names (Miss, Misses, Mr., Messrs.).

The outer envelope has the formal names of the principal guests (no children's names). No abbreviations are used except with common titles. Include the street address and ZIP code. Streets and states are always spelled out.

The inner envelope has the names of the guests and, if children are invited, the children's names on the next line. If you are close to the guest, you may use his or her nickname or loving name: Bobby and Missy or Grandma. There is no address on this envelope.

WHO RECEIVES INVITATIONS?

Married couples receive one invitation. Nonmarried couples receive individual invitations. If a couple is living together, you can either send one invitation addressed to both or send separate invitations. Experts are divided on how to handle this. Consider the relationship of the couple: do they function as a married couple or are they free spirits living together out of convenience? Use your discretion.

Single guests receive their own invitations. If you would like your single guest to invite a guest, add "and Guest" to the inner envelope. As a courtesy, young adults (16 and over) can receive their own invitations even if the whole family is invited and all are living together. Older family members (grandparents, great-aunts) receive their own invitations even if they live with the family. Children don't receive individual invitations; their first names are added below their parents' names on the inner envelope.

PUTTING IT ALL TOGETHER

The larger formal invitation is first folded across the middle. Extra enclosures (such as response cards, reception cards, and pew cards) are placed in the fold of the invitation.

Printers used to place a tissue next to the engraving to prevent smudging. If it is in place when you receive the order, leave it there. Otherwise it is not necessary to put it in.

Once all the enclosures are in place, slip the folded invitation into the inner invitation with the fold side down and front facing up. The inner envelope should

CHAPTER 5

not be sealed. Place the inner envelope so that the names will appear first when the guest opens the envelope.

WHEN TO MAIL INVITATIONS

Mail invitations four to six weeks before your wedding. If the ceremony will take place during a holiday season or a three-day weekend, mail invitations eight weeks ahead. This will allow guests to plan their weekends and holidays around your wedding date.

Send all wedding invitations at the same time. If you've given sealed invitations to your mother or the groom's mother, let them know the date you plan to send the invitations so they can send them on the same date.

DEATH IN THE IMMEDIATE FAMILY

If someone close to you (parent, sibling, grandparent) dies suddenly, postpone your wedding. Your wedding should be a happy celebration. You, your family, and close friends will be in mourning, which will ruin your big day. If you've already sent invitations, send a printed card recalling the wedding invitations if time allows. If the death occurs close to the wedding date, ask your attendants to help you call guests to postpone the wedding until further notice.

If you are aware that a family member or close friend is terminally ill, try to arrange your wedding date early so that he or she may attend the wedding. If the person will not be with you for long, set the date for a future date to allow enough time for mourning.

Often, a sick or dying family member may request that the wedding *not* be postponed because of his or her illness or death. In that case, continue the plans and celebrate your wedding as scheduled. During the ceremony or reception you may have a moment of silence or prayer in remembrance of this special person.

Printed Recall Cards

> *Mr. and Mrs. Adam Craig*
> *regret that due to a death in the family*
> *the invitation to*
> *their daughter's wedding*
> *(names optional)*
> *on Saturday, the thirteenth of July*
> *must be recalled*

WEDDING PROGRAMS

Guests often wonder who is officiating the ceremony or who is in the wedding party. By providing a wedding program, ushers can hand them out as the guests are seated, and guests can read through the program while they wait for the ceremony to begin. The wedding program lists the members of the bridal party and the series of ceremonial events. It is like a play; it lists the cast of characters and the acts. Guests enjoy knowing who is reading the selected poems and the program is a nice memento for the guests to take home. See the Sample Wedding Program on page 92.

PRINTED NAPKINS

Dinner or luncheon napkins help personalize the reception. Cocktail napkins add a nice touch at the bar. They usually list both of your names and the date of the wedding. There may be an imprint of wedding bells, two doves, wedding rings, or a similar line drawing above the names.

PARTY FAVORS

Placing mints or party favors at each guest's place setting at the reception can be a small thank-you gesture for joining the celebration.

These party favors can be purchased from stationery or party supply stores. If you have a creative flair, consider making them with your friends and attendants. Most materials can be purchased at craft and hobby stores. Here are some suggestions:

- Soft mints or Jordan almonds wrapped in netting and tied off with ribbons
- Champagne glasses with the names of the bride and groom, and also the wedding date.
- Ornamental boxes filled with candies
- Satin roses with the names of the bride and groom, and the wedding date printed on the ribbon tied to the stems.
- Miniature picture frames with engraving
- Ethnic trinkets
- Religious offerings

WEDDING PARTY

Maid of Honor . . . . Deborah Stevens

Bridesmaids . . . . Gail Gordon

Lorraine Coleman

Best Man . . . . Robert Dresser

Ushers . . . . William Dante

James Edwards

Flower Girl . . . . Nicole Wells

Ring Bearer . . . . Ross Smith

Guest Book . . . . Brittany Adams

Page 4

THE MARRIAGE SERVICE OF

Jaclyn Ann Roberts

and

Craig Steven Thompson

On Saturday, September 3, 2000

At 2:00 P.M.

Holy Cross Church

Santa Cruz, California

Page 1

OFFICIATING

Father Rusty Morell

PRELUDE

Adagio . . . . Albinoni

PROCESSIONAL

Wedding March . . . . Wagner

GREETING

PENITENTIAL RITE

LITURGY OF THE WORD

First Reading . . . . Colossians 3:12-17

Michael James

Responsorial Psalm . . . . Set Me Like a Seal

Ms. Jenny Wells

EXCHANGE OF VOWS

BLESSING AND EXCHANGE OF RINGS

Page 2

SOLOIST

Air from Suite. No. 3 . . . . Bach

OFFERTORY

LITURGY OF THE EUCHARIST

NUPTIAL BLESSING

RECESSIONAL . . . . Wedding March

PARENTS OF THE BRIDE

Mr. and Mrs. John Roberts

PARENTS OF THE GROOM

Mr. and Mrs. Paul Thompson

ORGANIST . . . . Dorothy Ward

SOLOIST . . . . Benjamin Hill

Page 3

Wedding Attire

THE BRIDE

WEDDING GOWN AND ACCESSORIES

You will be the center of attention on your glorious day and the gown you wear will set the tone for your wedding. It will determine the style for the groom's attire, your attendant's gowns, and the ushers' attire. Traditionally, white is worn to indicate purity and virginity, and it is still the most popular color for first-time brides. Review the Traditional Wedding Attire form on page 95 for a helpful overview of suggested attire for the wedding party.

ANYTHING GOES!

You can wear wild colors, styles, and lengths. Red, off-white, and even black are worn by brides today. If your favorite color is teal, wear teal! Sexy necklines and bold styles are worn to fit the personality of the bride. You can be creative. There are no guidelines except that your attire should be in good taste.

Try on all kinds of gowns. You'll know when you've tried on the right one—you'll feel gorgeous!

TIPS ON HOW TO BUY YOUR WEDDING GOWN

Magazines: Browse through bridal magazines or web pages to see what styles are available. Make copies of the designs you like best and save them. You will then be able to inform salespeople of the kind of designs that appeal to you so they can show you gowns that are close to your tastes.

Friend: Invite a friend, your mother, or your fiancé to accompany you when you try on gowns. It's best to invite just one person to avoid crowding. Bring a camera along to capture your favorite styles. Quickly develop the film and show the pictures to close friends and family to get opinions. Save the pictures for your "Pre-wedding album."

Appointments: To ensure good service, make appointments with several bridal stores. Start looking for your gown at least six months before your wedding date to allow enough time to make sure you will be able to get the perfect dress. Be up front about your budget so the salesperson won't show you gowns you can't afford.

What to Bring: Bring shoes with the same size heels you plan to wear at the wedding. Wear a strapless bra so you can get the full effect of each gown. Wear your hair the way you'd like to wear it at the wedding. Bring bobby pins so you can play with your hair when trying on different headpieces.

Deposits: Discuss the store's cancellation policy before leaving a deposit. Ask about charges for alterations or style changes. Always pay with a credit card. Use the Wedding Gown Worksheet on page 96 to keep track of choices, fitting dates, payment schedules, and other important information.

ABOUT LACES AND EMBROIDERY

Most wedding gowns have lace or embroidery to give the bride a romantic, feminine aura. Gowns usually have labels that list fabric content and cleaning instructions. Read the labels carefully. Few manufacturers give instructions about how to care for the lace and embroidery on the gown. Ask your salesperson for details and cleaning instructions.

RESTORED GOWNS

Not all wedding gowns are worn only once. Many brides carefully store their gowns for their daughters and granddaughters to wear. Wearing your mother's or grandmother's gown can make your wedding special. It is a sentimental gesture that the giver will appreciate.

TRADITIONAL WEDDING ATTIRE

TYPE OF WEDDING	BRIDE	MEN	BRIDESMAIDS	MOTHERS
Formal Daytime	*Bridal Gown:* White, ivory, or soft pastel. Chapel train or cathedral train. *Headpiece:* Long veil to cover train or to make train. If veil is shorter than fingertips, should be very full. *Accessories:* Bouquet or prayer book. Shoes to match. Long gloves with short sleeve (gloves optional). Simple jewelry.	*Traditional:* Oxford gray or black cutaway coat with striped waist coat, wing collared shirt, and a striped ascot. *Contemporary:* Long or short (black/gray/colors) contoured jacket, striped trousers, wing collared white shirt, gray vest (optional).	*Dress:* Floor length. Colors matching or harmonizing with other bridesmaids' dresses in style and color. *Headpiece:* Cap or hat. *Accessories:* Long or short gloves in white or pale tint. Bouquet, Jewelry.	*Dress:* Floor length or shorter with fashion trends. *Headpiece:* Matching or contrasting colored hat. *Accessories:* White or pale tint gloves. Corsage. Purse.
Formal Evening	*Bridal Gown:* Same for daytime but sleeves should be long and fabric more elaborate.	*Traditional:* Tailcoat, matching trousers, waist-coat, wing-collared shirt, bow tie. *Ultra formal:* Black tails and white tie. *Contemporary:* Long or short contoured jacket, matching trousers, wing-collared shirt, vest and	*Dress:* Long dresses. Fabric more elaborate. *Accessories:* Same as daytime.	*Dress:* Long dresses. *Headpiece:* Small head covering. *Accessories:* Furs. Jewelry.
Semiformal Daytime	*Bridal Gown:* White or pastel floor length dress. *Headpiece:* Elbow length or shorter veil. *Accessories:* Same as formal wedding.	*Traditional:* Gray or black stroller, striped trousers, gray vest, white soft collar shirt, gray and white striped tie. *Contemporary:* Formal suit, matching or contrasting trousers, white or collared shirt. Bow tie, vest, or cummerbund.	*Dress:* Same as formal. Cut and fabric can be simpler.	*Dress:* Same as formal.
Semiformal Evening	*Bridal Gown:* Same as daytime. Fabric can be more elaborate.	*Traditional:* Black dinner jacket/tuxedo, matching trousers, black vest or cummerbund, white dress shirt, black bow tie. In warm weather, white or ivory jacket. *Contemporary:* Formal suit (dark/light depending on seasons), matching or contrasting trousers. Bow tie to match vest or cummerbund.	*Dress:* Long *Accessories:* Same as for evening.	*Dress:* Same as formal
Informal Daytime or Evening	*Bridal Gown:* White or pastel floor length dress or short dress or suit. *Headpiece:* Short veil or bridal type hat. *Accessories:* Small bouquet, corsage, or prayer book. Suitable gloves and complimentary shoes.	*Contemporary:* Dark business suit for cold seasons, light suits for warm seasons.	*Dress:* Same length as bride's dress if bride's dress is short. If bride's dress if floor length, dress may be shorter. *Accessories:* Simple.	*Dress:* Street length.

WEDDING GOWN WORKSHEET

Bridal Shop/Seamstress: _____

Hours: _____

Salesperson: _____

Deposit Due: _____

Balance Due/Date: _____

Gown

Designer: _____

Style: _____

Color: _____ Size: _____

Style Alterations: _____

                         Cost: _____

Veil/Headpiece

Designer: _____

Style: _____

Color: _____ Size: _____

Style Alterations: _____

                         Cost: _____

Gloves

Designer: _____

Style: _____

Color: _____ Size: _____

Style Alterations: _____

                         Cost: _____

Shoes

Designer: _____

Style: _____

Color: _____ Size: _____

Style Alterations: _____

                         Cost: _____

Handkerchief

Designer: _____

Style: _____

Color: _____ Size: _____

Style Alterations: _____

                         Cost: _____

Bouquet

Style: _____

Colors: _____

                         Cost: _____

            TOTAL COSTS: _____

Address: _____

Phone: _____ Hours: _____

Date Ordered: _____

Expected Arrival: _____

First Fitting: _____

Second Fitting: _____

Final Fitting: _____

Instructions on Cleaning: _____

_____

Sketches

Person responsible for taking the gown to the cleaners: _____

Professionally store gown in box: _____

Restoring an old gown takes special skill and usually a great deal of money. Reducing the size or shortening a gown is easy but enlarging or lengthening gowns can be challenging. Fabric can be taken from hidden tiers or the back if more material is needed. Tea-dying new fabric is often done to match the faded fabric. Wrinkles in satin are difficult to get out but pressurized irons can do the job. Lace is fragile and may need to be replaced. Restoring a family heirloom may be expensive but most consider it money well spent.

Styles of yesterday can bring back a nostalgic feeling, making your gown special and beautiful. If the gown looks outdated or if you feel uncomfortable wearing it, be honest with the giver and wear what you like.

SECOND MARRIAGES

A bride's gown is a statement about who she is for her first as well as her second wedding. If you didn't wear white the first time around and you've always wanted to wear white, then wear white for your second wedding.

Many brides wear bright colors and accent them with a bridal touch (white pearls, white bouquet or corsage). Cream and off-white colors are typically worn for twice-around brides but don't let tradition set your style. If you look best in a champagne color, then select a champagne colored gown, suit, or dress.

Second-time brides often find their wedding attire in evening-wear shops instead of bridal salons. Antique dresses look best on the younger bride (under thirty-five) and classic suits on the bride over thirty-five. Select a dress that you can wear again.

ON THE WILD SIDE

Setting traditions aside, why not make your wedding attire bold and unique? Many brides are becoming trendsetters by breaking the "rules," and wedding etiquette has evolved to include these changes. If wearing a white, lacy formal wedding gown is too ordinary, go ahead and wear something flashy.

One bride wore a scarlet red, satin dress above the knee with her back bare. She carried a dozen long-stemmed white roses. Brides are wearing sexy dresses with low-cut necks and backs.

Those who marry in unusual places such as a ski slope, underwater, or in mid-air parachuting are likely to wear unconventional wedding attire. The skiers may be dressed in a tuxedo and traditional gown but they're wearing ski boots and sunglasses! The scuba divers may wear wetsuits and tanks with a

garter. The parachutists may sail down in matching jumpsuits with the bride carrying a bouquet or a bible!

If you are one-of-a-kind and you want your wedding to be a mirror image—as long as everything is tasteful and inoffensive—the sky's the limit.

PREGNANT BRIDES

Maternity bridal fashions vary depending on how far along you are in your pregnancy. If you have the ceremony while you are in your first or second trimester, you can wear most bridal styles. Once you're in the third trimester though, you'll need maternity gowns that allow breathing space for you and your belly. Bridal shops carry maternity lines. Call ahead to see which shops have gowns to try on and which have catalogues to choose from. A salesperson can help you determine what size gown to order. Your final alterations will need to be done close to your wedding date to make sure you don't outgrow your gown.

ALTERNATIVES TO BUYING A NEW GOWN

Renting: Grooms rent, why not brides? Bridal gowns can cost anywhere from $200 to $10,000 and they're usually worn only once. If you're on a tight budget you may wish to consider renting your gown. Call local formal wear shops. They usually have a good selection to choose from and alterations are taken care of on site.

Another alternative is to check secondhand shops for bridal gowns. To save time and energy, call all the secondhand stores in your area to see who has bridal gowns. Ask for descriptions, conditions, sizes, and styles to avoid wasted trips. You may be surprised to find a beautiful gown that, with minor alterations, fits you perfectly. Even with simple changes, such as tailoring sleeves and adding lace or trim, the savings will be substantial.

Sewing: Have the gown of your dreams sewn by a seamstress, a relative, or yourself. The cost of materials and labor is often cheaper than the high cost of designer gowns. Check bridal magazines for the style you like best and take it to a seamstress. If you're sewing the gown yourself, buy a pattern similar in style to work from. You may need to buy several patterns to mix and match necklines, sleeves, and bodices to create a design that's perfect for you. Words of advice—sew your own gown only if you are an experienced seamstress or your gown may end up looking like an "irregular garment" in a discount store.

ON-LINE RESOURCES

The Internet has come to provide excellent resources for shopping for and purchasing wedding gowns. There are hundreds of sites available offering new designer dresses, vintage dresses, novelty wedding dresses, bridesmaid dresses, accessories, and most anything else that could be imagined. Search headings to look under for wedding attire would include wedding gowns, bridal wear, formal wear, and designer gowns.

There are several ways to shop for wedding gowns over the Internet. If you don't know exactly what you are looking for, you can look for sites for wedding gowns and simply browse through web pages to find companies and styles that appeal to you. If you know of a particular designer you like, you can look up the designer's web page, which will give you descriptions of the designer's dresses and will also link you to stores in your area that carry their dresses. If there is a particular dress you want to buy, you can go to multiple web sites to ask for their best price quotes. Many web companies have automated price inquiries to help you price particular dresses.

The Internet offers a very convenient and inexpensive method for finding wedding attire. Through the Internet you can avoid much of the difficulty of traveling around to any number of bridal stores and having to deal with annoying salespeople. Also, many Internet companies are able to keep costs down since they don't have to pay expensive store rents, sales commissions, or mark-ups to individual dealers. Always use a credit card for Internet purchases to insure your purchase. Most companies offer guarantees on their merchandise but make sure you read the details of any purchase agreement. Many Internet companies also offer rush services and priority shipping to help you avoid long waiting periods.

CLEANING AND STORING YOUR GOWN

After you select your gown, ask the salesperson for a list of the gown's fabrics and materials. Manufacturers usually list the type of fabric on the label but they don't always list the type of lace, embroidery, and lining. Ask about cleaning instructions for the gown. You'll need to know how to handle emergency touch-ups on your wedding day and more detailed cleaning instructions for after the wedding.

Water-Soluble Stains: These include champagne, wine, perspiration, and beverages. Clean the stain with a water-based solution of water and vinegar or water and detergent. Put a towel under the fabric and blot it with a damp cloth. For wine stains, rub damp salt on the spot. Allow it to dry and then scrape away the residue.

Greasy Stains: These include lipstick, perfume, salad dressing, chocolate, and frosting. Clean these stains with dry cleaning solvents or spray-on spot removers. Hair spray also works well. Place the stained side down on paper towels and go over it using the cleaning solution with a clean cloth. Clean from the center to the edges. Be careful with delicate fabrics, silk, and taffeta, which wrinkles easily and permanently.

Professional Cleaners: Have your gown cleaned professionally after the wedding. Even though it may appear clean, unnoticed marks will surface and perspiration will damage the gown later. The gown should be cleaned within two days of the wedding to prevent stains from becoming permanent.

Storage: Fold the gown carefully into a large box using white tissues to help prevent wrinkling around the folds and the edges. Seal the box carefully to prevent moisture from seeping in. Do not put your gown in a plastic bag—it could be damaged by humidity and mildew.

If you choose not to seal and store your gown, don't hang it on a hanger. The weight of the gown can damage the lace and other delicate fabrics.

Professional dry cleaners can store your gown in specially made boxes or cabinets that will keep indefinitely. Choose a dry cleaner with a good reputation and tape the receipt on the box in case there is a problem later.

HAIRSTYLES

Try new hairstyles and haircuts six months before your wedding date to allow time for mistakes to grow out or straighten out. Don't try a new permanent or dye color a few weeks before the wedding. The chances of liking the new look are not worth the anxiety of hoping for miracles to correct a disaster. Browse through magazines to find unique ways to style your hair. Select a stylist and have him do your "wedding-day hair" two months ahead of time. If you like what he has done, set up a wedding day appointment. Although it is less expensive and more convenient for the stylist to meet you at the salon, some stylists will come to your home for an additional fee. Allow enough time to have your hair washed, set, and styled; leave enough time to apply make-up and to RELAX! You'll find a Hairstyle Checklist on page 101.

HAIRSTYLE CHECKLIST

Bride's Hairstyle

Beauty Salon: _____

Stylist: _____

Address: _____

Salon Phone No.: _____

Home Phone No.: _____

First Appointment: _____

   Time: _____

   Date: _____

               Cost: _____

Wedding Day Appointment:

   Time: _____

   Date: _____

   Location: _____

   Services: _____

     Wash: _____

     Set: _____

     Style: _____

     Facial: _____

     Manicure: _____

     Pedicure: _____

     Massage: _____

               Cost: _____

Style for Wedding Day: _____

_____

_____

Set: _____

_____

Comments: _____

_____

_____

Sketch

Attendants' Hairstyles

Attendant: _____

   Hairstyle: _____

   Accessories: _____

   Headpiece: _____

   Nails: _____

Attendant: _____

   Hairstyle: _____

   Accessories: _____

   Headpiece: _____

   Nails: _____

Attendant: _____

   Hairstyle: _____

   Accessories: _____

   Headpiece: _____

   Nails: _____

Attendant: _____

   Hairstyle: _____

   Accessories: _____

   Headpiece: _____

   Nails: _____

Attendant: _____

   Hairstyle: _____

   Accessories: _____

   Headpiece: _____

   Nails: _____

Attendant: _____

   Hairstyle: _____

   Accessories: _____

   Headpiece: _____

   Nails: _____

MAKE-UP

The right make-up can make you look gorgeous on your wedding day. There are two make-up applications to consider for your big day: (1) what the guests will see and (2) what the camera will see.

WHAT THE GUESTS WILL SEE

Professional Cosmetologists: A professional cosmetologist can do your bridal make-up for you. Have a session sometime before your wedding so you can find another cosmetologist if you don't like your new look.

Most cosmetologists will meet you at the wedding site to do your make-up. They supply all the make-up; all you do is sit back and enjoy the pampering. Set the date and time of the appointment in advance to make sure that the cosmetologist is available.

Department Store Cosmetologists: If you'd like to do your make-up yourself, visit the cosmetic departments of large department stores for free make-up sessions. Cosmetologists representing different make-up lines are trained to apply make-up and sell their products. Call ahead to schedule an appointment for a make-up session. If you like the look, purchase the make-up so you can practice at home.

TIPS ON MAKE-UP:

Foundation: Use a foundation base to give uniform color to your face. Select a base that matches your skin. Remember to blend the foundation from your face down to your neck and collar bone if they are exposed. If you have dark circles under your eyes, apply a concealer to cover dark areas.

Blushes: Blush emphasizes cheek bones and gives your face color and vitality. Pat on color and then swirl the brush in circles to blend.

Eyes: Shadows and liners emphasize and opens up the eyes. Mascara on the eyelashes widens the eyes.

Lips: Use a pencil to outline your lips and give them shape. Fill them in with a small brush with creams. Finish your lips with a gloss.

Powder. Finish your face with a neutral matte powder. This gives your face an even glow and helps absorb oils and perspiration.

WHAT THE CAMERA WILL SEE

Professional photographers are using better quality film than they have in years past. Brides used to need two totally different make-up applications: one for the guests and the other for the camera.

TIPS ON MAKE-UP:

Foundation: Use liquid or cream matte. Apply the same as above. Powder lightly. Shiny skin creates a glare.

Blushes: Be careful with blush if you are shooting a black and white photograph. The blush may look like a dark shadow instead of rosy cheeks.

Eyes: Highlight eyes and wear a lot of mascara. Eyes wash out in photographs. Avoid pale or frosted eyeliners and shadows.

Lips: Wear medium to deep tones with a gloss to finish.

Use the Bride's Wedding Day Checklist on page 104 to help keep track of attire and makeup details.

THE ATTENDANTS

The bride chooses the style, color, and material of the attendants' dresses to complement her own gown. Consider the attendants' heights, weights, figures, and ages. A full-figured woman won't feel comfortable wearing a clingy jersey; an older maid of honor might feel self-conscious in a short dress.

If you want all shoes dyed to match the gowns, ask the attendants to have the shoes dyed at the same shop to be sure the color lot is the same. Have out-of-town attendants mail their shoes to you. Having them wear white, gray, silver, or gold shoes can save on costs and prevent headaches.

Select a gown that your attendants can afford. If you're trying to keep down costs, select a dress that they can sew instead of choosing a designer gown. The bridesmaids can sew the gowns themselves or have it professionally made.

If your attendants can't afford to buy the dresses and can't sew, you may opt to buy the dresses yourself or split the costs with them. If you do this for one, do it for all.

Attendants' gowns are usually the same. The maid of honor may wear a different gown in coordinating colors so she stands out. Indicate the maid of honor's gown on the Attendants' Gown Checklist on page 105.

BRIDE'S WEDDING DAY CHECKLIST

DESCRIPTION OF ITEMS AND THINGS TO DO	DONE
Wedding Gown	
Headpiece and Veil	
Bra, Slip, Panties (extras too)	
Hosiery (two pairs)	
Shoes	
Jewelry	
Gloves	
Make-Up, Nail Polish	
Cotton Balls, Cotton Swabs	
Brush, Comb, Hair Spray, Bobby Pins	
Curling Iron and Blow Dryer	
Mirror	
Sewing Kit	
Iron and Ironing Board	
Cleaning Kit	
Perfume	
Bag to Put Gown In	
Going Away Clothes	
Accessories	
The Working Woman's Wedding Planner !	

ATTENDANTS' GOWN CHECKLIST

ATTENDANTS' NAMES	MEASUREMENTS	PHONE	SIZE	BUDGET

Store-Bought Gowns

Bridal Shop: _____

Address: _____

Phone: _____ Hours: _____

Salesperson: _____

Designer: _____

    Style: _____

    Color: _____

    Sizes: _____

             Cost Per Gown: _____

Date Ordered: _____

Expected Arrival: _____

First Fitting: _____

Final Fitting: _____

Accessories: _____

Deposit/Balance Due: _____

Headpieces

    Store: _____

    Designer/Style: _____

    Color: _____

    Quantity/Sizes to Order: _____

             Costs: _____

Gloves

    Store: _____

    Designer/Style: _____

    Color: _____

    Quantity/Sizes to Order: _____

             Costs: _____

Homemade Gowns

Fabric Shop: _____

Seamstress: _____

Phone: _____ Hours: _____

Designer: _____

    Style: _____

    Color: _____

    Sizes: _____

    Pattern No.: _____

    Fabric: _____

    Yardage/Gown: _____

    Accessories: _____

    Made By: _____

    Seamstress Fees: _____ Material Cost: _____

First Fitting: _____

Final Fitting: _____

Shoes

    Store: _____

    Style: _____

    Color: _____ Dye Lot: _____

    Quantity/Sizes to Order: _____

             Costs: _____

Bouquets

    Store: _____

    Colors: _____

             Costs: _____

GROOM'S WEDDING DAY CHECKLIST

DESCRIPTION OF ITEMS AND THINGS TO DO	DONE
Coat and Overcoat	
Trousers	
Shirt	
Vest	
Tie	
Ascot	
Cummerbund	
Gloves	
Shoes	
Suspenders	
Jewelry (Cuff Links)	
Underwear	
Hose	
Handkerchief	
Comb, Brush, Styling Mousse, Hair Spray	
Cologne	
Skin Cream or Lotion	
Going Away Clothes	
Accessories	
Storage Bag in Which to Return Formal Wear	

THE GROOM

The groom usually rents his formal wear. He can choose from traditional to contemporary designer tuxedos. Browse through bridal magazines to get a feel for the type of attire that you and your fiancé like. Make sure his attire complements yours.

The contemporary groom may wear a popular designer tuxedo with a shirt to match the bridal party's color. He may wear an old fashioned tuxedo with a top hat to accent your antique gown. You may both wear white to make you both stand out together. The groom should be comfortable with whatever attire you select.

Order his attire two to three months ahead of time. Schedule the fitting dates and enter it on his calendar. Have him try on the complete outfit to make sure it fits. His shirt collar should hug his neck and his cuff sleeves should extend one-half to one inch past his jacket sleeve. His trousers should touch his shoe tops. Socks and shoes should blend in with the rest of his attire. Make sure he has a copy of the Groom's Wedding Day Checklist on page 106.

THE BEST MAN AND USHERS

The best man's and ushers' attire should be similar in style and color to the groom's. Select the ushers' attire after you have selected the groom's and bridesmaids'. Traditionally, the ushers wear the same tuxedos as the groom except for something slightly different (for example, the groom should wear a different boutonniere, tails, or top hat).

The groom should stand out. When the groom wears the same color and style tuxedo as the ushers, guests may confuse him as an usher. Some ushers wear the same color shirt or cummerbund as the bridesmaids' dresses while the groom wears a different color. Select a style that complements the bride, groom, and attendants.

The ushers are responsible for paying for all their attire. Ask the formal-wear shop to fill out cards for each usher listing style, pieces, colors, and sizes. The complete attire from the tuxedo to the shoes can be rented from the same store. Contact the ushers to let them know where to go for measurements and fittings. Check with the manager periodically to make sure that all the ushers have been measured. With procrastinators, call them yourself; politely remind them to get their measurements.

If you have an usher who lives out of town, get a measurement card from your formal-wear store and send it to the usher. Ask him to go to a local formal-wear

shop to be measured. The shop will complete the measurement card and the usher should mail it to you. Send it to your formal-wear shop. The usher will need to come into town a few days early for his final fitting.

The Men's Attire Worksheet on page 109 will help you keep track of all the details.

THE FLOWER GIRL

The flower girl can wear a miniature version of the bridesmaids' attire from the headpiece to the stockings or she can wear a lacy Sunday dress. Some brides dress their flower girls in miniature bridal gowns with ribbons or a sash to match the bridal party.

Since children have growth spurts at unpredictable times, order the flower girl's dress ahead of time but wait until two weeks before the wedding to do the alterations. Ask a salesperson for help in ordering the correct size. The flower girl will need to be measured by the salesperson or seamstress. If she lives out-of-town, she can have the measurements taken at a local shop and then send them to you.

The flower girl's parents usually pay for her attire. If their finances are a problem, suggest that they sew the dress or offer to help out with the cost. If they opt to sew the dress, make sure the seamstress is reliable and proficient. Give them a copy of the Flower Girl's Gown Checklist on page 110 to help them keep track of everything.

Ask the flower girl to start breaking in her shoes a few weeks before the wedding to avoid blisters and a flower girl who walks down the aisle in her stocking feet.

THE RING BEARER/PAGES

The ring bearer wears a tuxedo or a suit to match the ushers or groom. He will be paired off with the flower girl so his attire should complement the flower girl's (if you have one).

If the ring bearer is under the age of four, you might put him in short trousers with a jacket for a hot summer wedding. He may also look charming in a tuxedo with tails if the groom is wearing tails.

The ring bearer carries a cushion with two fake rings sewn on it. This cushion can be purchased at bridal salons or stationery stores. If you have a creative vein, try making one to custom fit your wedding ceremony. Use the Ring Bearer's Cushion form on page 111 to record the details.

MEN'S ATTIRE WORKSHEET

NAME	ADDRESS	PHONE	SHOE SIZE	MEASUREMENTS				BUDGET
				NECK	ARM	WAIST	INSEAM	

Store: _____ Address: _____

Phone No.: _____ Hours: _____ Salesperson: _____

First Fitting: _____ Deposit Due: _____ Balance Due/Date: _____

Final Fitting: _____ Cancellation Policy: _____ Return Policy: _____

Date/Time to Pick Up: _____ Date to Return: _____ Damage/Stain Policy: _____

Person in Charge of Returning Men's Attire: _____

DESCRIPTION	GROOM	USHERS	NO.	RING BOY/PAGES	BR. FATHER	GR. FATHER
Style						
Coat Style Color Size						
Trouser Style Color Size						
Vest Style Color Size						
Shirt Style Color Size						
Cummerbund Style Color Size						
Tie Style Color Size						
Jewelry Cuff Links Accessories						
Shoe Style Color Size						
Hose Style Color Size						
Overcoat Style Color Size						
Boutonniere Flower/Color						

FLOWER GIRL'S GOWN CHECKLIST

Flower Girl: _____   Address: _____

Phone Number: _____   Age: _____

Budget: _____   Size: _____

<table>
<tr><td>

Store-Bought Gown

Store: _____

Address: _____

Phone: _____ Hours: _____

Salesperson: _____

Designer: _____

   Style: _____

   Color: _____

   Size: _____

             Cost: _____

Date Ordered: _____

Expected Arrival: _____

First Fitting: _____

Final Fitting: _____

Accessories: _____

Deposit Due: _____

Balance Due/Date: _____

Cancellation Policy: _____

</td><td>

Homemade Gown

Fabric Shop: _____

Seamstress: _____

Phone: _____ Hours: _____

Designer: _____

   Style: _____

   Color: _____

   Size: _____

   Pattern No.: _____

   Fabric: _____

   Yardage/Gown: _____

   Notions: _____

   Made By: _____

   Seamstress Fees: _____ Material Cost: _____

First Fitting: _____

Final Fitting: _____

   Accessories: _____

</td></tr>
</table>

Headpiece

   Store: _____

   Style: _____

   Color: _____

   Size: _____

             Cost: _____

Gloves

   Store: _____

   Style: _____

   Color: _____

   Size: _____

             Cost: _____

Shoes

   Store: _____

   Style: _____

   Color: _____

   Size: _____

             Cost: _____

Basket

   Style: _____

   Colors: _____

See Flower Girl's Basket, page 165.

Sketch

RING BEARER'S CUSHION

Design/Select Cushion Style: _____

Colors/Description: _____

Store-Bought Cushion	Homemade Cushion

Store-Bought Cushion

Store: _____

Address: _____

Phone: _____ Hours: _____

Salesperson: _____

Designer: _____

Style: _____

Color: _____

Cost: _____

Homemade Cushion

Fabric Shop: _____

Seamstress: _____

Phone: _____ Hours: _____

Designer: _____

Style: _____

Color: _____

Pattern No.: _____

Fabric: _____

Yardage: _____

Lace: _____

Yardage: _____

Notions: _____

Seamstress Fees: _____ Material Cost: _____

Sketch

Person responsible for bringing ring cushion to ceremony: _____

THE PARENTS

THE BRIDE'S MOTHER

The bride's mother traditionally wears a color to complement the bridal party. She informs the groom's mother of her choice of color, dress length, and accessories/jewelry.

Your mother should wear a color and style that looks good on her. Encourage her to choose colors that complement the bridal party, though the colors shouldn't dictate what she will wear. Let her wear what she feels best in. Etiquette experts suggest staying away from black or white: black is for funerals and white is for the bride.

GROOM'S MOTHER

In the past, the groom's mother would wait to hear from the bride's mother about what color, dress length, and jewelry she should try to match. The groom's mother made sure that she didn't outdo the bride's mother. Her colors were to match or complement the bride's mother's and the bridal party's dresses. Like your mother, the groom's mother should, of course, try to wear what she feels looks best on her. It's her big day too. Her son is getting married just as your mother's daughter is getting married. It would be a nice gesture for your mother to call the groom's mother to discuss their attire together. Again, no black or white for the mothers.

FATHERS

The father usually wears a tuxedo or a nice suit. The tuxedos can be the same style and jacket colors of the ushers. The shirt color can be the same as the bridal party but it is usually a different color. The fathers can wear the same style tuxedo or wear suits showing their distinct styles.

ACCESSORIES

Bridal accessories can be purchased from bridal shops or stationery stores. The guest book with all the signatures and comments from your guests is nice to have as a memento. Toasting goblets and cake knives can have your names and wedding date engraved on them. See Cake Knife and Cake Server on page 133 for details about engraving. To help organize your list of accessories to buy, see the Bride and Groom's Accessories Checklist on page 113.

BRIDE AND GROOM'S ACCESSORIES CHECKLIST

GUEST BOOK

Store:	Hours:
Address:	Phone:
Style/Color:	Cost:

GARTER

Store:	Hours:
Address:	Phone:
Style/Color:	Cost:

MARRIAGE CERTIFICATE HOLDER

Store:	Hours:
Address:	Phone:
Style/Color:	Cost:

TOASTING GOBLETS

Store:	Hours:
Address:	Phone:
Engraving:	
Cost of Engraving:	Date Complete:
Style/Color:	Cost:

BRIDAL GOWN BAG/BOX

Store:	Hours:
Address:	Phone:
Style/Color:	Cost:

BRIDE'S PURSE

Store:	Hours:
Address:	Phone:
Style/Color:	Cost:

DECORATIONS

Store:	Hours:
Address:	Phone:
Style/Color:	Cost:

OTHER:

Store:	Hours:
Address:	Phone:
Style/Color:	Cost:

The Caterer and the Bar

After deciding what type of wedding ceremony and reception you will have, it's time to select the caterer. According to experts on wedding etiquette, all that is essentially required at a wedding reception is the wedding cake and something bubbly to toast with. Receptions can range from a simple potluck dinner to a cocktail party with hors d'oeuvres to a formal seven-course dinner. It's up to you.

SELECTING A CATERER

RECOMMENDATIONS

Ask your friends for recommendations for caterers they have previously used for weddings, parties, and business functions. Check with the local Better Business Bureau to see if there have been any complaints lodged against the company. Use the Cater Possibility Checklist on page 116 to compare the caterers you interview. After selecting the caterer, use the Wedding Reception Caterer form on page 117 to note all the necessary data.

DATE AND TIME

Before launching into specific questions about the menu or company policies, check to make sure the caterer is available on your wedding date at your preferred

time. Request the caterer to allow enough time between your wedding and the next event so that he or she can stay longer if necessary.

CATERING YOUR OWN WEDDING

If your wedding will have less than fifty guests, catering it yourself is possible. You wouldn't want to cater your own wedding if you have a larger group. You will be so exhausted from preparing the meals and keeping an eye on the details that you won't enjoy your big day.

Plan your menu so that it can be prepared weeks in advance. Try a sample run of the whole menu and then freeze it for two weeks. Thaw it out and sample it again. If it stored well and tastes great, include it on your wedding day menu.

Hire servers and a bartender. Once the wedding starts, you should be free from responsibilities in the kitchen and bar. The servers should know where all the food and backups are. Give them a timetable to circulate hors d'oeuvres and champagne. Have the bar stocked well so that the bartender has all he needs to mix drinks. Make sure you have enough ice.

Tell the servers what you expect them to wear so there won't be any surprises.

Ask the servers and bartender to arrive thirty minutes early and clean up after the festivities. Be clear on where items need to be placed or returned.

Order your cake at least three weeks ahead. See Chapter Eight for more information.

Set the food tables and bar up at least four hours ahead of time. The dining tables should also be set up ahead of time. If the ceremony and reception will take place in the same area, have the tables set in an area away from the flow of traffic. After the ceremony, have your helpers move the tables to their appropriate locations.

BEVERAGES AND BUBBLY

Your liquor costs can easily exceed your meal costs. Carefully calculate the estimated amount of your bar tab and then check your budget.

You probably have a good hunch about the drinking habits of your guests. Depending upon your budget and your guests, you should decide whether you'll offer a hosted bar, no bar at all, or tray service.

CATERER POSSIBILITY CHECKLIST

QUESTIONS	POSSIBILITY	POSSIBILITY	POSSIBILITY
Caterer			
Manager			
Phone			
Address			
Hours			
Price per person?			
Breakdown: Food, service, and rentals?			
Does price include cake?			
Is there a cake cutting charge?			
Will caterer serve liquor?			
Is there a corkage fee?			
What is the ratio of servers to guests?			
What is the attire for servers?			
What is the condition of equipment?			
How will food be served/displayed?			
Can you observe an affair they are catering?			
Can you taste samples of menu?			
Is sales tax included?			
Are gratuities included?			
Is there an overtime charge?			
Cancellation policy?			
References?			
Will caterer feed the band/photographer?			
Initial deposit due date?			
Balance due date?			
Other:			

WEDDING RECEPTION CATERER

Caterer:	Manager:
Address:	
Phone:	Manager's Home Phone:
Store Hours:	Hours Available at Reception:
Last Date to Give Head Count:	
Reception Location:	Room Reserved:
Date: Set-up Time:	
Total Head Count: Cost per Person:	
Total Cost: Deposit Due Date: Balance Due/Date:	

COST WORK SHEET

ITEM	AMOUNT	SELECTION	COST ESTIMATE	ACTUAL COST
Hors d'oeuvres				
Lunch/Dinner				
Dessert				
Cake				
Fruit Punch				
Coffee/Tea				
Cake Cut Fees				
Decorations				
Taxes				
Gratuities				
Overtime Charges				
Total Food				

NONALCOHOLIC BEVERAGES

Always have nonalcoholic beverages available for your guests. They can be served in a decorative fountain or a punch bowl. Sparkling apple cider or grape juice has the same appeal as champagne without the alcohol. Serve it in champagne glasses so juice-drinking guests can toast along with the rest of the guests. Servers may pour soft drinks, sparkling water, or fruit juice at the table or at the bar. Coffee and tea are usually available after the meal.

ALCOHOLIC BEVERAGES

The cost of liquor at the reception can be your highest expense. Fine wines with dinner, topped off with the best champagne for the toast can add up. If you're looking to limit the cost of alcoholic beverages, premixed drinks served from pitchers and champagne punches served in a fountain or punch bowls may be a good option. Some guests enjoy the fruity zest of champagne punch. Other guests may prefer a glass of champagne. If your budget allows, offer both.

CHAMPAGNE

Champagne is the traditional beverage of weddings. It is usually served for the toast to the newlyweds and can be served throughout the entire reception—if your budget allows.

Champagne is a sparkling white wine made in the region of Champagne, France. It is fermented in the same bottle in which it is sold and served. According to French laws, sparkling white wine can only be called "champagne" if it is made in Champagne, France. Even so, the United States and other European countries are producing champagne with amazingly good results. Try a few different brands or go to some tasting rooms before you select the champagne for your reception.

WINE

Formal or gourmet dinners served with a selection of fine wine offers the finest in culinary delights. Consider your menu and your guests when selecting the wine. You can leave two different bottles on each table so the guests can serve themselves or the servers can pour.

Select a few bottles of fine wine to serve to special people at the parents' table and at your table. It's a kind gesture to those who appreciate good wine.

LIQUOR AND MIXES

Stocking a full bar requires a variety of liquor and mixes. Consider the guests, the season, and the time of day. The younger generation prefers white wine and blended drinks made with vodka, light rum, and gin. The older generation may request scotch, bourbon, and dry martinis. The lighter mixes are popular in the summer and the darker drinks may be favored in the winter.

Most liquor stores will give refunds for unopened bottles, so stock up on a wide variety. Ask your parents and the groom's parents for insights about their guests' liquor preferences. Combine their list with your friends' preferences and you'll have a good foundation on which to begin stocking your bar.

Have a good selection of mixers available for your guests. This will allow the bartender to whip up a variety of drinks for both your drinkers and your non-drinkers.

AFTER-DINNER DRINKS

After a formal dinner, you may offer after-dinner drinks. Your servers can circulate with bottles of brandies and liqueurs. If your budget allows, place a few selected bottles at each table for the guests to enjoy.

TRAY SERVICE

If a hosted bar is out of your budget, offer your guests mixed drinks with tray service. Select a few mixed drinks you think your guests will enjoy and ask the servers to offer them at the tables or as they mingle.

If you are concerned that the servers may offer more drinks than your budget allows, give them a schedule to serve drinks. Have them serve champagne as the guests arrive at the reception. After the toast, have them serve one round of drinks while dinner is being served. Serve the next round of drinks after dinner and continue until the cake cutting. The guests will then be distracted with the cake cutting, bouquet, and garter ceremonies and won't notice that the servers have stopped circulating drinks. When you and the groom slip into your going away clothes, your grand departure signifies the end of the reception.

If you plan to have dancing long after the bouquet toss, you should have the servers continue offering drinks to the guests who remain. There's a fine line between being a gracious hostess and a cheap one. Use discretion when scheduling rounds of tray service.

CORKAGE FEE

If your wedding reception will take place in a hotel or restaurant, the management usually requires that you purchase all the liquor from them. If you insist on bringing your own liquor, they may charge a corkage fee. This fee is a per bottle charge that covers the servers opening and pouring the bottles for the guests. Some establishments will let you bring your own liquor only if you have selected brands they cannot get, such as from private wineries.

Find out what the corkage fee is before buying your liquor. Sometimes, buying the bottles yourself ends up costing more when you add the corkage fees. If you have a large wedding, you may be able to negotiate the corkage fee or the number of bottles they'll charge for.

CALCULATING LIQUOR AMOUNTS

Calculating the amount of liquor consumed at a wedding reception requires insight on the guests invited. Once you have a good feel for the preferences of most of your guests, you can start playing with the numbers to get a ballpark figure. Order more than you need from a liquor store that is willing to buy back unopened bottles. If you are having the reception catered by a restaurant or hotel, they will stock the bar for you and charge you for all opened bottles.

The average guest will have between two to five drinks for the length of the reception. This, of course, depends on whether you're having a brunch or a formal sit-down dinner. Each drink has 1-1/2 ounces of liquor, so every quart will make twenty drinks and a fifth will make eighteen drinks. Guests who drink wine throughout the reception may drink one or more bottles each. If you offer champagne just for the toast, you'll need one bottle for every eight guests. After evaluating your guests' preferences, you can multiply the numbers to get a good estimate of quantities needed. Use the same formula to figure out quantities of mixes and drinks for your nondrinkers. Mixes, juices, and sodas are harder to calculate since they are used in mixed drinks as well as straight. Order more than you think you'll need to be on the safe side. Use the Worksheet for Estimating Liquor/Beverage Amounts on pages 121–122 to figure out how much to order. Then, use the Bar/Liquor Checklist on pages 123–124 to keep track of everything.

WORKSHEET FOR ESTIMATING LIQUOR/BEVERAGE AMOUNTS

Item	Number of Guests	× Number of Drinks	= Total Drinks	÷ 20 Drinks/Qt 18 Drinks/Fifth	= Total Quarts/ Fifths to Buy
Vodka					
Gin					
Light Rum					
Dark Rum					
Scotch					
Bourbon					
Whiskey					
Dry Vermouth					
Sweet Vermouth					
Dry Sherry					
Sweet Sherry					
Tequila					
White Wine		× Number of Bottles		Not applicable	
Red Wine		× Number of Bottles		Not applicable	
Rose		× Number of Bottles		Not applicable	
Brandy					
Liqueurs					
Champagne				÷ 8 Servings/ Bottle	
Other:					
Other:					
Other:					
Beer				÷ 24 =	__ Number of Cases
Club Soda				÷ 24 =	__ Number of Cases
Seltzer				÷ 24 =	__ Number of Cases
Tonic Water				÷24 =	__ Number of Cases
Triple Sec					
Lime Juice					

WORKSHEET FOR ESTIMATING
LIQUOR/BEVERAGE AMOUNTS (continued)

Item	Number of Guests	× Number of Drinks	= Total Drinks	÷ 20 Drinks/Qt 18 Drinks/Fifth	= Total Quarts/ Fifths to Buy
Grenadine					
Ginger Ale				÷ 24 =	__ Number of Cases
Lemon Lime Soda				÷ 24 =	__ Number of Cases
Seltzer				÷ 24 =	__ Number of Cases
Cola				÷ 24 =	__ Number of Cases
Root Beer				÷ 24 =	__ Number of Cases
Diet Soda				÷ 24 =	__ Number of Cases
Tomato Juice					
Orange Juice					
Grapefruit Juice					
Cranberry Juice					
Sparkling Apple Juice					
Sparkling Grape Juice					
Mineral Water				÷ 24 =	__ Number of Cases

BAR/LIQUOR CHECKLIST

Liquor Store:	Manager:

Address:

Unopened Bottle Return Policy:

Date Ordered:	Deposit Due/Date:
Total Cost:	Balance Due/Date:

Pickup Liquor Date/Time:

Person Responsible for Delivering Liquor:

Location to Deliver Liquor:

Does Store Manager Have the List of Items to Be Chilled?

Person Responsible for Returning Unopened Bottles to the Store:

Person Responsible for Storing Leftover Liquor/Accessories:

Location to Store Liquor/Accessories:

ITEM	QUANTITY	COST EACH	EXTENDED COSTS	CHILLED	RETURNS	ACTUAL COSTS
Vodka						
Gin						
Light Rum						
Dark Rum						
Scotch						
Bourbon						
Whiskey						
Dry Vermouth						
Sweet Vermouth						
Dry Sherry						
Sweet Sherry						
Tequila						
White Wine						
Red Wine						
Rose						
Brandy						
Liqueur						
Champagne						
Beer						

BAR/LIQUOR CHECKLIST (continued)

ITEM	QUANTITY	COST EACH	EXTENDED COSTS	CHILLED	RETURNS	ACTUAL COSTS
Club Soda						
Seltzer						
Tonic Water						
Triple Sec						
Lime Juice						
Grenadine						
Ginger Ale						
Lemon Lime Soda						
Cola						
Root Beer						
Diet Soda						
Tomato Juice						
Orange Juice						
Grapefruit Juice						
Cranberry Juice						
Sparkling Apple Cider						
Sparkling Grape Juice						
Mineral Water						
Limes						
Lemon and Lemon Peels						
Maraschino Cherries						
Cocktail Olives						
Sliced Fruit						
Angostura Bitters						
Superfine Sugar						
Salt						
Ice						
TOTAL						

CATERING EQUIPMENT

If your reception will be held in a restaurant or hotel, the equipment is usually included in your per person rate. Most caterers also include equipment in the per person rates. This is a convenient service and makes your planning much easier. Discuss all the details about equipment with your caterer, including napkin and tablecloth colors, table sizes and shapes, and large equipment like chafing dishes and fountains. Ask to see their equipment. Make sure that serving dishes and displays are clean and polished. The linen should be clean, pressed, and in good shape (not faded or marred with holes or tears). Use the helpful Caterer's Equipment Checklist on pages 126–129.

Avoid using paper plates, plastic drinking glasses, and plastic utensils for a self-catered reception. Renting dishes, glasses, and silverware is inexpensive enough and the food presentation is much more appealing.

PARTY RENTAL SHOPS

Party rental shops carry everything from fine glasses and silver-plated utensils to tents. Some carry linen tablecloths and napkins and provide lace on special request. Call around to see what services are available to you. Many offer brochures listing the supplies they carry as well as their rental policies.

Order in advance to assure getting the best selection and all your supplies from one rental store. You don't want to be running around town mixing and matching supplies because your order can't be filled in one shop.

When you place your order, be prepared to leave a deposit of 10 to 50 percent of the total cost. Ask about the policies on cancellation of orders, late returns, and broken or missing items. Double-check the order for quantity, sizes, pickup or delivery date and time, and any other stipulations you have requested. Your order will be packed in heavy-duty cartons when it arrives and it will need to be repacked into the cartons after the reception. Read through the contract and make sure you understand the terms.

CATERER'S EQUIPMENT CHECKLIST

Party Rental Store: Manager:

Address:

Phone: Hours:

Delivery Date/Time: Pickup Date/Time:

Cancellation Policy: Broken/Damaged Goods Policy:

Total Rental Costs: Deposit Due/Date:

Balance Due/Date:

ITEM	QTY	DESCRIPTION	COST EACH	EXTENDED COST	PERSON PICK UP/ RETURN
TABLES: Round (Size)					
Long (Size)					
Custom:					
CHAIRS					
LINEN: Round Tables					
Long Tables					
Custom:					
Napkins					
Serving Napkins					
Kitchen Towels					
Aprons					
Other:					
DINNERWARE: Dinner Plates					
Salad Plates					
Bread Plates					
Soup Bowls					
Luncheon Plates					
Cake Plates					
Coffee Cups/Saucers					
Demitasse Cups/Saucers					
Other:					

CATERER'S EQUIPMENT CHECKLIST (continued)

ITEM	Q'TY	DESCRIPTION	COST EACH	EXTENDED COST	PERSON PICK UP/ RETURN
SILVERWARE:					
Dinner Forks					
Salad Forks					
Dinner Knives					
Steak Knives					
Butter Knives					
Teaspoons					
Soup Spoons					
Dessert Spoons/Forks					
Demitasse Spoons					
Serving Forks/Spoons					
Cake Knife					
Cake Server					
Other:					
GLASSWARE:					
Wine, 10-1/2 oz.					
Wine, 8 oz.					
Goblet					
Champagne, Fluted					
Champagne, Saucer					
Highball					
Double Rocks					
Snifter					
Water					
Juice					
Punch Cup					
Other:					
TRAYS:					
Round, 12"					
Round, 14"					
Round, 16"					

ITEM	QTY	DESCRIPTION	COST EACH	EXTENDED COST	PERSON PICK UP/ RETURN
Meat Platters					
Oval, 13" × 21"					
Oval, 15" × 24"					
Oblong, 10" × 17"					
Oblong, 14" × 22"					
Oblong, 17" × 23"					
Bread Baskets					
Condiments Trays					
Other:					
KITCHEN:					
Chafing Dish, 2 Qt					
Chafing Dish, 4 Qt					
Chafing Dish, 8 Qt					
Hot Plates					
Microwave					
Barbeque Grill					
Lighter Fluid or Gas					
Sterno					
Coolers					
Ice Chest					
Waiters' Stands/Trays					
Trash Cans/Liners					
Other:					
MISCELLANEOUS:					
Coffee Maker, 35 Cups					
Coffee Maker, 50 Cups					
Coffee Maker, 100 Cups					
Insulated Coffee Pitchers					
Silver Coffee and Tea Service Set					
Creamer/Sugar					

ITEM	QTY	DESCRIPTION	COST EACH	EXTENDED COST	PERSON PICK UP/ RETURN
Punch Bowl, 3 Gallons					
Punch Fountain, 7 Gallons					
Salt/Pepper Sets					
Table Candles					
Table No. Stands					
Ashtrays					
Coat Racks					
Hangers/Cards					
Other:					
BAR: Corkscrews					
Bottle/Can Openers					
Strainers					
Cocktail Shakers					
Electric Blenders					
Ice Buckets					
Ice Tubs					
Knives					
Spoons					
Serving Trays					
Water Pitcher					
Specialty Drink Pitcher					
Condiments Trays					
Stirring Sticks					
Cocktail Napkins					
Cocktail Recipe Book					
Floor Protector, Plastic/Carpet					
TOTAL EQUIPMENT COST					

Wedding Cake

BRIDE'S CAKE

The bride's cake is a traditional white, tiered wedding cake. The wedding cake is symbolically very important at a wedding reception. This will be the first food that you share together as husband and wife. The wedding cake usually has its own table decorated with flowers and lace. Before the cake ceremony, you both stand in front of the cake for toasts and pictures.

The number of tiers depends on the size of your guest list. Although the icing is usually white, the inside of the cake doesn't have to be the typical white cake. You can have mocha, chocolate with almonds, carrot cake with a cream cheese frosting, amaretto nut—be creative! European wedding cakes are also popular. They resemble a torte: five to six thin layers of cake separated by filling and soaked in liquor. European cakes are richer and lighter than the traditional white cake. For a variety, have different flavored cakes for each tier so you can offer a selection to your guests.

The icing can be as elaborate or as simple as you wish. It can be decorated with colors to match your bridal party. Some bakers add fresh flowers to add natural colors and beauty.

GROOM'S CAKE

The groom's cake, sometimes known as the bride and groom's cake, is a smaller cake of chocolate or spice, something different from the bride's white, tiered cake. It sits next to the bride's cake on the cake table at the reception. The groom's cake is a Southern tradition. Almost all weddings in the South feature the groom's cake.

The groom's cake is cut and placed into tiny boxes and given to your guests to take home. You can also seal the groom's cake in a tin with brandy, freeze it, and eat it for your anniversary.

CAKE-CUTTING CEREMONY

The bride's cake is used for the cake-cutting ceremony. Guests gather around and watch as you both cut the first piece of cake together. The groom puts his hand over yours as you cut the bottom layer of the cake. You feed a small piece of cake to the groom and the groom feeds you. Then you serve cake to the groom's parents and the groom serves your parents. The servers cut the rest of the cake and serve the guests.

TIPS ON SELECTING A BAKERY

Ask friends and family for recommendations if you don't know a good bakery. Make sure the bakery is reliable. Check the Better Business Bureau and Consumer Affairs in your area to see if there are any claims against the bakery. The bakery should be experienced in handling wedding cakes. Ask about delivery and cancellation policies.

Take photos or magazine clippings of the cake design you like. Most bakeries have a portfolio you can look through for ideas. Once you have selected the cake, fillings, decorations, number of tiers, and cake top, ask for a copy of the order. Make sure that all the details are included. Ask to sample the cake and fillings that you choose.

Discuss the cake setup time and location with the bakery. Get the name and home phone number of the person responsible for delivering and setting up the cake. The cake stands are usually included in the price of the cake, but some bakeries only rent them to you. If you keep them, there is an additional charge. Inquire about the bakery's policies. Ask how accidents are handled, such as the delivery person dropping the cake. Are backup cakes available? Use the Wedding Cake worksheet on page 132 to keep track of all the details.

CHAPTER 8

WEDDING CAKE

Bakery: _____

Address: _____ Phone: _____

Manager: _____ Hours: _____

Cake Style

Type of Cake: _____

Type of Filling: _____

Type of Icing: _____

Flavor of Icing: _____

Date to Taste Samples: _____

Cake Accessories

Cake Top: _____

Cake Flowers: _____

Cake Decorations: _____

Cake Stands: _____

Cake Boxes: _____

Cake Knife: _____

Description of Cake

_____

_____

_____

Part to Save for Bride and Groom: _____

_____

Person in Charge of Saving and Freezing the
Cake: _____

Person Responsible for Storing the Cake Top,
Cake Knife, and Server: _____

Details: _____

_____

Return Cake Stand to Bakery: _____

Cake Costs

Total Cake Costs: _____

Delivery Charge: _____

Cake Stand Rental Cost: _____

Cake Knife and Server Rental Cost: _____

Deposit Due/Date: _____

Balance Due/Date: _____

Sketch

Setup Time

Location: _____

How to Decorate Cake Table: _____

How to Cut Cake

CUTTING THE CAKE

Use a sharp, thin knife or a serrated knife. If the cake sticks to the knife, wipe the blade with a cool, wet towel after each slice. Use a cake server to place the cake on each plate. The cuts differ depending on how many pieces you want to serve and the shape of the cake.

CAKE KNIFE AND CAKE SERVER

The cake knife and the cake server are usually displayed on the cake table, along with the toasting goblets. They can be silver, silver-plated, stainless steel, or a variety of materials. The bakery or the florist usually dresses them up with ribbons and flowers. If you would like to keep the cake knife and server as a memento, you should have them engraved with your names and the date of your wedding.

Have them engraved at least two months ahead of time to allow for errors to be corrected. If a cake knife or server is not important to you, the bakery, the caterer, or the party rental store should be able to supply you with a cake knife for your wedding day.

CAKE TOPS

For an elegant cake top, blown glass is beautiful. The traditional cake top has a miniature bride and groom standing at the altar. Some use wedding symbols like bells, doves, or rings. You can even make your own cake top. Craft stores have all the supplies and accessories you need to put together the perfect cake top for your wedding.

ON-LINE SERVICES

The Internet can provide you with several special options for wedding cakes. First you will have to locate the web pages of companies in your area. Once you have found companies near you, you can view their web pages and see pictures and descriptions of particular wedding cakes they offer. Many companies will let you custom order your cake if you have special instructions or tastes. You could have a vegan wedding cake if you so desired. On-line services will let you choose your flavors and designs in advance before negotiating with the companies over costs and delivery.

Photographer and Videographer

SELECTING A PHOTOGRAPHER

Your wedding celebration will be over in hours and all you will have to remember this joyous occasion by, other than your memories and stories told by friends, are your wedding photographs. These photographs taken at your wedding will be looked at for a lifetime and will become an heirloom for future generations. Select a photographer who specializes in weddings and comes recommended by people you trust. The best photographers have their schedules booked as far as a year in advance, so start interviewing as soon as you can.

INTERVIEW

After you have asked friends and family about photographers they might recommend, start calling the photographers to inquire about their services. Ask to speak to the photographer so you could get a feel for his or her personality over the phone. Check to see if they are available on the date and time of your wedding. Set up appointments with at least two photographers so you can compare their portfolios and policies.

Visit their studios so you can see their daily operations. Look through their portfolios and wall portraits. If you want romantic photographs of you and your

groom in a park setting with special effects and you don't see any similar sample photographs displayed, ask the photographer if he has done anything like that before. It would be helpful if you brought in photographs in the style you're looking for. Discuss the types of pictures and special effects or features you'd like. If you don't feel completely comfortable and confident in the photographer you are interviewing, go on to your next appointment.

POLICIES

Most wedding photographers have a brochure describing their services, policies, packages and prices. Review the policies carefully and question anything that isn't stated on the brochures or contracts. Ask about their cancellation policy. Will you get your deposit back? Will the photographer whom you are interviewing be the photographer at your wedding? Find out how many photographers and assistants there will be at your wedding. What happens if he or she gets sick? What will the staff be wearing? You wouldn't want them running around in shorts and tank tops! Is their staff professionally trained to handle large groups of people for portraits? Do they know what to expect at weddings and where to be so they don't miss any important shots? See the Photographer Possibilities Checklist on pages 136–137.

COSTS

Wedding photography can be very expensive. Find out all costs ahead of time so you're not surprised after the wedding when you have no recourse. Don't be fooled by the bridal packages photographers offer for $200.00. That may include the photograph for the ceremony and reception and a bridal album of 10–20 photographs but it doesn't include all the extra photographs you'll want to purchase for the parents, bridal party, relatives, etc. The photographer usually retains ownership of the negatives so you are at his or her mercy when it comes time to order.

Some photographers offer complete bridal packages which include albums for the parents and all the attendants. Get a price list for the additional pictures you may want to order. Ask about quantity discounts. If you order five to ten of the same family portraits, will you receive a discount? Who keeps the proofs? Can you purchase the negatives? Find out what your photographer's position is on all of your questions *before* you sign the contract.

PHOTOGRAPHER POSSIBILITIES CHECKLIST

QUESTIONS	POSSIBILITY 1	POSSIBILITY 2	POSSIBILITY 3
Photographer			
Address			
Contact Person			
Office Phone			
Home Phone			
Interview Date/Time			
Photographer's Style			
Special Effects Offered			

Wedding Package Includes:
    Sessions:
    Length of Time:
    Bride's Album:
       Total Number of
       Photographs and Sizes:
Number of Parents' Albums:
    Total Number of
    Photographs and
    Sizes for Each:
Complementary:
Cost of Package:			

Individual Portraits:
    Bridal Portrait:
    Engagement Portrait:
    Newspaper Portrait:			

Extra Photo Costs:
    16" × 20" :
    11" × 14" :
    8" × 10" :
    5" × 7" :
    4" × 5" :
    Wallets:
    Proofs:
    Negatives:
    Other:
    Quantity Discounts:			

QUESTIONS	POSSIBILITY 1	POSSIBILITY 2	POSSIBILITY 3
Cancellation Policy			
Who Will Be the Photographer			
How Many Photographers and Assistants			
Staff Attire			
Staff Knowledge of Weddings			

PHOTOGRAPHER POSSIBILITIES CHECKLIST (continued)

SCHEDULING PHOTO SESSIONS

Decide which photo sessions you would like to have as part of your photo package and set up your schedule with the photographer. Use the Photo Session Schedule on page 139. Make a copy of this schedule and give it to the photographer. You may not have all the time schedules at this time. Don't worry—you can call the photographer with updated details once you prepare a list of guests to be included in the wedding day photos.

BRIDAL PORTRAIT

The bridal portrait can be a photograph with you alone or you with the groom. This will be your first photo in your gown, and it is the photo that will go in the newspapers for the announcement. It is usually taken weeks in advance at the photographer's studio. Ask if your bridal salon will allow you to take your bridal portrait in the salon's dressing room; this will eliminate the problem of transporting your gown and veil all over town.

The bridal portrait usually takes about an hour. The photographer shoots about ten to twenty poses. You'll choose your bridal portrait and newspaper announcement photograph from the proofs.

Take all accessories needed for the bridal portrait. You want the portrait to look as if it had been taken on your wedding day.

If you can part with your glasses, take them off for the portrait photographs. Glasses cover your face and reflect light that can ruin your portraits. If you feel naked without your glasses, you might want to remove the lenses for the photograph so your eyes will be photographed more clearly.

WEDDING DAY PORTRAITS

BEFORE OR AFTER?

Photographers prefer taking all formal portraits before the wedding ceremony when the bridal party is fresh. The old superstition that the groom shouldn't see the bride until she walks down the aisle has been dismissed in favor of getting all posed portraits taken before the festivities so the bridal party can enjoy the celebration with the guests. Trying to get the posed portraits taken between the ceremony and reception takes a long time, often leaving the guests unattended for an hour or more. Discuss the time for your posed photographs with your photographer.

PHOTO SESSION SCHEDULE

Formal Bridal Portrait

Date/Time: _____

Location: _____

Photograph for the Newspaper: _____

Photograph to Include: _____

_____

_____

Park Setting

Date/Time: _____

Location: _____

Photograph to Include: _____

_____

_____

Before the Ceremony

Date/Time: _____

Location: _____

Photograph to Include: _____

_____

_____

During the Ceremony

Date/Time: _____

Location: _____

Photograph to Include: _____

_____

_____

After the Ceremony

Date/Time: _____

Location: _____

Photograph to Include: _____

_____

_____

Before the Reception

Date/Time: _____

Location: _____

Photograph to Include: _____

_____

_____

During the Reception

Date/Time: _____

Location: _____

Photograph to Include: _____

_____

_____

Other Sessions

Date/Time: _____

Location: _____

Photograph to Include: _____

_____

_____

INFORM THOSE TO BE INCLUDED IN FAMILY PORTRAITS

Tell the guests who are to be included in family portraits all the pertinent information about time and location so you won't be delayed waiting for them to arrive. Let the photographer know whom to call up for each photograph. This can speed up the process. If the photographer knows in advance the guests' names and relationship to the bride and groom, the photo session will be more personal and run more efficiently.

DIVORCED PARENTS: WHO SHOULD BE IN FAMILY PORTRAITS?

Family portraits with the bride and groom make up a good percentage of the formal photographs. If you have parents or in-laws who are divorced, separated, or living with a friend, deciding who stands in family portraits can be a sensitive issue. Abigail Van Buren, in *Dear Abby on Planning Your Wedding*, says that the bride and groom should make the final decision and their wishes should be respected by the parents and stepparents. She says that the bridal couple should carefully consider all family members and their feelings. If you want a picture with your natural parents together, be diplomatic and also have portraits taken of your parents with their new families.

Family portraits with divorced parents are controversial. If the bride or groom wants a photograph of his or her natural parents and siblings together for one special moment, parents and stepparents should oblige.

Others argue that a family photograph should depict the present picture, not the past. They believe that the parents should stand next to their new spouses and families. Consider the feelings of those involved, and then make the decision that makes you feel most comfortable and happy. These portraits will be for you and your future family to enjoy.

FIANCÉS: SHOULD THEY BE INCLUDED IN FAMILY PORTRAITS?

Should fiancés be included in family portraits? This is another sensitive issue that may be best answered by a story. One bride wanted her brother and his fiancé to stand in her family portrait. They were going to be married the following year so

she felt that it was just a technicality. Their engagement was called off six months later and her brother married another woman. Now this bride has a family portrait with a woman who isn't part of the family and never legally was.

If you are wary of including fiancés in your wedding portrait but receive pressure from family members to have them included, why not take two pictures? Take one with your family the way you'd prefer and then take another with the fiancé to keep peace in the family.

CEREMONY AND RECEPTION PHOTOGRAPHS

Ask the clergymember if flash photography is allowed at the ceremony site and reception facility. Some churches and museums don't allow flashbulbs or cameras. Even if the facility does allow flashbulbs, ask your photographer if he'll permit guests to take pictures with a flashbulb when he shoots the posed photos. If your guests are using their flashbulbs at the same time the photographer takes a picture, it changes the light in the room and may ruin his pictures.

Most photographers are familiar with the traditional posed photographs (you getting ready with your mother, cutting the cake, and so forth). The Photographer's Checklist of Wedding Candids on page 142 lists all of the traditional poses with space available for you to add any special requests. If you would like a picture of you with your college roommates, just add that to your list so the photographer is sure to get the shot. Review the checklist and mark off all poses you want taken.

During the reception while the band takes a break, you might want to call up different groups of people to take a group picture on the dance floor. If you have high school friends, fellow business associates, or club members at your wedding, it makes a nice memento to have a posed picture of those special groups.

While the guests are seated and enjoying their meal, walk around with the groom to each table for a photograph. This gives you the opportunity to greet guests and thank them for attending, along with getting pictures of all of the guests. If you can't visit each table before more festivities take place, ask the photographer to continue to shoot each table. You'll appreciate seeing all of your guests in photographs after the wedding. Traditional wedding photographs include primarily pictures of the bride and groom alone. It's nice to remember who was there and how they looked that day.

PHOTOGRAPHER'S CHECKLIST OF WEDDING CANDIDS

Inform appropriate people of photo session dates and times. Give a copy of this page to your photographer.

Before the Ceremony:
_____ Bride in dress
_____ Bride with mother
_____ Bride with father
_____ Bride with both parents
_____ Bride with honor attendant
_____ Bride with maids
_____ Bride with grandparents
_____ Everyone getting flowers

At the Ceremony:
_____ Guests outside church
_____ Bride and father getting out of car
_____ Bride and father going into church
_____ Ushers escorting guests
_____ Groom's parents being seated
_____ Soloist and organist
_____ Groom and ushers at altar
_____ Giving-away ceremony
_____ Bride/groom exchanging vows
_____ Ring ceremony
_____ Bridesmaids coming down aisle

Posed Photos Before Reception (may be taken before ceremony):
_____ Bridesmaids looking at rings
_____ Bride's and groom's hands
_____ Bride and groom together
_____ Groom with parents
_____ Bride with parents
_____ Bride and groom with honor attendants
_____ Bride and groom with children

At the Reception:
_____ Bride and groom arriving
_____ Bride and groom getting out of car
_____ Bride and groom going into reception
_____ The receiving line
_____ Bride/groom in receiving line
_____ Bride's mother in receiving line
_____ Groom's parents in receiving line
_____ Buffet table
_____ Friends serving punch
_____ Bride/groom at bride's table
_____ Parent's table
_____ Bride and groom dancing
_____ Bride dancing with father
_____ Groom dancing with mother
_____ The musicians
_____ Bride and groom talking with guests
_____ Signing the guest book
_____ Bride and groom at each guest table

_____ Bride at gift table
_____ Bride leaving house
_____ Bride and father getting in car
_____ Groom alone
_____ Groom with best man
_____ Ushers getting boutonnieres
_____ Bride touching up make-up
_____ _____

_____ Maid or matron of honor
_____ Flower girl and ring bearer
_____ Bride and father
_____ Groom meeting bride
_____ The kiss
_____ Bride and groom in recessional
_____ Bride and groom among guests
_____ Bride and groom in back seat of car
_____ Bride, groom, and bride's family
_____ Bride, groom, and groom's family
_____ _____

_____ Bride with her attendants
_____ Groom with his attendants
_____ Bride, groom, and wedding party
_____ Bride, groom, and family
_____ Bride, groom, and clergy
_____ _____
_____ _____

_____ Bride/groom feeding cake
_____ Bride/groom toasting
_____ Throwing/catching bouquet
_____ Groom taking off garter
_____ Throwing/catching garter
_____ Wedding party decorating car
_____ Bride and groom in going-away clothes
_____ Bride/groom saying good-bye to parents
_____ Bride/groom ready to leave
_____ Guests throwing rice
_____ Bridegroom getting into car
_____ Guests waving goodbye
_____ Rear of car speeding off
_____ Other reception fun
_____ Cake table
_____ Bride and groom cutting cake
_____ _____
_____ _____

AMATEUR PHOTOGRAPHERS

Your professional photographer will be busy taking all of the posed, traditional pictures for your album and may miss some of the great spontaneous shots. If friends and family offer to take candid pictures, encourage them to do so. You may want to provide the rolls of film to use so they just give you the rolls for developing. Then if you get pictures that you want duplicates of, you won't have to ask for the negatives—you'll already have them.

Avoid using friends who are amateur photographers to take your wedding photographs. You will probably be disappointed with the results. Even if you are on a tight budget, have a professional photographer take the portraits for your album. Then rely on your amateur photographers to shoot all of the candids. That will take the pressure off your amateur photographer guest so he or she can also enjoy the celebration.

GUEST PHOTOGRAPHERS

One increasingly popular idea for capturing candid shots is to place a disposable camera at each of the tables at the reception for the guests to use throughout the celebration. The cameras can then be placed in a collection box at the end of the night and developed later. You will then have any number of wonderful candid photographs to keep for yourself or send to your guests.

ORDERING PHOTOGRAPHS

Ask the photographer for the date by which the proofs will be ready. Proofs are regular-sized pictures taken from the negatives. They aren't touched up so you may see small blemishes that can be removed on the final portraits. The proofs are numbered on the back for ordering.

Make a list of guests who will receive gifts of photographs (parents, attendants, family). Write the proof number, description, and size for each photograph you order for each person. If guests want to order photographs themselves, either take their order or have them order directly from the photographer.

ON-LINE SERVICES

Most major photographers now have web pages where you can browse through the services they offer and what special wedding packages they have available. Most photographers will also place portions of their portfolios on-line for you to view their work without having to come into their offices beforehand. The Internet is an excellent way to find possible photographers for your wedding. You will still want to contact photographers personally before making any commitments in order to find out more specific information and details about their services.

ON-LINE WEDDINGS

With the advent of recent technology it is even possible for you to broadcast your wedding on-line. Special cameras can be linked to computers to provide live video of your wedding to distant friends and family.

Some people have started to create their own web pages specifically for their weddings. There are even companies that will set up these web pages for you. On these web pages you can place information about you and the groom, place pictures of all your prewedding and postwedding events, and even write personal messages to your close friends and family. Another popular feature of these wedding pages is the on-line guestbook where the people who visit your wedding page can leave you personal messages if they will not be able to attend the actual wedding or even if they just want to send you words of support before joining you on your big day.

SELECTING A VIDEOGRAPHER

Videotaping offers a new way of preserving your wedding memories. Years from now you can look at the videotape, relive your exchange of vows, and watch everyone dancing at your reception. Videotaping captures the essence of the whole wedding celebration. You'll cry as you remember the toast the best man gave, and laugh at Uncle Frank as he dances the Irish jig with greatgrandmother Myrtle.

Only twenty years ago, having a videotape of your wedding was only for the rich and famous. With the cost of video cameras coming down over the years, videotaping your wedding has become an affordable option for many. If your budget allows, hire a professional videographer. A videographer shoots hours of tape and edits the production so you can receive a high-quality videotape.

Your videographer, like your photographer, will be shooting once-in-a-lifetime events. Base your selection on his or her experience, reliability, amount of raw footage to be taped, and the amount of time you can allow for editing. Make sure he or she has done at least fifty weddings. The videographer's job is a difficult one: he or she is producing a film live. There are no retakes at a wedding. The art of videotaping is complex; adding the chaos and emotions of the wedding ceremony and reception makes it even more difficult.

INTERVIEW

Ask for recommendations from friends and family you trust. Set up an interview with the videographer at his studio. Inquire about the number of cameras, videographers, and assistants the videographer plans to have for a wedding of your size. Ask to see videos of weddings he or she has done. Take the videos home and review them. This will give you insight as to the quality of the production—transitions, music, blends, voice-overs, etc.

Ask what quality and size tape the videographer uses. Most videographers work with Super VHS or digital camcorders. However, unless you have SVHS or digital equipment to view the production, it will have to be recorded on standard VHS tape at a lower resolution. Ask how many hours of raw footage will be shot, how many hours will be spent editing the tape, and how long the final tape will be when it is completed. Can the videographer shoot in low light for a candlelight ceremony and how will the videographer encourage guests to participate at the reception?

Things to keep in mind when interviewing videographers include: how simple or complex you want the project to be from *your* perspective, what will the venue permit, and how much you want to spend. Ask about package deals and editing costs. Make sure that you cover all aspects of the production so you don't get surprised by hidden costs you didn't know about. Use the Videographer Possibilities Checklist on pages 147–148 to help make your choice easier.

POLICIES

Find out what the videographer will guarantee (raw footage and editing). Ask if you can have the raw footage. You may find some funny bloopers that wouldn't be included in your professional videotape. Review the policy for cancellation and guarantee on the quality of the work.

Cost

Review the costs with the videographer to be sure you understand what is covered. Inquire about the costs of additional tapes and any extra services you may require, such as photographs of your parents' wedding portraits or pre-wedding activities.

EVENTS TO VIDEOTAPE

The videographer usually shoots the same classic wedding events that the professional photographer takes. Use the Events to Videotape Worksheet on page 149 to decide which events you would like included and add any special requests now. Once you've decided what you want, make a copy of the worksheet and give it to the videographer.

Extras

1. Give the videographer pictures of you and the groom when you were growing up from birth to when you first met. The videographer can put the photographs to music or you can give a brief history for a narration. The pictures are fun to look at and it is a unique way to start the wedding video.
2. Have the video start off with pictures of both of your parents' wedding photographs.
3. Include pre-wedding parties in the wedding video: bridal showers, bachelor parties, and rehearsals.

AMATEUR VIDEOGRAPHERS

If the professional videographer's services are out of your budget, ask a friend or relative with a video camera if he or she would tape certain parts of your wedding. It's best to get several volunteers to cover different parts of the wedding so they can still enjoy the wedding themselves. This offers variety and a little insurance in case one of your volunteers forgets the camcorder, runs out of tape, or if the camera's batteries go dead.

When you receive the videotapes from friends you can edit them yourself or have a service put the tapes together for you. Your wedding video will be like a live show hosted or narrated by your friends and family.

VIDEOGRAPHER POSSIBILITIES CHECKLIST

QUESTIONS	POSSIBILITY 1	POSSIBILITY 2	POSSIBILITY 3
Videographer			
Address			
Contact Person			
Office Phone			
Home Phone			
Interview Date/Time			
Videographer's Style			
Special Effects Offered			
Who Will Videotape			
Number of Videographers			
Number of Assistants			
Staff Attire			
Number of Weddings Done			
Videotaping Session Included: At Home: Before Ceremony: Ceremony: Receiving Line: Reception: Driving Away:			
Hours of Raw Footage			
Hours of Editing			
Type of Tape Used			
Ability to Tape in Low Light			
Who Keeps Raw Footage			
Quality of Sample Wedding Videos			
Personality of Videographer			

VIDEOGRAPHER POSSIBILITIES CHECKLIST (continued)

QUESTIONS	POSSIBILITY 1	POSSIBILITY 2	POSSIBILITY 3
Videographer Costs			
Cost of Extra Tapes			
Other Costs			
Sales Tax			
Total Due/Date			

EVENTS TO VIDEOTAPE WORKSHEET

Engagement Party
Date: _____ Time: _____
Location: _____
Special Requests: _____
_____
_____

Bride Getting Dressed at Home
Date: _____ Time: _____
Location: _____
Special Requests: _____
_____

Ceremony
Date: _____ Time: _____
Location: _____
Guests Arriving: _____
Ceremony: _____
_____

Guests Leaving: _____
Special Requests: _____
_____
_____
_____

Reception
Date: _____ Time: _____
Location: _____
Guests Arriving: _____
Announcing Newlyweds and Bridal Party: _____
_____
Toasts: _____
_____
First Dance: _____
Cake-Cutting Ceremony: _____
Bouquet and Garter Ceremonies: _____
Guests Dancing: _____
Guests at the Dining Table: _____
Bride and Groom Bidding Farewell and Thanks to Parents: _____
_____
Bride and Groom Getaway: _____
Special Requests: _____
_____
_____
_____

10

Wedding Music

The music at the ceremony and the reception sets the atmosphere for your wedding. The ceremony music is the grand, majestic music that accompanies the processional and recessional of the bride and groom and the wedding party. The reception music consists of the background music during the banquet and the entertaining music for dancing. Classical music will give a peaceful, serene ambiance while rock and roll will give an upbeat, dancing mood. There are versatile musicians who can play at both the ceremony and reception, or you may opt for using prerecorded music. Otherwise, you may need to have two different sets of musicians for the ceremony and reception.

CEREMONY MUSIC

The organist and soloist are traditionally the musicians at the ceremony. A guitar, harpsichord, or saxophone can add a new flair to your ceremony if you prefer a different sound. Check with the facilities manager to see what is allowed. Some churches do not permit musical instruments, allowing only a soloist. Give a copy of the Ceremony Music Worksheet on page 153 to the musician. If you're on a tight budget, play prerecorded music.

Prelude: The prelude takes place during the last half hour before the processional. You set the tone of the wedding ceremony by the music you select. Guests are seated at this time and anxiously await the processional.

Processional: The music for the processional should be different from the prelude music to indicate that the prelude is over and the processional is about to begin. It is usually upbeat but formal, with an even beat, making it easy for the bridal party to walk to it. The music changes again after all the attendants are in place at the altar. This signifies that you are about to make your entrance and signals the guests to rise.

Ceremony: Most ceremonies are conducted without music. This allows the voices to be heard with ease by all. Some musicians may play soft background music to provide atmosphere. You might ask the musician to practice during the rehearsal to see if the music is soft enough. Check with the clergymember before making decisions on music during the ceremony.

Recessional: The recessional music indicates that the ceremony is over and that you and the groom are now husband and wife. This music is usually triumphant with a faster tempo. You walk down the aisle, arm in arm, followed by the attendants. The recessional ends after the last attendant walks down the aisle.

Postlude: The postlude is the background music that is played while the guests leave from the ceremony site. The guests usually exit row by row starting with the first row.

Selecting the Musicians

Once you've decided on the type of music to be played for the ceremony, start interviewing musicians. If you know exactly what you want played or sung throughout the ceremony, your questions will be easy to formulate and you'll know when you have found the right person or persons. If you've decided on a general mood but haven't selected the pieces or songs yet, ask the musician for recommendations. Borrow a wedding cassette tape or videotape of the musician's performances. Ask if you can see an upcoming appearance. Select a soloist with experience—friends or family can make the ceremony more personal but they may choke at the last minute.

Make sure the musician is available on the date of your wedding. Discuss the style, number, and length of sets and breaks, and any special requests you may have. Use the Ceremony Musician Possibilities Checklist on page 154 to remind you of questions you may want to ask.

Prerecorded Ceremony Music

The performance quality of prerecorded music is excellent. When putting together your music for all phases of the ceremony, use a good quality tape (ninety minutes

on both sides). Cheaper quality tape tends to be thinner and breaks easily. Or use a CD recorder to make a custom wedding CD.

Check the sound system ahead of time to make sure there is a good balance and the acoustics are satisfactory. You may want to use auxiliary speakers and experiment with their placement for the best effect.

RECEPTION MUSIC

Music sets the tone for the reception. Base selections on your personal preferences, keeping in mind the tastes of the guests you've invited. You may want to find a versatile band that can play a waltz, jazz, rock and roll, and popular music for all of your guests' desires. If you have favorite ethnic dances you'd like your guests to participate in, give the music to the band ahead of time so they can become familiar with it. Disc jockeys play the music of the original artists and can play a wide selection of music. If you're having a gourmet feast with fine wines, and you prefer a serene atmosphere of good conversations, a classical guitarist or a string quartet would be more appropriate than a rock-and-roll band.

SELECTING RECEPTION MUSICIANS AND DISC JOCKEYS

Set up interviews with the musicians or disc jockeys to see the organization of their group and where they practice. Ask to see them perform live if they have a wedding coming up or view a videotape of a wedding they've done. The lead singer's or the disc jockey's stage personality is crucial in getting guests to participate in ethnic dances, bouquet and garter tossing, and all the events at the reception. A polished speaker can get the guests involved and make the reception more enjoyable.

Use the Reception Musician/Disc Jockey Possibilities Checklist on page 155 to help get all the pertinent information during the interview. Find out what restrictions the reception facility may have on music. Ask the band to go to the reception site to check acoustics and equipment available to make sure that the facility has ample room to house them. Once you have selected the musicians or disc jockey, fill in the Reception Music Worksheet on pages 156–157. List what you want played during every event of the reception. Decide whether you would like the band or the best man to announce all the events taking place during the reception: first dance, toast, cake-cutting, bouquet and garter toss, and newlywed getaway. Discuss the background music, if any, during these events. When the band takes a break, who puts on the background prerecorded music? Give the disc jockey or musicians a copy of this worksheet so they will be prepared.

CEREMONY MUSIC WORKSHEET

Wedding Site:

Address:

Phone:

Date:

Set-up Time:

INSTRUMENTALIST	PHONE NUMBER
SOLOIST	PHONE NUMBER

PRELUDE

SONG/PIECE	MUSICIAN

PROCESSIONAL

SONG/PIECE	MUSICIAN

CEREMONY

SONG/PIECE	MUSICIAN

RECESSIONAL

SONG/PIECE	MUSICIAN

POSTLUDE

SONG/PIECE	MUSICIAN

Give copies to musicians

CEREMONY MUSICIAN POSSIBILITIES CHECKLIST

QUESTIONS	POSSIBILITY 1	POSSIBILITY 2	POSSIBILITY 3
Name			
Address			
Office Phone			
Home Phone			
Manager			
Interview Date/Time			
Instruments Used			
Fees			
Hours of Performance			
Length of Each Set			
Number of Sets			
Length of Breaks			
Number of Breaks			
Who Will Perform			
What Equipment Needed: Electrical Outlets / Microphones / Amplifiers / Music Stands / Chair/Stool			
Song List			
Musician Attire			
Cancellation Policy			
Special Requests			
Special Requests Charges			
Overtime Charges			
Musician Fees			
Deposit Due/Date			
Balance Due/Date			

RECEPTION MUSICIAN/DISC JOCKEY POSSIBILITIES CHECKLIST

QUESTIONS	POSSIBILITY 1	POSSIBILITY 2	POSSIBILITY 3
Name			
Address			
Office Phone			
Home Phone			
Interview Date/Time			
Instruments Used			
Hours of Performance			
Length of Each Set			
Number of Sets			
Length of Breaks			
Number of Breaks			
Who Will Perform			
Special Equipment Needed:			
Song List			
Overtime Charges			
Musician Attire			
Cancellation Policy			
Musician Fees			
Special Requests			
Special Requests Charges			
Deposit Due/Date			
Balance Due/Date			
Personality of Announcer			
Facility Appropriate for Musicians			

RECEPTION MUSIC WORKSHEET

Reception Site:

Address:

Phone:

Date:

Setup Time:

Hours of Music

Music to Begin: Music to End:

Number of Breaks: Length of Breaks:

Will Band Play Prerecorded Music During Breaks?

Who Will Supply the Tapes?

Is Band Invited for Meal?

Total Cost of Reception Music:

Overtime Rate:

Total Due:

Deposit Due/Date:

Balance Due/Date:

Other:

MUSIC EQUIPMENT NEEDED

ITEM	RESPONSIBILITY		
	BRIDE/GROOM'S	MUSICIAN'S	FACILITY'S
Instruments			
Microphones/Stands			
Amplifiers			
Stage			
Tape Deck			
CD Player			
Prerecorded Tapes			
Chairs/Stools			
Music Stands			
Lighting			
Electrical Outlets			

RECEPTION MUSIC SELECTIONS

	TIME	MUSIC SELECTIONS
Arrival of Newlyweds		
Announce Wedding Party		
Other:		
Receiving Line		
Banquet Background Music		
Other:		
First Dance		
Toasts		
Dancing: (Make selections or give guidelines)		
Ethnic Dances: (Give instructions to band ahead of time.)		
Cake-Cutting		
Tossing the Bouquet		
Throwing the Garter		
Newlyweds' Getaway		
Last Dance		
Other:		

WEDDING MUSIC SUGGESTIONS

Wedding music is very personal. It is difficult to list suggestions that will appeal to all types of weddings. Select music that will set the mood for the type of wedding you're planning to have. Michael Tatsui, a wedding music specialist, has made the following recommendations on page 159. If you don't recognize the music listed here, go to a music store that specializes in classical music. The sales staff is usually very knowledgeable about music and can also offer suggestions; he can play pieces that he knows and offer other ideas.

WEDDING MUSIC SELECTIONS

	Composer	Title	Performed By
Prelude	Albinoni	Adagio	
	J. S. Bach	Allegro from Brandenburg Concerto Number 4	
	Chopin	Nocturne in E flat, Op 9 No. 2	
	Tchaikovsky	Waltz (from *Sleeping Beauty* Act I)	
Processional	Wagner	Bridal March from *Lohengrin* (Here Comes the Bride)	
	Telemann	Heroic Marches	
	Charpentier	Processional to *Te Deum*	
	Beethoven	Midnight Blue	
Interlude	Vivaldi	Spring from *The Four Seasons*	
	Schubert	Ave Maria	
	Grieg	Hymn - Finlandia	
	Puccini	"Quando Men'uo" (Musetta's Waltz from *La Bohème*)	
Recessional	J.S. Bach	Prelude and Fugue in C Major	
	Beethoven	Ode to Joy	
	Vivaldi	Autumn from *The Four Seasons*	
	Tartini	Sonata in G	
First Dance		Crazy for You	Madonna
(vocals)		The Way You Look Tonight	Frank Sinatra
		In Your Eyes	Peter Gabriel
		Just a Lifetime	Edward Ka-Spel
		Unforgettable	Nat King Cole
First Dance			
(instrumental)		Theme from *Somewhere in Time*	John Barry
		Theme from *Summer of '42*	Michel Legrand
		Theme from *Romeo and Juliet* (1968)	Nino Rota

11

Wedding Flowers

Flowers, just as the music, set the tone for the ceremony and reception. Elaborate flower arrangements give an aura of fantasy and romance. Exotic flower arrangements can accent the style you've chosen for your wedding. Florists can have your flowers dyed to match the colors of the bridal party. The possibilities are endless, but if your budget isn't, there are creative ways to use your colors and create the perfect atmosphere without taking a second job.

SELECTING A FLORIST

The florist will be working on her own to create the floral atmosphere at the ceremony and reception sites. She will also use her talents to turn a bunch of cut flowers into gorgeous bouquets and centerpieces. Select a responsive florist who listens to you and offers her suggestions based on your budget and style.

Interview several florists to get a good overview of the possibilities and price ranges available to you. Ask to see a wedding site they will be doing in the near future or look through their portfolios. Use the Florist Possibilities Checklist on page 161 while interviewing florists. Enter some of your special preferences under "Special Requests" so you can get quotes from all possibilities. When comparing prices, make sure you are comparing "roses to roses"!

FLORIST POSSIBILITIES CHECKLIST

QUESTIONS	POSSIBILITY 1	POSSIBILITY 2	POSSIBILITY 3
Florist			
Address			
Phone			
Hours			
Person to Decorate Site			
Charges for Travel Time to Wedding and Reception Sites			
Types of Flowers Available (In-Season) for your Wedding			
Special Requests			
Price Sheets: (If they don't have price sheets, use this hypothetical list to get prices.) —Bride's Cascade of White Roses and Stephanotis —Usher's White Carnation —Mother's Corsage with Two Gardenias —Potted Plants			
Quantity Discounts			
Wedding Packages			
Rent Tablepiece Vases			
Silk Flowers Available			
Consulting Fees			
Cancellation Policy			
Has Florist Ever Done Your Ceremony or Reception Site Before?			
Will Florist Visit the Sites to Make Recommendations for You?			
Deposit Due/Date			
Balance Due/Date			

TIPS ON CUTTING COSTS

Seasonal Flowers: Ask which flowers will be in season on your wedding date so you can base your selections on seasonal flowers.

Potted Plants: Instead of using cut flowers, use potted plants for the altar and table centerpieces. Order flowering perennials so you can plant them in your garden or give them away as gifts after the wedding.

Greenery and Baby's Breath: Foliage interspersed with baby's breath and a few flowers can help stretch your dollar without giving up fresh flowers. The huppah (canopy) at a Jewish wedding can be covered with ivy and speckled with flowers instead of covering the entire huppah with freshly cut flowers. Using more greenery at the altar, pews, bride's table, guests' tables, and cake table adds a cool, natural beauty to the atmosphere.

Share Altar and Pew Flowers: Many churches and chapels book more than one wedding on the same day. Consider sharing the altar and pew flowers with the other brides to save expenses. Ask the manager in charge for the phone numbers and call the brides whose ceremonies are before and after your wedding. If you select a white flower arrangement for the whole ceremony site, it will most likely work well with the other brides' colors. Discuss your budget with the other brides. You can either cut your costs in half or thirds, or you can get two or three times the number of flower arrangements for the same cost.

Silk Flowers: Imitation flowers are made so well that you may have to touch them to determine if they are real. Silk flowers are the nicest and resemble real flowers the most, but they are more expensive. Use silk flowers in arrangements at the altar, pews, and in places where they are viewed from a distance.

Wholesale Flowers: Buying your flowers wholesale through the Internet or from local, specialized dealers can save you a great deal of money on all kinds of flowers. If there are specific flowers or arrangements you would like for your wedding, and you need them in large quantities, you will probably be able to save money by buying them wholesale.

Cut Your Own Flowers: Grow flowers in your garden or in pots in a greenhouse specifically for your wedding. Have a few friends with green thumbs help cut and arrange the flowers at the ceremony and reception sites. The altar, pews, and centerpieces are fairly easy to arrange. Purchase the supplies at a home and garden center or from a florist. Have the traditional bouquets (unless your friends have experience making bouquets) made by a florist.

Cutting Wild Flowers: Wild flower arrangements can add the perfect final touch to an outdoor, garden wedding. The wide array of colors and scents make beautiful centerpieces and altar decorations. Make sure you get permission from the land owner if the patch of wild flowers you locate is not on your property.

Simple Arrangements: A simple carnation or rose in a rented vase on each guest table makes a lovely centerpiece. It is not necessary to have expensive floral arrangements on each table. Most florists will rent vases, this will reduce the cost of your centerpieces.

Rented Potted Plants: Most nurseries will rent large potted plants for weddings. This will help reduce your costs if you need more greenery to create atmosphere and boundaries. Some nurseries or florists will even deliver and pick up the plants.

Edible Centerpieces: The centerpieces on the guests' tables can become an appetizer or dessert. A vegetable tray filled with carrots, radishes, green and red peppers, olives, and miniature corn with a clam dip in the center makes a colorful, edible centerpiece that everyone can enjoy. Fresh strawberries, bananas, and spongecake cut into bite-sized pieces and served around a chocolate fondue will be the highlight of the table as the aroma of melting chocolate fills the room.

BOUQUETS

The bouquet adds the final touch to your attire, completing the traditional bridal picture. A bridesmaid without a bouquet can look like a guest—the bouquet makes the bridesmaid stand out. It also gives you and the bridesmaids something to do with your hands as you stroll down the aisle.

Alternatives: Wedding bouquets are not a must. Some brides carry a Bible instead. Others may carry a single rose or a dozen long-stemmed roses. Your style may help determine what type of bouquet you carry. The bridesmaids usually carry a similar style bouquet.

Composition: The bouquet is made up of flowers, fillers (baby's breath), and greens (ivy, ferns, leaves). The proportion of flowers to fillers and greens will determine the cost of the bouquet. Traditional flowers are white roses, orchids, carnations, stephanotis, lilies of the valley, and gardenias.

Style: The style of a formal bouquet can be an elegant cascade, a spray, or a long-stemmed arm arrangement. A simple bouquet can be made of a few flowers immersed in a flowing sea of ivy or of a single flower. Consider your gown and your figure. A formal gown on a petite bride is usually complemented by an elaborate small cascade.

Ribbons: The florist can use ribbons to match your bridal party color scheme. You may want to supply the ribbons to make sure the match is right. Most fabric stores have a wide selection of ribbons.

Wire Wrap: Ask the florist to wire wrap your bouquet so it stays together through all the events. The plastic holders are cumbersome to hold and may drip water on your gown.

Second-Time Brides: Bouquets for second-time brides are usually brighter, deeper tones. The same styles are appropriate depending on the style of the gown and the bride's figure.

Bouquet Toss: If you plan to preserve your bouquet, have a smaller replica made up for the bouquet tossing ceremony. The florist can make up a version of your bouquet for a fraction of the cost.

BOUTONNIERES/CORSAGES

The groom can wear a lapel spray taken from your bouquet or a traditional boutonniere (rose, sprig of stephanotis, lilies of the valley). The lapel spray helps the groom stand out from the ushers, especially if they are wearing the same tuxedos. The boutonniere is always worn on the left lapel.

The ushers usually wear a boutonniere of a single carnation or a rose. The flower can be white or it can match the colors of the bridal party.

Mothers and grandmothers traditionally receive corsages. The corsage can be as simple as a single rose with baby's breath and a little greenery or an elegant gardenia spray. Consider the dress style, jewelry, and figure when selecting each corsage.

Some dresses won't support a customary corsage because of the fabric content (lace, chiffon). Select a corsage that can be worn on the wrist or taped to a cane. Each corsage should be personalized to complement each mother.

Traditionally the mothers of the bride and groom discuss their wedding attire and try to match styles, colors, and accessories. This eliminates the possibility of one mother feeling cheated if the other receives a larger, more elaborate corsage to complement her dress. Again, the mothers should wear what they like

and not make selections based on what the other mother is wearing or the colors of the bridal party.

Special people and guests who help should also receive corsages. These corsages don't need to be personalized and should be smaller and less elaborate than the mothers' and grandmothers'.

FLOWER GIRL'S BASKET

The flower girl carries a little basket filled with flowers and baby's breath. The colors of the flowers can match that of the bridal party or can be an assortment of colors. Customary flowers are rosebuds, violets, lilies of the valley, and seasonal dainty blossoms.

Traditionally, the flower girl carried a basket filled with loose flower petals to strew in the bride's path. This custom proved to be dangerous as brides slipped on the petals; it is rarely done today.

Have the basket arranged uniformly so the flower girl can carry it any way. She will have a lot on her mind and may not remember to hold the basket a certain way.

CEREMONY FLOWERS

Pew: Ceremony flowers add life and romance to your site. They consist of flowers decorating the altar and the pews. Consider the time of day and the lighting. If you are having an evening wedding, use light-colored flowers. The focus should be on the altar. Flower arrangements on both sides of the altar are usually enough. The larger the flowers, the more visible they are from the pews. The height and design of the arrangement should be determined by the ceremony site.

Huppah: If you are having a Jewish ceremony, you can decorate the huppah with flowers and greenery. Your budget will determine the proportion of flowers to greenery.

Share with Reception: The ceremony flowers tend to be less elaborate than the reception flowers. The ceremony is usually over in less than an hour and the reception generally goes on for hours. Have the flowers moved after the ceremony to the reception site. This will help avoid duplicating some costs.

RECEPTION FLOWERS

Focal Tables: The reception is a more involved event than the ceremony. You have a banquet with tables for the bridal party, guests, cake, gifts, punch, and bar. Your table usually has the most elaborate centerpiece. Keep it low so the guests can see you while you're seated.

The focal tables during the ceremony should have some color and greenery. The cake can be encircled by a ring of ivy with baby roses. Put potted flowering plants on the gift table and guest book table. Flower arrangements can add flair to windows and columns.

Guests' Tables: The guests' tables have centerpieces of flowers or candles. You can be creative when selecting the centerpieces. Some brides include the table number stands in the floral arrangements. Others use silk flowers that can be saved as a memento. Candles in hurricane lamps surrounded by flowers and greenery give the table a warm glow for evening receptions. Oriental flower arrangements using flowers and branches in an elegant balance between color and space offer a unique centerpiece.

Plants to Section off Room: Large potted plants or trees can be used to section off a room that is too large. This is an effective way to create a comfortable atmosphere. Using a large room for a small reception can create an empty feeling that detracts from the spirit of the wedding.

Use the Flowers Checklist on pages 168–169 to record your selections and all pertinent details.

PRESERVING FLOWERS

Flowers can be preserved as a memento. The bridal bouquet is typically the only flower arrangement that is preserved.

PROFESSIONAL FLORIST

Florists have several techniques for preserving flowers. Look through their portfolio of preserved bouquets so you know what you are ordering. Discuss the costs ahead of time and arrange to have the bouquet dropped off within two days of the reception. Make sure the bouquet is refrigerated immediately after the reception.

HOME TECHNIQUES

Potpourri: Hang your bouquet upside down in a cool, dry place for about two weeks. When the petals are dried, peel them off the stems and place them in a glass container. You can mix the petals with spices and scents to fill a lace pillow to add fragrance to your drawers.

Pressed Flower Arrangement: Take your bouquet apart. Take larger flowers apart petal by petal. Press the petals and small flowers between clean paper under heavy weights for about two months. After the flowers have dried completely, carefully peel them off the paper. Place them on parchment paper to be framed behind glass. You can arrange the flowers in a pattern to resemble your bouquet or just create a new pattern.

GIFTS OF FLOWERS TO YOUR GUESTS

If you have purchased all parts of the guests' centerpieces and nothing needs to be returned to the florist, offer the centerpieces to the guests. The best man can make an announcement to that effect after his toast. Since you have one centerpiece per eight to ten guests, create a little contest to determine who takes the flowers home. The guest whose birthday is closest to the wedding date can be the lucky winner.

You may prefer to donate the flowers and arrangements to charity. The flowers will last for another couple of days so others will enjoy them.

FLOWERS CHECKLIST

ITEM	AMOUNT	DESCRIPTION (STYLE, FLOWERS)	DELIVERY LOCATION	COST
BRIDAL PARTY				
Bride's Bouquet				
Bride's Throw-Away Bouquet				
Bride's Going-Away Corsage				
Maid of Honor				
Bridesmaids				
Groom's Boutonniere				
Best Man				
Ushers				
Flower Girl's Basket				
Ring Bearer/Page Boutonniere Names:				
Bridal Party Total				
FAMILY				
Bride's Mother				
Groom's Mother				
Bride's Father				
Groom's Father				
Grandparents				
Other:				
Family Total				
HELPERS				
Coordinator				
Guest Book Attendant				
Gift Attendant				
Officiant				
Soloists				
Musicians				
Cake Server				
Other:				
Helpers Total				
CEREMONY				
Altar/Canopy				

FLOWERS CHECKLIST(continued)

ITEM	AMOUNT	DESCRIPTION (STYLE, FLOWERS)	DELIVERY LOCATION	COST
Candelabras				
Candlelighters				
Pews				
Aisles				
Windows				
Other:				
Ceremony total				
RECEPTION				
Bride's Table				
Parents' Tables				
Guests' Tables				
Cake Table				
Champagne/Punch Table				
Gift Table				
Guest Book Table				
Receiving Line				
Ladies' Room				
Other:				
Reception Total				

TOTAL FLORIST CATEGORIES	COSTS
Bridal Party Flowers	
Family Flowers	
Helpers Flowers	
Ceremony Flowers	
Reception Flowers	
Total Flowers	
Sales Tax	
Total	
Deposit Due/Date	
Balance Due/Date	
Person Responsible for Giving Flowers to Bridal Party and Guests:	
Person Responsible for Taking Ceremony Flowers to Reception Site:	
Person Responsible for Taking Reception Flowers to Wedding Suite:	
Person Responsible for Getting Bouquet Preserved:	
Person Responsible for Returning Rented Equipment to Florist:	

12

Wedding Rings

The engagement ring custom originated when a groom would purchase his bride. He offered an engagement ring as partial payment and as a token of his good intentions as a future husband and provider. Today the engagement ring is offered as a token of love and commitment to marriage. The wedding band is a symbol of marriage. It tells all those who see the band that you are married.

The ceremony and reception are over in hours, but your wedding rings will be the most enduring memento from your wedding day.

SELECTING A JEWELER

Choose a jeweler who comes highly recommended from a reliable source. He or she should be a certified gemologist with the Gemological Institute of America. Check with the Better Business Bureau to help make sure you are not dealing with a dishonest company. You'll be relying on the integrity of your jeweler unless you know about precious stones. If you have any doubts about the quality of the diamonds you have purchased, get a second appraisal while you still have recourse. Your insurance company may require an appraisal to insure your rings.

There are wholesale gemologists who sell precious stones to the public. You can get a good buy on your diamonds and order your setting from a jeweler. Wholesalers can be found in some metropolitan cities and also on the Internet.

SELECTING YOUR RINGS

The groom traditionally selects the engagement ring and surprises the bride with the proposal and ring. This is exciting and romantic but the groom's taste in rings may be different from yours. When the marriage proposal comes before the engagement ring, and if you are particular about your jewelry, suggest that you select your rings together. Use the Jewelry Worksheet on page 175 to record all necessary details. You can also use this for insurance purposes.

STYLE

The traditional engagement ring is a single band with a solitary diamond. The wedding band is a single band made of the same material as the engagement ring.

Matching ring sets are very popular. You both wear the same style wedding band. Your ring is a smaller version of the groom's. If you want matching wedding bands but don't want to give up the diamonds, wear an engagement ring that complements your wedding band.

Choose a style that complements your hands and fingers. Narrow bands with a single stone look great on petite hands. The bold designs with wide bands look best on larger hands. If you plan to wear your ring every day, select a stone and setting that will withstand the daily abuse of household work and sporting activities. Avoid pearls placed in high settings.

COST

Some experts suggest that the wedding ring budget be no more than both of your salaries for two months. Others say that the cost of the rings should be equivalent to three weeks' salary. These are just guidelines, not rules. Make your decision based on your financial picture. If you choose to buy an inexpensive ring now, consider adding stones on each anniversary or design a new ring for your tenth anniversary when you will be able to afford something more expensive.

HEIRLOOM

You may receive a stone or a wedding set from your favorite grandparent that has been passed along for generations. If you want a contemporary wedding ring set, have it remounted in a setting of your choice. Adding different-sized stones to the heirloom will allow you to design your own rings using the new and the old.

RING FROM A PREVIOUS MARRIAGE

Rings from prior marriages carry much history with them, usually not very fond memories, and generally are not used in the new wedding ring set. If you have children from your first marriage, save it for them and give the ring to the first to marry. If you are friendly with your ex-spouse, have it remounted into a cocktail ring or brooch. When there is anger towards your ex-spouse, sell the ring so there are no old ties and use the money for something you want.

DIAMONDS

DETERMINING QUALITY

Precious stones are evaluated by the four "C"s: cut, clarity, color, and carat. Make sure you get a good price for the quality stone you purchase. Larger isn't necessarily more valuable. Small, fine diamonds may cost more than larger, inferior diamonds.

Cut: The gem's cut is an important factor in determining the quality of the stone. The cut can be round and smooth, like an opal, or faceted with angular cuts, like a diamond. The faceted stones display their brilliance through the many sides. Stones can be cut in many shapes: brilliant (round), emerald (square/rectangular), oval, teardrop (pear), and marquise (oval with two points). Full cut diamonds have 58 facets (sides). The "perfect cut" diamond is perfectly proportioned and angled.

Clarity: Flawless diamonds are very rare. Most diamonds have inclusions (flaws) ranging from tiny spots to large carbon spots. The fewer the flaws, the better the quality the diamond is considered to be. With a good quality diamond, you shouldn't see specks or bubbles with the naked eye. Flawless diamonds can be magnified ten times with no signs of imperfections.

Color: The perfect diamond is colorless. Most diamonds have a hint of yellow or brown. The color of the diamond is considered to be one of the most important factors in evaluating its quality.

Carat: The carat is the weight of the stone. One carat has one hundred points and weighs 1/142 ounce. The price of the stone is determined by the number of points.

Caring for Diamonds

Wedding rings worn daily get abused by soaps, lotions, oils in the skin, and normal wear. Wash your rings once a month to restore their brilliance and beauty.

Detergent and Water: Bathe rings in a warm solution of dishwashing detergent and water. Brush gently with a small brush to loosen the dried-on films. Rinse in a tea strainer to protect them. Make sure the drain pipe is closed to avoid accidentally dropping the rings down the pipe. Dry them with a soft cloth.

Ammonia and Cold Water: Bathe rings in a solution of half ammonia and half water. Soak diamonds for thirty minutes. Lift them out and dry them with a soft cloth.

Ultrasonic Cleaners: Jewelers carry ultrasonic cleaners that work wonders in just a few minutes. They work by using high frequency vibrations to loosen the dirt as the rings sit in a cleaning solution. Follow the directions for use.

Be Careful: If you are involved in rough sports or heavy work, your diamonds may get chipped or the prongs may become loose. Take your rings off and store them in a safe place while you're engaged in heavy work. Have your jeweler check the mountings once a year. Some household cleaners such as chlorine bleach can pit or discolor the ring mountings. Wear rubber gloves or remove rings while cleaning.

Diamonds can scratch other diamonds. Separate jewelry when traveling and store it wrapped in a soft cloth or tissue paper to avoid scratches.

Other Precious Stones

Although diamonds are the most popular stone used for engagement and wedding rings, some brides are breaking away from that tradition. Princess Diana, for instance, chose a sapphire to complement her blue eyes. It is also common for brides to use their birthstones.

January—garnet

February—amethyst

March—bloodstone, aquamarine, or jasper

April—diamond

May—emerald or agate

June—pearl, moonstone, or emerald

July—ruby or onyx

August—sardonyx, peridot, or carnelian

September—sapphire

October—opal, aquamarine, or tourmaline

November—topaz

December—turquoise, zircon, or ruby

PRECIOUS METALS

Wedding bands are made of gold or platinum. *Gold* is the most popular metal used in rings. It is either yellow or white in color. Most rings are made of 14K or 18K gold. The gold is mixed with a stronger metal to add strength to the band. Pure gold is 24K and is too soft to be used for rings.

Platinum is the strongest metal used for rings. It is white in color. The prongs are often made of platinum to ensure the fit of the stone.

INSURING YOUR RINGS

Wedding rings are an asset that increases in value with time. Get an appraisal of your rings along with a close-up photograph to put in a safe deposit box. Contact your insurance agent to see what type of coverage you can get for your rings. They will usually want an appraisal at the time of a claim, so get it done now.

Read the fine print on your policy to be sure that you are getting optimum coverage. Many insurance policies don't cover lost stones unless the entire ring is lost. Others give a cash settlement only for the appraised value at the time of purchase. If you lose your ring twenty years later, your settlement may be half of what it will cost to replace the same ring at that time. Make sure that you get full replacement coverage. That means that no matter when you lose your rings, the insurance company will cover all costs to replace the exact ring to your specifications.

Please see Chapter 21, Insurance.

JEWELRY WORKSHEET

Bride's Engagement Ring

Jeweler: _____

Address: _____

Phone: _____ Hours: _____

Ring Style: _____

    Setting: _____

    Stone: _____

    Engravings: _____

    Comments: _____

    Tax: _____

    Deposit: _____

Total Cost: _____

    Balance Due/Date: _____

    Payment Terms: _____

Fitting Date: _____

Ring Ready: _____

Insurance Co.: _____

    Agent: _____ Policy Number: _____

Bride's Wedding Ring

Jeweler: _____

Address: _____

Phone: _____ Hours: _____

Ring Style: _____

    Setting: _____

    Stone: _____

    Engravings: _____

    Comments: _____

    Tax: _____

    Deposit: _____

Total Cost: _____

    Balance Due/Date: _____

    Payment Terms: _____

Fitting Date: _____

Ring Ready: _____

Insurance Co.: _____

    Agent: _____ Policy Number: _____

Groom's Wedding Ring

Jeweler: _____

Address: _____

Phone: _____ Hours: _____

Ring Style: _____

    Setting: _____

    Stone: _____

    Engravings: _____

    Comments: _____

    Tax: _____

    Deposit: _____

Total Cost: _____

    Balance Due/Date: _____

    Payment Terms: _____

Fitting Date: _____

Ring Ready: _____

Insurance Co.: _____

    Agent: _____ Policy Number: _____

Sketch

13

Transportation and Out-of-Town Guests

BRIDAL PARTY TRANSPORTATION

Discuss the mode of transportation for you and your parents, the bridesmaids, the groom, the ushers, and the groom's parents. The location of both ceremony and reception sites may determine the form of transportation. If you're having the ceremony and reception in your parents' garden, the bridal party will drive themselves. If your formal wedding will be held at a church and the reception site is at least a few miles away, a dramatic departure after the ceremony adds to the excitement of the wedding day.

First, set up a time schedule listing all the events to take place on your wedding date. Figure the time you need to be at each location; for example, 12:00 P.M. at home for the getting-ready pictures and 1:00 P.M. at the ceremony site for the family portraits. Determine who needs to be where at what time.

If you are providing transportation for the bridal party, organize the place and time for the bride's attendants and the groom's attendants to meet. If time and distance allow, each attendant can be picked up at his or her home. See the Wedding Day Events Schedule on page 177.

WEDDING DAY EVENTS SCHEDULE

Time	Event	Who Needs to Be There	Transportation	Pick-up/Time/Place

LIMOUSINES

Limousines are popular for transporting the wedding party. They accommodate the most people and offer comfort and relaxation.

Refer to the yellow pages of your local phone book or the Internet to find limousine companies. Inquire about rates and the minimum number of hours you need to rent each vehicle. If you are booking more than one limousine, ask about quantity discounts.

You should also find out about the year and make of the limousine. Get proof of insurance from the company. Ask about the qualifications and driving records of their chauffeurs. Discuss the attire of the chauffeurs.

Check the Better Business Bureau and Consumer Affairs records of particular limousine companies. Get references from the companies themselves. You'll be depending on their punctuality and the reliability of their vehicles.

OTHER MODES OF TRANSPORTATION

If you want a unique mode of transportation, consider an antique car. Check with antique car clubs in your area for contacts. You may have to rent directly from the owner and provide your own chauffeur. Make sure both the vehicle and drivers are properly insured.

A horse and buggy adds a new dimension to wedding transportation. This may be difficult to arrange in a metropolitan city but they have them in New York City's Central Park! Check your resources for other unique ideas. Use the Transportation Possibilities Checklist on page 179 to compare your options.

PARKING

For large weddings in congested areas or large hotels, parking attendants help ease the confusion and long distance walks to the ceremony and/or reception. If your wedding coincides with a holiday or special event, contact the local police department for possible assistance with traffic control.

PARKING ATTENDANTS

If you are hiring an independent parking attendant, make sure he is insured and licensed to drive for pay. You are trusting your guests' cars and valuables inside their cars to these attendants.

TRANSPORTATION POSSIBILITIES CHECKLIST

QUESTIONS	POSSIBILITY 1	POSSIBILITY 2	POSSIBILITY 3
Type of Vehicle			
Name of Company			
Address			
Manager			
Phone			
Hours			
Make of Vehicle			
Year of Vehicle			
Number of Vehicles			
Insurance Policy			
Proof of Insurance			
Chauffeur Qualifications			
Chauffeur Attire			
Backup Vehicles			
Better Business Bureau Rating			
Consumer Affairs			
Cost			
Minimum Number of Hours			
Gratuities			
Deposit Due/Date			
Balance Due/Date			

Wedding Ceremony

Attendant's Name: _____

Address: _____

Phone: _____ Age: _____ Driver's License No.: _____

Union: _____ Insurance Co.: _____

Time of Arrival: _____ Proof of Insurance: _____

Attendant's Attire: _____ Time of Departure: _____

Fees: _____ Tips/Tax: _____

Overtime: _____ Sign Posted if Tip Prepaid: _____

Cancellation Policy: _____

Deposit Due/Date: _____ Balance Due/Date: _____

_____

_____

_____

_____

_____

Wedding Reception

Attendant's Name: _____

Address: _____

Phone: _____ Age: _____ Driver's License No.: _____

Union: _____ Insurance Co.: _____

Time of Arrival: _____ Proof of Insurance: _____

Attendant's Attire: _____ Time of Departure: _____

Fees: _____ Tips/Tax: _____

Overtime: _____ Sign Posted if Tip Prepaid: _____

Cancellation Policy: _____

Deposit Due/Date: _____ Balance Due/Date: _____

_____

_____

_____

_____

Discuss the rates and gratuities. Some companies charge based on the number of guests you have and others on the actual number of cars parked. Negotiate fees for large groups. Inquire about the number of attendants (valets) per site. Most companies include gratuities in the fees. If gratuities are prepaid, the parking attendant should post a sign to that effect so guests will know that the gratuities have been taken care of.

Enter the information on the Parking Attendant Checklist on page 180. Get a copy of the proof of insurance before you sign the contract and pay a deposit.

VALET PARKING

If your wedding or reception is at a fine hotel or restaurant, it may have valet parking available. Discuss rates per car and gratuities. For large parties negotiate a reduction in per car fees. Hotels often subcontract the valet parking services out to other companies. Check for proof of insurance to be safe.

PARKING GARAGES

If the ceremony or reception does not have parking available, reserve space in a nearby parking garage. Indicate which parking garage to use if you've reserved space ahead of time. If you are paying for spaces for your guests, the parking facility should post a sign to that effect to inform guests.

OUT-OF-TOWN GUESTS

Send an itinerary of parties to out-of-town guests with the invitation. This will help them plan their travel time so they can attend the various pre-wedding parties. See Entertainment for Out-of-Town Guests on page 184 for pre-wedding itineraries.

HOUSING/HOTEL ACCOMMODATIONS

Friends and family may offer special accommodations for your guests. This helps your guests feel more welcome and also helps cut back on their expenses. Enter the guests' names on the worksheet for Housing/Hotel Accommodations for Out-of-Town Guests on page 182.

Some guests will feel more comfortable staying in a nearby hotel. You can offer to book their reservations for them. Suggest hotels in different price ranges. Once you book their hotels, let them know the details about check-in and check-out times. If you have several guests staying in hotels, suggest the same hotel so they can share transportation and company. If your reception is in a hotel, guests may prefer to stay in that hotel for convenience.

HOUSING/HOTEL ACCOMMODATIONS
FOR OUT-OF-TOWN GUESTS

FRIENDS'/RELATIVES' HOUSE ACCOMMODATIONS

GUEST	HOST/ADDRESS	PHONE	DATES

HOTEL ACCOMMODATIONS

GUEST	HOTEL/LOCATION	PHONE	DATES	CHECK-IN/OUT	COST

TRANSPORTATION FOR OUT-OF-TOWN GUESTS

If transportation will be provided for out-of-town guests, use this chart to help coordinate trips.

GUEST	ARRIVAL TIME/LOCATION	DRIVER/VEHICLE	DEPARTURE TIME/LOCATION	DRIVER/VEHICLE

TRANSPORTATION

Out-of-town guests can find driving around town a frustrating experience. Some guests rent cars and enjoy their independence. Other guests appreciate door-to-door hospitality. Providing transportation for these guests is a kind gesture.

Try to discuss travel arrival timetables with your out-of-town guests before they book their flights. If you have many out-of-town guests it would be easier for you if they arrived at designated times such as 7:00 P.M. Guests could arrange their flights so they arrive as close to that time as possible. You could visit with the guests who arrive first while you wait for the other flights to arrive. Otherwise, you might be driving back and forth from the airport for several days as different guests arrive.

If friends volunteer to help, ask them to help with the transportation of out-of-town guests to and from the airport. Some guests will be able to arrange their transportation to the ceremony with the hosts they are staying with. Other guests staying in hotels may need transportation on the wedding day. List all of your out-of-town guests on the Transportation for Out-of-Town Guests worksheet on page 183. This will help you organize transportation schedules and drivers. Call or write your out-of-town guests to give them their transportation information. Enter the details for the drivers on the Bridal Party's Checklist on page 23.

ENTERTAINMENT FOR OUT-OF-TOWN GUESTS

Most engaged couples used to come from the same hometowns. Planning a guest list was simple because everybody lived nearby. Now, with college students moving all over the country to continue their education or couples relocating for better jobs, 20 to 50 percent of the guest list may consist of out-of-town friends and relatives.

When you have a large number of guests coming from out of the area to join you for your nuptials, it would be nice to spend some time with them before or after your wedding. You might plan to have lunch or dinner at your favorite restaurant. If you have many out-of-town guests and family visiting, it might be best to plan an itinerary of activities for guests. Then the guests will be able to join you at their convenience. Use the Pre-Wedding Itinerary form on page 186 to outline your activities.

Send a copy of your pre-wedding itinerary to out-of-town guests with the invitation. This will let them know your plans before and after the ceremony so they won't miss any activities they would like to participate in. Ask them to indicate which activities they will attend. You may want to invite your close friends to meet your out-of-town friends and family. If they know that you are setting time aside to

spend with friends and family from out-of-town, they may be more inclined to join you. Guests often travel for hours and spend considerable money on transportation and lodging only to spend a few minutes with their friends at the ceremony. Use the Guest List for Pre-Wedding Activities form on page 187. Be sure to let each host/hostess know how many guests to expect.

You may prefer to plan an itinerary that is simpler or more elaborate than the sample shown. Consider your energy level and the stress you'll be under as the countdown begins. Be organized and plan your activities ahead so you won't be pulled in all directions by guests, friends, and family.

CHAPTER 13

SAMPLE PRE-WEDDING ITINERARY					
TUESDAY	WEDNESDAY	THURSDAY	FRIDAY	SATURDAY	SUNDAY
				11:00 A.M. Breakfast at Aunt Lori's (We will not be there.)	11:00 A.M. Breakfast with the Families
		2:00 P.M. Day at the Beach Picnic	12:00 NOON Champagne Brunch at Debbie's		2:00 P.M. Gift Opening at Nicole's
7:00 P.M. Barbeque Party with Fresh Strawberry Daiquiris	7:00 P.M. Bachelor Party at Alan's Bridesmaids' Dinner at Charthouse	6:00 P.M. Rehearsal and Rehearsal Dinner at Queen Mary		6:00 P.M. Wedding Ceremony and Reception	

_____ (BRIDE) & (GROOM) _____'s

PRE-WEDDING ITINERARY

TUESDAY	WEDNESDAY	THURSDAY	FRIDAY	SATURDAY	SUNDAY

GUEST LIST FOR PRE-WEDDING ACTIVITIES

DATE	TIME	ACTIVITY	LOCATION	GUEST R.S.V.P.

14

Wedding Gifts

Wedding gifts are given by the guests to help you start your new lives together. It's a tradition that started years ago when the bride and groom moved directly from their parents' homes to their new home as husband and wife. They didn't have any furnishings or kitchenware. It was easy for the guests to buy gifts since couples were starting off with nothing.

Couples are getting married later in life today. It is becoming harder to shop for wedding gifts now that so many couples have acquired the essentials while they lived on their own. The bride and groom may have gone off to college and lived on their own for several years. Those who have lived together prior to marriage and those getting married for the second time have all the necessities. Guests are often at a loss trying to buy a gift that the couple doesn't already have. Contemporary wedding gifts tend to be luxuries and not basic necessities (kitchen, bath, and bed items).

CONTEMPORARY GIFT IDEAS

Here are some suggestions when guests ask you what you'd like for a wedding present.

Bed and Breakfast: Request a night at a bed and breakfast inn. Select a place that is within driving distance so you don't have to spend a fortune to get there. Add flowers and a bottle of champagne and you'll have a wonderful, romantic evening.

Dinner for Two: Enjoy a special dinner-for-two gift certificate at your favorite restaurant.

Wine: If you and your groom are lovers of wine, ask for an assortment of fine wines. For an extra-personalized touch, ask the gift giver to attach a card to each bottle with a description of the wine and a date for it to be opened.

Talents: If you have guests with special talents or skills, you might cherish a gift of their talents over a toaster oven. An amateur photographer might offer to put together a slide show of you and the groom, as you were growing up, or a collage of wedding pictures. A painter can offer his or her services to paint your new home. A musician can offer to play at your next party.

Joint Gift: Close friends usually know what the bride and groom need or want but it may cost more than their budgets will allow. If one person organizes a collection from several friends, they can pool their money together to buy that special gift. It takes a thoughtful person to organize this type of project.

Charities: For those who either feel uncomfortable receiving gifts or have everything they need, donating wedding gifts to charity is an option that allows everyone to win. According to proper etiquette, it isn't proper to mention gift choices on the invitations. Spread the word around that all gifts will be donated to charity.

Cash Gifts: Cash seems to be the most popular gift of recent times. Newlywed couples are eager to save money for a down payment on a house or car and often prefer to receive cash. If you are paying for the wedding celebration yourselves, cash gifts come in handy when paying the bills.

If you prefer cash gifts, get the word out to close friends and family. They will pass it along. Again, it's not proper to ask for cash gifts on the invitation itself or mention it to guests unless they ask first.

REGISTERED GIFTS

Registering gifts will make it easier for the gift giver to select a gift that he or she knows you will like. You won't receive as many duplicates and you won't get the perfect gift in the wrong color.

Most department stores and specialty shops have a bridal registry program. It is a big business for them and their trained staff will help you make a complete list of items to fit everyone's budget. Select your patterns in dinnerware, flatware, and glassware, along with individual items such as vases and kitchen items. Even if you

have the bare necessities, you can upgrade and get that new iron that turns itself off in ten minutes if you forget, or that Tiffany-style lamp you've had your eye on for months.

Guests will usually ask your parents or someone in the bridal party if you are registered. Get the word out to your family and friends so guests will shop only where you are registered. To follow proper etiquette, do not mention gift preferences, and especially do not print where you are registered on your invitations. Record your selections on the Registered Gift List on pages 191–192. Use the list to keep track of what you have received, and what you still need to get.

RECORDING GIFTS

You will start receiving gifts soon after you send invitations until months after your wedding. To make sure that you don't mix up gifts or forget to document the gift, enter the information on the Wedding Invitation and Gift List (starting on page 52) as soon as you open the gift. List the gift and the store it was purchased from (in case it will be returned). Write a description of the gift on the wedding card you receive as a backup.

If you receive many gifts, number the invitation list and stick corresponding numbers on each gift to avoid confusing similar gifts.

WHEN TO OPEN WEDDING GIFTS

Open gifts as they arrive before your wedding. This gives you a chance to appreciate each gift and makes it easier for you to write a meaningful thank-you note right away. Gifts that you receive at the ceremony and reception should be opened before you take off for your honeymoon. If you have an afternoon reception, open the gifts that evening before you leave on your honeymoon. Open the gifts the following day if your reception is at night. Don't wait until you get back from your honeymoon to open the gifts. The cards may get lost or the gifts may get misplaced or lost. Open them and record the gifts right away.

The families and close friends may want to watch you open your gifts. They enjoy seeing the gifts you receive. It's nice to have help recording the gifts and throwing away the wrapping and packing materials.

Take your *Working Woman's Wedding Planner* and stationery with you on your honeymoon so you can write thank-you notes during your quiet times.

REGISTERED GIFT LIST

FINE CHINA:

Pattern	Qty	Rec'd
Dinner Plate		
Salads		
Bread/Butter		
Tea cup/saucer		
Soup Bowls		
Cereal Bowls		
Fruit Bowls		
Cream Soup		
Demitasse		
Sugar Bowl		
Creamer		
Vegetable Dish		
Covered Casserole		
Platter 12"		
Platter 14"		
Platter 16"		
Salad Bowl		
Soup Tureen		
Coffeepot		
Teapot		
Gravy Boat		
Salt/Pepper		

INFORMAL DINNERWARE:

Pattern	Qty	Rec'd
Dinner Plate	12	
Salads		
Bread/Butter		
Tea cup/saucer		
Soup Bowls		
Cereal Bowls		
Fruit Bowls		
Cream Soup		
Demitasse		
Sugar Bowl		
Creamer		
Vegetable Dish		
Covered Casserole		
Platter 12"		
Platter 14"		
Platter 16"		
Salad Bowl		
Soup Tureen		
Coffeepot		
Teapot		
Gravy Boat		
Salt/Pepper		

FLATWARE/SILVER:

Pattern	Qty	Rec'd
Knives		
Forks		
Teaspoons		
Salad Forks		
Place Spoons		
Butter Spreader		

	Qty	Rec'd
Cream Soups		
Iced Tea Spoons		
Tablespoons		
Cold Meat Fork		
Pierced Tablespoon		
Butter Knife		
Gravy Ladle		
Pickle Fork		
Sugar Spoon		
Cocktail Fork		
Cheese Knife		
Pie Server		
Silver Chest		

FLATWARE/STAINLESS:

Pattern	Qty	Rec'd
Knives		
Forks		
Teaspoons		
Salad Forks		
Place Spoons		
Butter Spreader		
Cream Soups		
Iced Tea Spoons		
Tablespoons		
Cold Meat Fork		
Pierced Tablespoon		
Butter Knife		
Gravy Ladle		
Pickle Fork		
Sugar Spoon		
Steak Knives		
Carving Set		

FINE CRYSTAL:

Pattern	Qty	Rec'd
Goblets		
Champagne		
Wines		
On-the-Rocks		
Highball		
Juices		
Cordials		
Iced Teas		
Brandy Snifter		
Liqueurs		
Pilseners		
Decanters		
Pitchers		
Punch Bowl		
Dessert Bowls		
Candy Dish		

CASUAL GLASS:

Pattern	Qty	Rec'd
Goblets		
Champagne		

	Qty	Rec'd
Wines		
On-the-Rocks		
Highball		
Juices		
Iced Teas		
Brandy Snifters		
Liqueurs		
Beers		
Decanters		
Pitchers		
Punch Bowl		
Cruets		
Dessert Plates		

SERVING ACCESSORIES:

Pattern	Qty	Rec'd
Compote		
Coffee Service		
Tea Service		
Serving Trays		
Candlesticks		
Candelabra		
Carafe		
Serving Cart		
Trivets		
Vase		
Baskets		
Serving Platter		
Buffet Dishes		
Chafing Dish		
Salad Bowl Set		
Warming Tray		
Pepper Mill		
Coasters		

COOK. EQUIP:

Pattern/Model	Qty	Rec'd
Saucepan __ qt.		
Saucepan __ qt.		
Saucepan __ qt.		
Skillet 8"		
Skillet 10"		
Skillet 12"		
Covered Casserole __ qt.		
Covered Casserole __ qt.		
Covered Casserole __ qt.		
Baking Dish __		
Baking Dish __		
Double Boiler		
Dutch Oven		
Tea Kettle		
Coffee Pot		
Mixing Bowl Set		
Roaster/Rack		
Pressure Cooker		
Egg Poacher		

COOK. EQUIP: Pattern/Model

	Qty	Rec'd
Utensil Set		
Cutting Board		
Molds		
Wok		

KITCHEN WARE

	Qty	Rec'd
Cutlery Set		
Canister Set		
Nonstick Cookware		
Fondue Pans		
Muffin Tins		
Cookie Sheet		
Pie Pans		
Meas. Spoons		
Meas. Cups		
Bread Knife		
Egg Beater		
Thermometer		
Food Scale		
Whisks		
Timer		
Grater		
Strainers		
Veg. Peeler		
Corkscrew		
Ice Bucket		
Baster		
Colander		
Food Chopper		
Spice Rack		
Ice Cream Scoop		
Kitchen Clock		
Cookbooks		

LINENS

	Mfr Qty	Rec'd
Table:		
Tablecloths		
Napkins		
Placemats		
Kitchen:		
Dish Towels		
Dish Cloths		
Pot Holders		
Apron		
Appliance Covers		
Bath:		
Bath Towels		
Hand Towels		
Washcloths		
Guest Towels		
Bath Mat		
Rug/Lid Set		
Shower Curtain		
Scale		
Hamper		

Bedroom:

	Mfr Qty	Rec'd
Flat Sheets		
Fitted Sheets		
Pillow Cases		
Pillows		
Blanket/Light		
Blanket/Heavy		
Electric Blanket		
Bedspread		
Comforter		
Mattress		

ELECTRICAL APPLIANCES

	Mfr	Rec'd
Toaster/Oven		
Mixer		
Blender		
Bread Baker		
Food Processor		
Juicer		
Frying Pan		
Rotisserie		
Waffle Grill		
Can Opener		
Electric Knife		
Slow Cooker		
Microwave		

HOME ENTERTAINMENT

	Mfr	Rec'd
Rugs		
Clocks		
Mirrors		
Card Table/Chairs		
Tray Tables		
TV-Video, etc.		
Clock Radio		
Sound System		
Photo Equipment		
Sewing Machine		
Desk		
Computer		
Magazine Rack		
Wall Hangings		
Planters		
Fireplace Equipment		
Bicycles		
B.B.Q. Equipment		
Patio Furniture		
Camping Gear		
Picnic Basket		
Smoke Alarm		

LUGGAGE: Style Name

	Mfr	Rec'd
Tote		
Overnighter		
Weekender		
Pullman		
Garment Bag		

HOUSEWARES

	Mfr	Rec'd
Vacuum Cleaner		
Dustpan/Brush		
Broom		
Mop		
Ironing Board		
Iron		
Garbage Pail		
Wastebaskets		
Step Stool		
Tool Kit		

FURNITURE: Basic Decorating Scheme

	Mfr	Rec'd
Living Room:		
Sofa/Sofabed		
Chairs		
End Tables		
Coffee Table		
Lamps		
Shelves		
Curt./Drapes		
Bedroom:		
Bed		
Mattress		
Night Tables		
Chest/Armoire		
Lamps		
Curt./Drapes		
Dining Room:		
Table		
Chairs		
Buffet/Storage		
Curt./Drapes		
Chandelier		

CLOSET ACCESS.

	Qty	Rec'd
Garment Bags		
Shoe Bag/Rack		
Hangers		
Linen Storage		

BAR ACCESS.

	Qty	Rec'd
Bar Table		
Decanters		
Ice Crusher		
Jiggers		
Cocktail Shaker		
Champagne Bucket		
Wine Rack		

OTHER

DISPLAYING GIFTS

Traditionally, you (or your parents) set up a gift table to display all the gifts as you receive them. Separate tables should be used to display different types of gifts: silver, crystal, kitchen items, household items, and fun items.

Some consider this tradition pretentious and awkward. If you feel uncomfortable displaying gifts, just bring out a few of your favorites when friends and family ask to see what you've received.

PROBLEMS WITH GIFTS

DAMAGED GIFTS

If your gift arrives damaged, and it was sent directly from the store, send it back for a replacement. If the gift was sent from the gift giver and the package was insured, call the gift giver and explain the situation. The sender will be reimbursed by the shipping company so a replacement can be acquired. If there was no indication of insurance on the package and it was shipped by the gift giver, do not mention the problem to the gift giver. He or she may feel obligated to purchase another gift.

EXCHANGING GIFTS

Exchange a gift only if the gift giver will not know. He or she may have used lots of time and energy to select the gift for you and may be offended to learn that the gift was exchanged for something else. Don't ask where the gift was purchased so you can return it and never mention the exchange in thank-you letters.

MISSING GIFT CARDS

Occasionally you will receive a gift without a gift card or the gift cards may fall off several gifts and you're not sure who the gift givers are. If a store sent the gift, you can call the store and ask for the name of the giver.

If the gift was brought to the ceremony or reception, you may have to play detective to figure out who the gift giver was. First, through the process of elimination, check your guest and gift lists to see who attended the wedding and hasn't had a gift recorded. If there is one guest, then you have found the gift giver. If there are several guests who haven't sent gifts, you may ask friends or family to try to find out what other guests gave you. Some guests send gifts late and will state that. You'll eventually narrow it down to one guest. Sometimes you'll be able to tell by the gift itself. If you've been admiring a friend's glassware, put two and two together and you may have found the answer without inquiring.

MONOGRAMMING

When Jaclyn Ann Silvers marries David William Miller, the monogram can read J M S or J S M. If there is only one letter monogrammed, the last name is usually used. You and the groom can use your first initials on either side of the larger capital letter.

CANCELED WEDDING

If your wedding has been canceled, send back all gifts, even those that have been monogrammed. Include a letter stating that the wedding will not take place and that you apologize for the inconvenience of returning the gift. You do not need to explain why the wedding has been called off.

    If your wedding is postponed until a later date, you may keep all the gifts. Send a brief note explaining why the wedding will be postponed and thank the giver for the gift.

THANK-YOU NOTES

Send thank-you notes immediately after you receive the gift. The gift giver is usually eager to learn if you received the gift and how you like it. If you are very busy with pre-wedding planning or post-wedding organization, send the letters as soon as possible, though no later than two or three months after the wedding.

GIFTS TO EACH OTHER

Traditionally the bride and groom give gifts to each other. Select something of permanence that will be treasured for years. Popular gifts are watches, jewelry, and silver frames. Many couples feel that the wedding rings and the wedding celebration are enough to give each other for their big day so they don't exchange gifts.

GIFTS TO THE BRIDAL PARTY

After you've planned all the details and gone over guidelines with all of the members of the bridal party, it's time to give gifts of thanks. It is traditional that the bride

give her attendants gifts and the groom give his ushers gifts. Gifts should be permanent items of a personal nature that somehow relate to the wedding. These items make nice mementos which they can keep to remember this special day that they shared with you.

Gift Ideas for Bride's Attendants

- Engraved jewelry (bracelet)
- Brass picture frame
- Engraved jewelry box
- Engraved jewelry stand
- Engraved pen

Gift Ideas for Groom's Best Man and Ushers

- Engraved pewter mug
- Engraved money clip
- Engraved pen
- Engraved belt buckle
- Engraved key ring

GIFTS TO PARENTS

Parents are often forgotten during the wedding preparation and celebration. There is so much to do. When the big day finally arrives, it seems to go by so quickly. You want to greet and thank all your guests for coming and before you know it, you're off on your honeymoon!

It is traditional for the bride and groom to give their parents gifts of thanks. This is especially true if the parents financed the wedding. Even if they don't finance the wedding, it is a nice statement to both families thanking them for all their support.

Gifts to parents should be permanent items that they can keep as mementos. Brass or beveled glass picture frames are good choices. Consider including your wedding portrait. Items that can be engraved with a thank-you message and your names and date of the wedding are especially nice. An especially nice gift would be the wedding album that parents usually order.

On the other hand, it can be fun to invite the parents over for a special dinner prepared by the newlyweds or take the parents out to dinner.

15

The Wedding
Ceremony

CEREMONY STYLE

Wedding ceremonies can be as unique as you are. They don't have to be the "traditional American Hollywood" ceremony. The style couples choose for their ceremony should reflect their own personalities and lifestyles.

PASSIVE

Not every bride likes to be the center of attention, even for her own wedding ceremony. Some brides cringe at the thought of marching up and down the aisle and sharing their personal vows in front of a large group of people. Many couples have private ceremonies and celebrate with their friends and family at the reception.

You can be married at City Hall in your town or have a rectory ceremony in your church. Some couples prefer to elope to ensure a completely private ceremony.

UNIQUE

Others prefer making a statement with their wedding ceremonies. They want a unique wedding that portrays characteristics of their personalities. Wearing a gown and a tuxedo and walking down the aisle of a church may be too ordinary. Sports enthusiasts have been married while scuba diving, skiing on snow-covered mountains, parachuting from planes, and water-skiing behind a boat. Others have been

married nude in nudist colonies, and some have even been married where they had spent most of their time together: at work!

TRADITIONAL

The traditional wedding usually takes place in a church or temple and is performed by a member of the clergy. There are many variations based on the traditional religious ceremony. Double weddings have been performed for years. A military ceremony is also considered traditional. See the section below on Types of Ceremonies for a description of different ceremonies.

CONTEMPORARY

Some couples prefer to have a wedding that is more personal but not extreme. Weddings in a favorite museum add a contemporary flair without shocking your guests. Holding the ceremony outdoors, among majestic redwood trees, or overlooking a spectacular ocean sunset, creates a romantic wedding atmosphere.

If your guests are willing to travel a few hours from your hometown, you may be able to use a historical site as your wedding location. Contact the historical societies in surrounding towns to see if special museums or mansions are available for weddings. Ask the Chamber of Commerce for other suggestions. They may have inside information that can lead you to the perfect setting.

Using someone's home garden for the ceremony adds a personal touch to the occasion. If you have an accommodating parent or friend, your ceremony can be more personal and special by sharing their home and garden for your big day.

TYPES OF CEREMONIES

CATHOLIC CEREMONY

REQUIREMENTS

Baptismal Certificate and Other Documentation: You will need to show documentation of your baptism within six months of the wedding date, and also a record of your Confirmation. You both need to receive a letter of free state issued by your parishes.

Catholic weddings are usually held in church. If the ceremony will be an interfaith marriage, the wedding can take place outside the church as long as the location is a place of worship. Catholic ceremonies are not celebrated in chapels

where the purpose of the site is commercial, not religious. Check with your parish to determine its requirements.

Wedding Date and Time: Catholic weddings are usually held during the day and scheduled before six o'clock, although evening weddings are permitted. Saturday is usually the preferred day. Wedding ceremonies are not permitted on Holy Thursday, Good Friday, Holy Saturday, or during regularly scheduled mass.

Preparation: You may be required to participate in a wedding preparation four months prior to the wedding date. This consists of three mandatory programs: (1) "Evenings for the Engaged" (six evening sessions), (2) personality testing and evaluation sessions, and (3) instruction in the faith.

The "Evenings for the Engaged" consists of six evening sessions designed to provide vocational preparation for the Sacrament of Marriage. Each couple is matched with a married couple and a priest who share with them their knowledge of the Sacrament of Marriage. These sessions take place in the homes of the married couple.

Another option for couples is the "Engagement Encounter." This is a weekend program for groups of brides and grooms, led by the married couples and priests. The couples discuss their philosophy on marriage, family, sexuality, and the church.

Couples examine their relationship through the personality test and evaluation sessions. After the test, the couple meets with the priest for three sessions. They discuss the test results in these counseling sessions. The priest helps the couple determine their strengths and weaknesses. If he feels strongly that the wedding should not take place, he'll make that recommendation.

If a Catholic marries a person who is a member of another Christian church or is agnostic, the Catholic church will allow this marriage to take place as long as the practicing person continues to be active in the Catholic faith and promises to raise future children in the belief of the Catholic Christian community.

Annulment: If you have been married before, you can be married in the Catholic church for your second wedding as long as you go through the annulment process. The Church Tribunal, after careful review, declares that the previous marriage was invalid because at least one of the essential elements binding the marriage was missing.

Each diocese has different procedures regarding annulment. Most have questionnaires for you to complete prior to your sessions. The priest will discuss your previous marriage in detail. He will ask you about your courtship, marriage, and breakup. It is important for the priest to understand what was happening around the time of the marriage in order to assess whether or not there are grounds for an annulment.

Your ex-spouse will be contacted and has a right to be part of the process. If he is unwilling to cooperate or his whereabouts are unknown, the annulment proceedings will continue without him. Witnesses will also be contacted to give more information regarding your past marriage.

Allow approximately one year to complete the process. The purpose of this annulment is to invalidate the previous marriage. This does not affect the legitimacy of the children from that marriage. The Catholic annulment is not a legal divorce. Your previous marriage will need to be terminated according to the laws of your state for a full divorce to be legally recognized.

CEREMONY DESCRIPTION

There are two traditional wedding ceremonies in the Catholic Church. The Rite of Marriage during mass is generally used between two practicing Catholics. The Rite of Marriage outside mass is appropriate for a Catholic marrying a person of a different Christian faith, Catholics who are not active in the church, and a Catholic marrying an unbaptized person.

Rite for Celebrating Marriage During Mass

1. Prelude
2. Processional
3. Penitential Rite
4. Gloria
5. Opening Prayer
6. Liturgy of the Word
   A. Old Testament Reading
   B. Responsorial Psalm
   C. New Testament Reading
   D. Gospel Acclamation
   E. Gospel
7. Homily
8. Marriage Rite
   A. Statement of Intentions
   B. Exchange of Vows and Consent
   C. Blessing and Exchange of Rings
   D. Meditation
   E. General Intercessions

    F. Preparation of the Gifts

    G. Eucharistic Prayer

    H. The Lord's Prayer

9. Nuptial Blessing

10. Sign of Peace

11. Breaking of the Bread

12. Communion

13. Prayer after Communion

14. Final Prayer and Blessing

15. Dismissal

16. Recessional

Rite for Celebrating Marriage Outside Mass

1. Prelude

2. Processional

3. Opening Prayer

4. Liturgy of the Word

    A. Old Testament Reading

    B. Responsorial Psalm

    C. New Testament Reading

    D. Gospel Acclamation

    E. Gospel

5. Homily

6. Rite of Marriage

    A. Statement of Intentions

    B. Exchange of Vows and Consent

    C. Blessing and Exchange of Rings

    D. Meditation

    E. General Intercessions

    F. The Lord's Prayer

7. Nuptial Blessing

8. Final Prayer and Blessing

9. Recessional

JEWISH CEREMONY

There are three denominations in the Jewish religion: Orthodox (traditional and very strict), Conservative (less strict), and Reform (lenient).

REQUIREMENTS

Interfaith Marriage: Orthodox or Conservative rabbis will not perform an interfaith ceremony. Some Reform rabbis will perform an interfaith ceremony.

Wedding Date: Wedding ceremonies cannot take place on Friday night, Saturday (the Sabbath), during Passover, or on other holy days. Most weddings are held in synagogues, but they can take place anywhere you prefer.

Male Witnesses: Two male witnesses are required at all Jewish weddings.

Skullcaps: In Orthodox and Conservative synagogues, all men are required to cover their heads to show respect. There are skullcaps available in the vestibule for those without hats. Women usually wear hats or cover their heads too.

Remarriage: Jews must obtain a "Get," which is a religious sanction of divorce. Without a "Get" a Jewish remarriage cannot take place. The "Get" is given by the husband to the wife; a wife may not divorce the husband.

WEDDING CEREMONIES

There are variations among the Orthodox, Conservative, and Reform denominations related to the bride's egalitarian participation in the ceremony. The wedding ceremony has three main components: (1) the Ketubah (wedding contract), (2) the ring, and (3) the huppah (canopy which symbolizes cohabitation and consummation).

Prior to the Ceremony

1. Oyfrufn
   A. The groom (or both of you) blesses the Torah in the synagogue on the Shabbat morning before the wedding.
   B. Candy is thrown at the bride and groom after the reading to symbolize a sweet life together.
2. Fasting: The bride and groom fast on the wedding day until the reception.
3. Tenaim: The bride and groom sign this legal document before the ceremony.
4. Kinyan: The groom takes a handkerchief given to him by the rabbi symbolizing his willingness to abide by the Ketubah.

5. Bedeken: The ushers dance around the groom as he approaches the bride to lift her veil, making sure that the bride is not an imposter.

The Ceremony

1. Processional: The attendants precede the groom with his parents, followed by the maid of honor and the flower girl, then you and your parents.
2. Circling the Groom: You circle the groom several (two to thirteen times is the tradition) times. Sometimes the mothers join you.
3. Wedding Service: The rabbi leads the wedding service through recitation of the passages from the Bible, hymns, and blessings. It includes the Shevah Berachot (Seven Blessings). You both share a goblet of wine while being blessed. Then the groom recites the vow of consecration and puts the wedding ring on your right index finger. In double-ring ceremonies, the bride repeats this procedure.
4. Ketubah: The rabbi reads the marriage contract.
5. Breaking the Glass: The groom breaks a wine glass with his foot.
6. Recessional
7. Yihud: You both have private, intimate time together before the reception begins.

The Protestant Ceremony

Requirements

Baptism: Either you or the groom, or both, must be baptized a Protestant of that sect. Interfaith marriages are acceptable.

Divorce: All that is necessary is proof of legal divorce. Some may require church "judgment" for second marriages. Check with your church.

Wedding Ceremony

The traditional Protestant ceremony is taken from *The Book of Common Prayer*. There are variations on the marriage vows depending on the sect.

1. Introduction
   A. Scriptural and Other Readings
   B. Homily or Sermon
2. Statement of Intentions
3. Exchange of Marriage Vows

4. Exchange of Rings
5. Prayers
6. Declaration of Marriage
   A. Lord's Prayer
   B. Holy Communion
7. Benediction
8. Recessional

EASTERN ORTHODOX CEREMONY

The Eastern Orthodox church is similar to the Roman Catholic church. The leadership of the Eastern Orthodox church is the Patriarch instead of the Pope for the Roman Catholic church. Mediterranean and Eastern countries (Greece, Romania, Russia, Lebanon) make up the membership of this religion. The wedding ceremony is very similar to the Roman Catholic ceremony with the differences discussed below.

REQUIREMENTS

Location: The wedding ceremony takes place in a church and during daylight hours.

Interfaith Marriages: Interfaith marriages are permitted as long as either the bride or groom is Eastern Orthodox.

Holy Communion: You are both required to receive Holy Communion on the Sunday before your wedding date. For interfaith marriages, only the Orthodox member receives Holy Communion.

Ecclesiastical Decree: Second marriages are permitted but the couple must satisfy the requirements of the church.

WEDDING CEREMONY

The wedding ceremony is similar to the Roman Catholic ceremony. Only the differences are listed below.

1. Office of Crowning: The priest places crowns (either flowers and leaves, gold, or silver) on your heads. You walk around the table in front of the Holy Doors three times in honor of the Trinity.
2. Candles: You both hold lit candles during the ceremony.
3. Wine: You both drink from the same glass of wine.

MORMON CEREMONY

The Church of Jesus Christ of Latter Day Saints has two types of wedding ceremonies: (1) the temple ceremony is for "life and eternity," and (2) the civil or church ceremony is for "life" only.

REQUIREMENTS FOR TEMPLE CEREMONY

The requirements are very strict for a temple ceremony. To be married in the temple is to be married for eternity. Only those members of the church in good standing are allowed into the temple to participate in the ceremony.

Baptism: You both must be baptized. Records of Baptism are on file in the church headquarters in Salt Lake City. The groom has to have been ordained an elder in the Melchizedek Priesthood. This does not apply to the bride.

Member in Good Standing: You both must be members in good standing. This is determined by the bishop and the stake president within your ward. Your bishop determines whether you are in good standing on an annual basis. To be a member in good standing, you must live your life according to the following standards:

1. No alcohol.
2. No smoking.
3. No tea, coffee, or other harsh substances.
4. Sustain church leadership.
5. Pay tithings (10 percent of your annual income must go to the church).
6. Live a good moral life.
7. Be honest in your dealings with fellow men.

Counsel: The bishop meets with you to prepare you for married life. He gives advice on keeping avenues of communication open. He encourages you to have daily prayer together and to tell each other "I love you" every day.

Divorce: The Mormon divorce rate is very low. The church tries to help couples work out their differences before discussing divorce. If you are divorced and you want to be remarried in the temple, you will both need to be members in good standing. Discuss this with your bishop.

Attire: You must wear special temple clothing for your ceremony. Everything must be white. The groom wears white trousers, shirt, and jacket. The bride wears a modest, white gown (no revealing necklines).

REQUIREMENTS FOR CIVIL/CHURCH CEREMONY

There are no requirements for a civil ceremony. The couple doesn't have to be Mormon nor do they have to be in good standing with the church. You are married for this life, not eternity. There are no fees.

Cultural Hall or Relief Society Room: Your ceremony takes place in the cultural hall or the relief society room of the church. It does not take place in the temple. Civil ceremonies can take place outside the church in a garden or recreation hall.

Counsel: The bishop meets with you and gives you advice for married life together. He reviews the ceremony description to make sure that you are both in agreement with the ceremony.

WEDDING CEREMONY

Temple Ceremony

1. Endowment Room in the Temple: Give your commitment to the Heavenly Father.
2. Sealing Room in the Temple
   A. You are married by the stake president or the temple sealers, not the bishop.
   B. Exchange of Rings.
   C. You both kneel across the altar holding hands.
   D. Advice about marriage.
   E. Witnesses sign the wedding certificate.
   F. Family members and close friends who have a Temple Recommendation are allowed to join you during the ceremony; it is not open to all your guests.
   G. Family and friends congratulate you.
   H. You do not have a processional or recessional.

Civil Ceremony

1. You are married by the bishop.
2. You both hold right hands.
3. Exchange of vows.
4. Announce marriage for mortal life.
5. Exchange of rings.
6. Bishop presents you to the congregation.

BUDDHIST CEREMONY

There are three denominations of the Buddhist religion: (1) Zen, (2) Jodo Shinshu, and (3) Nishi-ren. Each denomination has its own wedding ceremony.

REQUIREMENTS

Respect: The couple should pay respect to the Buddha, Dharma, and the Sangha. They should also attend the weekly services at the temple.

Interfaith Marriage: There are no regulations stipulating conversion if either of you are not Buddhist.

Location: The ceremony does not have to take place at the temple.

WEDDING CEREMONY

Jodo Shinshu: The Jodo Shinshu sect's wedding ceremony is patterned after the Protestant ceremony. It doesn't stress meditation like the Zen sect does.

1. Ringing of the temple bell (outside)
2. Minister enters
3. Ushers escort grandparents and parents
4. Ushers light candles
5. Wedding music
6. Groom and his attendants enter
7. Wedding march begins
8. Bridal party enters
9. Your father presents you to the groom
10. Best man and maid of honor present rings to the minister
11. Minister asks your names
12. Recite Three Treasures
13. Recite Nembutsu
14. Minister chants Sutra
15. Minister chants Three Treasures
16. Minister reads wedding text
17. Consent of vows
18. Exchange of rings
19. Minister presents marriage license to groom

20. Minister presents the Buddhist "ojuz" (rosary) to you and the groom
21. You both offer incense
22. Message by the minister
23. Wedding embrace
24. Minister and wedding party to gassho and bow together
25. Minister introduces the newlyweds
26. Recessional
27. Receiving line in the temple entrance area

MUSLIM WEDDING

REQUIREMENTS

Interfaith Weddings: It is forbidden for a Muslim woman to marry a non-Muslim man. A Muslim man, however, may marry a non-Muslim woman.

Witnesses: The witnesses need to be Muslim unless you are not Muslim. In that case the witnesses do not have to be Muslim.

WEDDING CEREMONY

1. Guests and witnesses are seated as you both stand facing each other holding your right hands.
2. Officiant offers prayer.
3. You make a statement of intention and promise to follow terms of marital agreement.
4. Groom makes a statement of intention and promises to follow terms of marital agreement.
5. You pledge obedience and faithfulness to the groom.
6. The groom pledges faithfulness and helpfulness to you.
7. Officiant offers final prayer and wishes.

ECUMENICAL (INTERFAITH) CEREMONY

REQUIREMENTS

Consult both churches: Each church may have different requirements in an interfaith ceremony. Discuss the requirements with the officiant of each church.

Location: Interfaith ceremonies are usually held on neutral grounds (neither place of worship) like a garden or home. Some religions allow interfaith weddings to take place in either a church or temple.

WEDDING CEREMONY

A clergymember from each church officiates at the ceremony. Decide how you would like to divide the ceremony procedures and discuss your plans with the clergy. Meet with both officiants together to review the whole wedding ceremony. Make sure that both churches are equally represented.

NONDENOMINATIONAL CEREMONY

REQUIREMENTS

The purpose of a nondenominational ceremony is to allow you to be married with a spiritual essence without the structure or dogma of one or two religions. There are no requirements for nondenominational ceremonies.

The ceremony can be offered by any willing church or by nondenominational societies.

WEDDING CEREMONY

The ceremony is usually similar to the traditional Protestant ceremony. You can add your own poems and vows.

CIVIL CEREMONY

REQUIREMENTS

For most civil marriages, all that is required is a marriage license.

WEDDING CEREMONY

Getting married at City Hall is fast, easy, and economical. First get the blood tests and marriage license. Call your local City Hall for details. Once you take care of the blood test and marriage license, the ceremony takes only a minute.

The judge or justice will also allow you to have a civil ceremony outside of City Hall. You can have as formal or as informal an affair as you like. The civil ceremony doesn't mean less romance, it just leaves out the religious doctrines and

rituals. Discuss your philosophy on marriage with the judge and he or she can help create a wedding ceremony of your dreams.

MILITARY CEREMONY

Commissioned Officers: Only commissioned officers may have the sword ceremony. There is no fee for use of the chapel or for the services of the military chaplain.

Uniform: Being in uniform is not required to have the traditional arch of sabers/swords at the end of your ceremony. Civilian tuxedos and gowns are allowed.

Club Facilities: The bride and groom can use the Officer's Club or the Enlisted Club on base for their reception. All that is required is proper identification. Use these facilities catered the same way as you would any other reception site.

WEDDING CEREMONY

The term "military ceremony" is a misnomer. There isn't a military wedding ceremony procedure. The ceremony is performed by the clergymember of your choice either in the church, temple, or chapel on base. The military chaplain can perform the ceremony in uniform or in robe and stole. After the ceremony (outside the church), the ushers (in uniform) face each other and arch their sabers (army) or draw their swords (navy). You both march under the arch as you leave the church.

WEDDING CHAPEL

The wedding chapel is a commercial wedding site. Its sole purpose is to marry couples from any denomination. It can be as elaborate as the wedding chapel on the Queen Mary or as simple as the wedding chapels in Reno (notorious for their quick weddings).

Some wedding chapels operate the same as any other wedding ceremony site. You rent the site for a fee and provide the clergymember, flowers, photographs, and musicians. Others have package deals that include all the above for one fee.

Wedding chapels are predominately found in California, Nevada, and the Southwestern United States. Most of these states have a confidential marriage certificate that allows the couple to get married without blood tests and public record of their marriage.

REQUIREMENTS

Clergymember: There are no requirements to be married in a wedding chapel unless you have a clergymember from your church officiating. The Catholic church won't allow weddings to take place in a wedding chapel because it is a commercial wedding establishment and not a place of worship. Check with your clergymember to be sure.

Marriage License: Quickie wedding chapels usually have wedding licenses available for your convenience. Other wedding chapels require that you obtain the wedding license prior to your wedding ceremony.

WEDDING CEREMONY

The wedding ceremony at quickie chapels is performed by the house officiant. It is a standard ceremony usually taken from *The Book of Common Prayer*. The ceremony is very short. You may have a few close friends or family there to join you for your nuptials.

If a clergymember officiates, the ceremony will be based on his or her religion. It can be as formal and as personal as you choose.

RECTORY WEDDING

The rectory wedding ceremony is for those who prefer a religious, private ceremony. The requirements are the same as for weddings in a public setting. Request a meeting with your clergymember to discuss requirements and procedures.

DOUBLE WEDDING

REQUIREMENTS

The requirements for a double wedding ceremony are the same as for a single wedding. Both couples decide on the type of ceremony and consult the clergymember about requirements.

WEDDING CEREMONY

A double wedding offers twice the fun and excitement while cutting down on the expense for both couples. If you want to have a personal wedding but want a double ceremony, consider having your own wedding ceremony with a double reception.

Attire: The two brides should wear similar gowns. One bride should not outshine the other. The attendants can wear different colors and styles as long as the colors don't clash. The groom and ushers can wear either the same colors or coordinating colors to match their bridal party.

Wedding Party: Both sets of brides and grooms select their own wedding attendants. Often the bride and groom will be the maid of honor and best man in each other's weddings.

Processional and Recessional: Traditionally the older of the two brides goes first. If there are two aisles, both brides can walk down them simultaneously. If the brides are sisters, the father can escort both down together, thus eliminating the need to decide who goes first.

Pews: The first pews are reserved for all of the parents. Both brides' parents sit in the first pew on the left and both grooms' parents sit in the first pew on the right.

Receiving Lines: If the brides are sisters, only one receiving line is necessary. The newlyweds along with the brides' parents and both sets of the grooms' parents stand in line. If the brides aren't related, have two separate receiving lines.

ELOPEMENT

The ceremony for elopement is usually performed at a rectory, City Hall, or a wedding chapel. The ceremony is usually simple and fast, but it can be as elaborate as you prefer. An elopement is a private ceremony that is usually a secret known only to the bride and groom. All of the ceremony requirements are the same, depending on the type of ceremony you select.

CEREMONY SITES

Once you decide on your wedding style, you'll need to select the location. If you're having a traditional wedding and you both belong to the same church, your decision is easy. On the other hand, if you want a unique or contemporary ceremony, you may need to explore various possibilities.

Call around and ask if your wedding date and time are available. Ask if the site will accommodate the number of guests you plan to invite. Many facilities have literature listing their policies about music, flash photography, rice, candlelight, and so forth. Use the Wedding Ceremony Site Possibilities Checklist on page 212 to help you consider all your possibilities. When you have selected the site, use the Wedding Ceremony Site Worksheet on page 213 to keep track of all the details.

WEDDING CEREMONY SITE POSSIBILITIES CHECKLIST

QUESTIONS	POSSIBILITY 1	POSSIBILITY 2	POSSIBILITY 3
Location			
Address			
Phone			
Manager			
Availability			
Length of Time			
Minimum/Maximum Number of Guests			
Denomination			
Organist/Soloist			
Other Music Allowed			
Photography Allowed			
Rice/Flower Throwing			
Candlelight Ceremony			
Floral Decorations			
Rehearsal Time			
Coat/Hat Room			
Dressing Room for Bridal Party			
Handicap Accessibility			
Special Church Requirements			
Do Vows Need to Be Approved?			
Fees			
Parking Availability			
Other Services at the Same Time			

WEDDING CEREMONY SITE WORKSHEET

Type of Ceremony: _____

Location: _____

_____

Address: _____

_____

Phone Number: _____

Manager: _____

Minimum Guests: _____

Maximum Guests: _____

Length of Time: _____

Date: _____

Time: _____

Earliest Arrival Time: _____

Fees/Due Date: _____

Floral Arrangements Setup Time: _____

Details: _____

_____

White Carpet Setup Time: _____

Candlelight Ceremony: _____

Rice/Flower Throwing: _____

Equipment/Costs: _____

Wedding Altar: _____

Wedding Arch: _____

Guest Book Stand: _____

Aisle Stanchions: _____

Chairs: _____

Candelabras: _____

Candles: _____

_____

Kneeling Bench: _____

Rehearsal Times: _____

Do Personal Vows Need to Be Approved: _____

Organist: _____

Soloist: _____

Other Musicians: _____

Denomination: _____

Clergy: _____

Dressing Room: _____

Photography Setup Time: _____

Videography Setup Time: _____

Audio Equipment/Cost: _____

Gift Table: _____

Guest Book with Pen: _____

Person in Charge of Guest Book: _____

Person to Pass Out Wedding
Programs: _____

Person to Move Flowers to
Reception Site: _____

Usher to Receive Seating Chart
for Pews: _____

Number of Seating Chart Copies: _____

People to Pass Out Flowers/Rice to Throw: _____

Person to Watch Gifts During Ceremony
and to Move to Reception: _____

Coat/Hat Room Attendant: _____

Fees Due/Date: _____

Fees for Janitor: _____

Other: _____

_____

_____

LONG-DISTANCE WEDDING SITES

If you're planning a long-distance wedding, you'll need to depend on a close friend or relative or travel yourself to check out the sites. Popular wedding sites may have Internet web pages set up to help you explore your possibilities. Get as much background information you can get on your desired site, make appointments to visit and reserve it as soon as possible.

CONFERENCE OR PICTUREPHONE™ WEDDING SITES

If your families and close friends live across the continent and the cost of flights inhibits their traveling, consider having a conference or PICTUREPHONE™ wedding. The wedding ceremony takes place in your town. With the conference call wedding, all parties are tied together over the phone lines so everyone hears the wedding ceremony live. They can all participate, offering prayers and blessings. With the PICTUREPHONE™ wedding, all parties need to have the PICTURE-PHONE™ or rent it from their telephone company. This is also live and allows the other parties to see the wedding via live video. Everybody can participate in the ceremony as well.

CEREMONY VOWS

Wedding vows are public pronouncements; you make promises to each other in front of all your guests. Wedding vows can be a beautiful combination of your family tradition and your contemporary beliefs. If you're having a religious ceremony, talk to your clergymember about the ceremony and vows. Read through the traditional vows to see if they reflect your true feelings. If there are phrases that are outdated or sexist, change the wording to make it more personal and appropriate for you.

Discuss the possibilities with your officiant. He or she is your best source of ideas. Browse through books at the bookstore, library, and church. Consider poetry and literature to include in special readings.

Your vows and ceremony should represent the way you feel about each other and what your marriage means to you. Use symbolism. Use special readings and symbols from other religions and ceremonies that feel right to you.

Involve friends and family by asking them to read special scriptures or poetry during the ceremony.

GUIDELINES FOR WRITING YOUR OWN VOWS

If you choose not to use the traditional wedding vows and want to write your own to personalize your ceremony, here are some guidelines:

1. Acknowledge all your guests.
2. Describe what is taking place (marriage).
3. Describe the important factors in your relationship (things that you like in each other).
4. Describe what you hope for in your future relationship (parenthood, friendship, companionship).
5. Describe your commitment to each other now and forever (despite problems with health, finances, or crises.)
6. Describe how your religion will be an integral part of your relationship (if applicable).
7. Restate your love and desire to be married.

SYMBOLIC CEREMONIES

WEDDING RING CEREMONY

The wedding ring ceremony is traditional in most weddings and mandatory in the Jewish wedding. The double ring ceremony is popular in the United States. The circular shape of the wedding ring symbolizes eternal love.

The best man usually carries both rings and hands them to the officiant during the ceremony. The officiant blesses the rings and briefly describes the history behind the custom. The groom places the ring on the bride's left hand, third finger. Then the bride places the groom's ring on his left hand, third finger.

WINE CEREMONY

The wine ceremony is part of many Christian wedding ceremonies. You share a glass of wine together to symbolize sharing your lives together and with God. The wine service is usually part of the wedding ceremony. When the Communion service follows the ceremony, wine and bread are offered to you and your guests.

WEDDING KISS

The traditional wedding kiss or embrace takes place just before the recessional. The maid of honor lifts the veil (if you're wearing one) over your face. You and the groom kiss to celebrate your new union and the guests cheer.

PROCESSIONAL AND RECESSIONAL

The wedding processional and recessional is an exciting event for the guests. They enjoy watching the bridesmaids and ushers in their beautiful gowns and tuxedos while anticipating your grand entrance. When the organist plays the bridal march, all guests rise. You walk down the aisle, escorted by your proud father in your gorgeous gown among your closest friends and family. The lilting music and array of flowers add to the majestic walk down the path to your groom.

The ushers should walk erectly and be careful not to bop or sway. During the rehearsal, practice the processional and recessional until everybody has the walk down smoothly. The ushers should walk slowly leaving four pews between them. They should start walking with the left foot. The bridesmaids follow the same pattern. They should look straight ahead and smile.

You start walking when there are eight pews between you and the last attendant. Walk slowly and enjoy every moment—all eyes are on you! Once you reach the chapel steps the music stops. Your father stands at your side until the officiant asks him to be seated.

The recessional traditionally is the reverse lineup of the processional. You and the groom make a grand exit followed by the flower girl and ring bearer, best man, and maid of honor, and then the pairs of bridesmaids and ushers. To add a special moment in the recessional you may stop and kiss your parents and the groom's parents or offer a gift of flowers to each.

The processional and recessional lineups are not cast in stone. You can create a processional that is comfortable for your attendants and ushers. The following suggestions are just guidelines.

CHRISTIAN WEDDINGS

PROCESSIONAL

The organist pauses for a moment and then plays the music for the processional. The groom and best man enter from a room off to the right. The ushers walk up the aisle in pairs starting with the shortest to the tallest. The bridesmaids follow in

pairs (if there are more than four) also starting with the shortest. If there is an uneven number of bridesmaids, the shortest walks alone before the pairs. If there are fewer than four bridesmaids, they walk singly. The maid of honor is next, followed by the ring bearer and the flower girl. The ring bearer can walk either before or with the flower girl.

The organist pauses again for a moment to indicate that you and your father will be entering. The music is majestic as you make your entrance. The guests all rise until the officiant asks the guests to be seated.

RECESSIONAL

The organist plays a happy march as you and the groom walk arm-in-arm down the aisle. The flower girl and ring bearer pair off and follow behind. Then the maid of honor and the best man pair off, followed by pairs of the bridesmaids and ushers. The officiant follows the last bridesmaid and usher.

After the recessional, the ushers return to the ceremony site and escort guests out. The ushers can untie the pew ribbons row by row indicating when each row is to exit.

AT THE ALTAR

The officiant stands at the altar with you on the left and the groom on the right. The best man stands next to the groom and the ring bearer is next. The ushers line up making a straight line. The maid of honor stands next to you and the flower girl stands next to her. The bridesmaids line up next to the flower girl.

To be sure that everyone is standing in the right position you might want to place a penny on the spot for each attendant. This will help avoid having attendants stand too closely together or creating a crooked line.

Have young flower girls and ring bearers sit in the first pew next to their parents during the ceremony. They can stand and join in the recessional at the appropriate time. Children four years old or younger may have difficulty standing still for any length of time.

JEWISH WEDDINGS

PROCESSIONAL

The beginning of the processional is sounded off by the uplifting music of the organist or other instrumentalists. The rabbi is the first to walk down the aisle (with the cantor if you have one). He or she is followed by the ushers. The ushers walk singly and the best man follows them. The groom is escorted by both of his

parents. The groom's father is on the left and the groom's mother is on the right. The bridesmaids follow single file. The maid of honor is next followed by the flower girl and the ring bearer. You are escorted by both of your parents. Your father is on your left and your mother is on your right.

RECESSIONAL

You and the groom lead the way down the aisle for the recessional. Your mother and father are next followed by the groom's mother and father. The ushers and bridesmaids pair off. The flower girl and ring bearer are next followed by the rabbi/cantor.

AT THE ALTAR

Both of you stand with the rabbi under the huppah. If there is room under the huppah, the groom's mother and father stand on the left side and your mother and father stand on the right side. If there is room, grandparents may also join you under the huppah. The bridesmaids and ushers stand outside the huppah.

YOUR ESCORT AND WHO GIVES YOU AWAY

DIVORCED PARENTS

If your parents are divorced and neither parent has remarried, your father will escort you. If your mother has recently remarried, your father should still escort you since your stepfather did not raise you.

If your parents divorced when you were a young child and your mother and stepfather raised you, this puts you in an awkward position. You can ask your stepfather to escort you down the aisle if your father played a passive role in your life and upbringing. If your father actively participated in raising you along with your mother and stepfather try involving them both in the ceremony. Maybe your stepfather could walk you down the aisle and your father could stand by the altar to give you away. Consider all the variables and try to make a decision that is fair to all.

DECEASED FATHER

Planning your wedding will bring up feelings of sadness and loss if your father is deceased. He was supposed to walk you down the aisle and give you away. One bride walked down the aisle with her mother and carried a framed picture of her

father as she walked during the processional. That's a good way to come to a closure with your father's death if it was recent. He raised you with your mother and symbolically he and your mother will give you away.

Others ask a brother, stepfather, uncle, or godfather to escort them down the aisle. Choose somebody to whom you feel close. It's a special honor for both of you.

CHOOSING THE CLERGYMEMBER

For some, choosing a clergymember is easy. If you have belonged to the same parish for over twenty years then there is only one person and place to consider. For others, this can be the beginning of an emotional tug of war. Those couples who have been faithful to different religions may experience a rude awakening when they need to choose which church will marry them. This may bring up all kinds of questions about your relationship that you may not have dealt with yet. Have you thought about how you will raise your children and under which faith?

Couples in this dilemma often compromise by having an interfaith wedding ceremony. You meet with each clergymember in their respective places of worship. You undergo all the requirements for each church or temple. Then you meet with both clergymembers to discuss the ceremony prayers, vows, and so forth. Interfaith relationships are happening at all socioeconomic levels. Ecumenical ceremonies are becoming commonplace in our society today.

Sometimes a couple doesn't practice their religion or doesn't have any religious ties. They don't want to have a City Hall ceremony and yet they don't want to be married under false pretenses with promises they can't keep. Couples who don't have strong religious ties, but want to have a spiritual ceremony, should check with the Unitarian church or ask friends for suggestions.

If you want a ceremony without any religious overtones, you'll need a judge or justice. Be clear with the officiant when you talk with him. State the type of ceremony you want and what you don't want. Ask to see the standard wedding ceremony and see how receptive he or she is to changes.

Once you've decided on who will marry you, check to make sure the schedule is open on your wedding date. You may need to change the date or the location if you are set on a particular clergymember. Use the Clergymember/Church Requirements worksheet on page 220 to help you inquire about all facets of the ceremony and special requirements.

CLERGYMEMBER/CHURCH REQUIREMENTS WORKSHEET

Clergymember: _____   Phone: _____

Address: _____

Denomination: _____

REQUIREMENTS	DATE COMPLETED
Clergymember Requirements:	
Church/Temple Requirements:	
Bride and Groom's Special Requirements: (Special readings or vows)	
Meeting Dates/Places:	
Rehearsal Dates/Places	
Clergymember Fees:	
Church/Temple Fees:	
Person in Charge of Giving Fees to Clergymember:	

MARRIAGE LICENSE

REGULAR MARRIAGE LICENSE

Most states require proof of citizenship, proof of age, state health certification, and proof of divorce if you were previously married. Gather all of these certificates before you go to the County Clerk's office to apply for the license. Most states require that the marriage license be applied for no more than thirty days before the ceremony.

If you are under eighteen years of age, you may need a written letter of consent from your parents to marry. Even with the consent from parents, most states won't allow a legal marriage under the age of sixteen. The laws are different for men and women in many states.

The state health certificate consists of blood test results. They screen for syphilis and rubella and in some states they check for genetically transmitted diseases. You should both have complete physical examinations so that you are both aware of each other's health factors. This information is vital for couples to know before they get married and start a family. Use the Bride's Health Record on pages 222–223 and the Groom's Health Record on pages 224–225 to note all vital medical information. The state health certificate is good for ninety days.

Call your County Clerk's office to set up an appointment. Be sure that your appointment date falls within the required period for your state. Take all necessary documentation to avoid a second trip. Don't forget your checkbook. There is a small fee to pay for the license. You and your fiancé are required to apply together. Use the Marriage License Checklist on page 226 to keep track of all the details.

CONFIDENTIAL MARRIAGE LICENSE

A confidential marriage license is kept under seal by the state. The state health certificate is not required but all other stipulations stand. This confidential marriage license was adopted when couples wanted to prevent their children from discovering their marriage dates. Pregnant brides could get married to protect their children's legitimacy and inheritance without public record of the wedding date.

One in three couples use the confidential marriage certificate. Those who don't support the health test requirements also choose this type of license. Check with the County Clerk's office for fees. The state will issue a certified copy of your confidential marriage certificate to you upon request, for a nominal fee.

BRIDE'S HEALTH RECORD

Full Married Name:	
Full Maiden Name:	

Birthday:	Birthplace:	
Weight at Birth:	Length at Birth:	

Mother's Name:
Father's Name:

Doctor:	Address:	Phone:
Gynecologist:	Address:	Phone:
Specialist:	Address:	Phone:
Dentist:	Address:	Phone:
Medical Insurance Co.:	Policy Number:	Phone:
Dental Insurance Co.:	Policy Number:	Phone:

PERSONAL INFORMATION		HAVE YOU EVER HAD?			
Blood Type		Rheumatic Fever		Arthritis	
Blood Rh		Heart Trouble		Headaches	
Present Weight		Tuberculosis		Numbness	
Height		Nervousness		Digestive Problems	
Blood Pressure		Dizziness		Allergies	
Cholesterol		Backaches		Anemia	
Vision (20/20)		Diabetes		Cancer	
Hearing		Sinus Trouble		Insomnia	
		Asthma		Sexually Transmitted Diseases	

IMMUNIZATIONS	DATE	IMMUNIZATIONS	DATE	MENSTRUAL CYCLE	
DTP		Rubella		Age/First Period	
Tetanus (adult)		Polio		Regular Cycles?	
Measles		Smallpox		Length of Cycle	
Mumps		Tuberculosis		No. Days/Period	
Hepatitis					

X-Rays:

Reason: Hospital: Date:

Reason: Hospital: Date:

Hospitalization:

Reason: Hospital: Date:

Reason: Hospital: Date:

Allergies:

Allergy: Reaction:

Allergy: Reaction:

Medications:

Name: For: Dosage:

Name: For: Dosage:

Name: For: Dosage:

Birth Control:

Other Health Problems:

FAMILY HISTORY

RELATIONSHIP	SERIOUS ILLNESS	IF DECEASED, AGE AT DEATH	CAUSE OF DEATH
Mother			
Father			
Maternal Grandmother			
Maternal Grandfather			
Paternal Grandmother			
Paternal Grandfather			
Brother			
Brother			
Sister			
Sister			
Other Relatives:			

GROOM'S HEALTH RECORD

Full Name:

Birthday: | Birthplace:

Weight at Birth: | Length at Birth:

Mother's Name:

Father's Name:

Doctor: | Address: | Phone:

Urologist: | Address: | Phone:

Specialist: | Address: | Phone:

Dentist: | Address: | Phone:

Medical Insurance Co.: | Policy Number: | Phone:

Dental Insurance Co.: | Policy Number: | Phone:

PERSONAL INFORMATION		HAVE YOU EVER HAD?			
Blood Type		Rheumatic Fever		Arthritis	
Blood Rh		Heart Trouble		Headaches	
Present Weight		Tuberculosis		Numbness	
Height		Nervousness		Digestive Problems	
Blood Pressure		Dizziness		Allergies	
Cholesterol		Backaches		Anemia	
Vision (20/20)		Diabetes		Cancer	
Hearing		Sinus Trouble		Insomnia	
		Asthma		Sexually Transmitted Diseases	
IMMUNIZATIONS	DATE	IMMUNIZATIONS	DATE		
DTP		Rubella			
Tetanus (adult)		Polio			
Measles		Smallpox			
Mumps		Tuberculosis			
Hepatitis					

X-Rays:

Reason:	Hospital:	Date:
Reason:	Hospital:	Date:

Hospitalization:

Reason:	Hospital:	Date:
Reason:	Hospital:	Date:

Allergies:

Allergy:	Reaction:
Allergy:	Reaction:

Medications:

Name:	For:	Dosage:
Name:	For:	Dosage:
Name:	For:	Dosage:

Birth Control:

Other Health Problems:

FAMILY HISTORY

RELATIONSHIP	SERIOUS ILLNESS	IF DECEASED, AGE AT DEATH	CAUSE OF DEATH
Mother			
Father			
Maternal Grandmother			
Maternal Grandfather			
Paternal Grandmother			
Paternal Grandfather			
Brother			
Brother			
Sister			
Sister			
Other Relatives:			

MARRIAGE LICENSE CHECKLIST

County Clerk's Address:	
County Clerk's Phone:	
County Clerk's Hours:	
State's Minimum Age of Marriage:	
Marriage License Fees:	
Waiting Period After Application:	
Marriage License Is Good for How Many Days:	
Appointment with County Clerk: (Less Than Thirty Days from Wedding)	
Bride's Doctor:	
Doctor's Address:	
Doctor's Phone:	
Doctor's Fees for Exam:	
Appointment Date:	
Groom's Doctor:	
Doctor's Address:	
Doctor's Phone:	
Doctor's Fees for Exam:	
Appointment Date:	

DOCUMENTS FOR COUNTY CLERK

Proof of Citizenship: (Driver's License)	
Proof of Age: (Birth Certificate)	
State Health Certificate:	
Proof of Divorce: (If Previously Married)	
Letters of Consent for Marriage of Minor:	
Other:	

CEREMONY SEATING

There should be enough seating for all of your guests to sit comfortably. If the ceremony site is too large with more seating than you need, try to section off an appropriate-sized area. This will create a cozy atmosphere instead of a wide open, empty feeling.

TRADITIONAL SEATING

Your guests sit on the left side and the groom's sit on the right. If either you or the groom have significantly more guests than the other, use the traditional seating for the reserved pews only. Ushers can seat guests on either side.

RESERVED SECTION SEATING (PEW)

Reserved Section Seating Cards: Mark the reserved pews off with ribbons and flowers so guests won't sit in the reserved sections. Send reserved pew seating cards to these special guests with their invitation so they can hand it to the usher when they arrive. This helps avoid a faux pas if an usher misses a special guests and seats him or her in the back. See the Reserved Section Checklist on page 228.

Traditional Seating: Your parents sit in the first pew on the left side. Your grandparents, siblings, or children can also sit in the first pew. Special aunts and uncles can sit in the second and third rows. The groom's family is seated in the same manner but on the right side.

Divorced Parents: If your parents or the groom's parents are divorced, the mother and her husband sit in the first pew and the father and his wife sit in the second or third pew.

If you live with your father and stepmother or if you were raised by them, they sit in the first pew and your mother and stepfather sit in the second or third pew.

RESERVED SECTION CHECKLIST

PEW NUMBER	BRIDE'S SECTION	GROOM'S SECTION
First Pew		
Second Pew		
Third Pew		

Head usher responsible for reserved section seating: _____
Make copies and give to the head usher and ushers along with the Bridal Party Checklist.

SPECIAL CIRCUMSTANCES

The Ozzie and Harriet marriage and family has fallen from being the norm. There are many twists in family trees. The following suggestions cover some of the special circumstances that may apply to your wedding. Use your good judgment when making decisions about handling special people. Remember, your wedding will raise many emotions, both good and bad, so be prepared to deal with them. Discuss your options with your fiancé. Consider all the variables and then make a decision. Let all those concerned know what you've decided so there are no surprises for them and for you on your wedding day.

SECOND MARRIAGE

People who have been married before tend to make their second wedding very personal. Their weddings depict their individual styles. If you want a traditional wedding, go ahead. Some brides have completely different weddings for their second time around. If you had a church service the first time, you may opt for something a little more wild and personal. On the other hand, if you had a unique wedding the first time, you may want to have a traditional religious ceremony for your second. Your wedding can be anything that makes you feel wonderful as long as it is done with taste.

STEPCHILDREN

It is important that children from previous marriages don't feel left out of your future plans. This is especially true for younger children. Their routine and stability are up in the air as all these changes are taking place. Make the children an integral part of your plans. If they are old enough, ask them to be honor attendants. If they are too young, they can be ring bearers, pages, or flower girls.

Some couples include the children in the marriage ceremony. They can read special poems and can even be included in the vows. Make your ceremony unique by including all of your children. After all, your marriage is creating a whole new family and the growth and dynamics of this new family can start on a good, healthy note by including everyone in your wedding day celebration.

REAFFIRMING VOWS

If you eloped and now regret it, reaffirm your vows with all the wedding frills. It's never too late to reaffirm your vows. Some couples were intimidated by the high cost of weddings and had small civil ceremonies. After a few years of saving, they decide to reaffirm vows and celebrate their marriage with the friends and family

members whom they couldn't invite the first time around. Pregnant brides often don't have time to plan an elaborate wedding so they marry at City Hall and then reaffirm their vows in a formal wedding after the baby is born.

CEREMONY REHEARSAL

WHOM TO INCLUDE

Invite the wedding party, clergymember, both sets of parents, ceremony musicians, altar boys, and anyone else who will be involved in the ceremony. Discourage spouses and friends from attending the rehearsal. Invite them to the rehearsal dinner or party after the rehearsal. Use the Ceremony Rehearsal Checklist on page 233 to make sure you bring what you need to the rehearsal.

WHAT TO WEAR

Wear a pretty, flowing dress to enhance the atmosphere. The attendants should also wear long dresses and dress shoes. The ushers should wear trousers and long sleeved shirts. Advise the wedding party of a respectful dress code if the rehearsal will take place in a church or temple. Have someone take pictures of the rehearsal. These photographs will later bring back fond memories.

INDIVIDUAL RESPONSIBILITIES

Complete a checklist for each attendant and helper. Fill in all of the pertinent information for the wedding party, parents, and helpers. Use the checklist in Chapter Two, Bridal Party's Checklist on page 23. As you make decisions for every facet of the ceremony and reception, fill in the person's name on that worksheet and enter the task on that person's checklist. Double-check your lists to make sure you don't forget anything.

Sometime during the rehearsal, meet with each attendant, parent, and helper individually. Go over their checklists with them. Ask each person to explain what he or she is responsible for so you can catch any misunderstandings. If you do all the explaining while they passively listen, important details may be overlooked. Make sure they understand where they need to be and what they need to do. Give each person a checklist along with a copy of the Ceremony and Reception Time Line worksheets on pages 234 and 235. The better informed everybody is, the less likely they will be to forget their responsibilities.

The coordinator should receive a copy of everybody's checklists along with the Ceremony and Reception Time Line worksheets. Give the coordinator her checklist with the wedding party's names and addresses and all the details about the services (florist, photographer, musicians, and so on) for the ceremony and reception. That way, if somebody forgets a task, the coordinator can remind him. Or, if the florist is late, she will have the numbers to call to take care of problems.

The coordinator will also be the person who tells the attendants when to start walking down the aisle. She makes sure that everybody looks perfect and keeps calm while they wait for the processional to begin.

WHAT TO REHEARSE

When everybody arrives, get their attention and review the ceremony time line. Have everybody stand in place at the altar. Use stickers or pennies to mark each attendant's spot. Then start from the beginning by having all the attendants pretend to arrive at the site. The bridesmaids go to the bride's dressing room and the ushers make sure the site is ready for guests. The clergymember and groom go off to the appropriate room to wait. Ask the organist to play the prelude music while the ushers practice escorting the guests. After the bride's mother is seated, the clergymember will walk up to the altar and signal the groom and best man to enter. The organist starts the processional music and the wedding party enters. After the maid of honor or flower girl enters, the organist plays the wedding march and the bride enters.

The clergymember will outline the ceremony and direct you and the groom. He or she acts as Master of Ceremonies. The clergymember can help if you are nervous by asking you to repeat your vows after him. If you have a wine ceremony, the clergymember will direct the best man to get the wine and lead you through each step. Turn around and smile at your guests for a moment and walk to the beat of the recessional. The wedding party follows in the reverse order of the processional. Your parents and the groom's parents exit next.

USHERS SEATING GUESTS

Ushers should be told to start seating guests as soon as they arrive. Eldest guests are seated first if a group of guests arrive at the same time. Ushers should offer female guests his right arm and escort them down the aisle to the appropriate side. He should ask the guest which side she should be seated on. If you have reserved pews, the usher will seat those special guests in the appropriate sections. If a woman arrives with her husband, he follows behind. If the guest is an elderly man, the usher offers his right arm to escort him to his seat.

The florist usually will set up pew ribbons if you are using them. If the florist doesn't, the ushers should put the ribbons up. Ask two ushers to be responsible for the pew ribbons and two ushers to lay the aisle carpet. The same ushers should remove the pew ribbons and aisle carpet after the ceremony.

Passing the Bouquet

After you reach the altar, your maid of honor will pass her bouquet to the next bridesmaid in line so she can adjust your gown and train. Then you pass your bouquet to her so you have your hands free during the ceremony. Just before the recessional, your maid of honor adjusts your gown so you can move with ease, hands you your bouquet, and off you and the groom go!

Passing the Rings

The best man holds the rings during the ceremony. At the appropriate time, he produces the rings and hands them to the clergymember. The clergymember hands the bride's ring to the groom with his palms up. This makes it easier for a nervous groom to grab. He does the same for the bride.

Ushers Signaling Guests to Leave After the Ceremony

To help avoid a traffic jam in the church, have the ushers signal guests to leave by rows, beginning with the first row. The ushers untie pew ribbons on each side simultaneously, one row at a time. They bow and motion to guests with their arms to exit. Have the ushers practice so their timing is uniform. The guests leave in an organized fashion. This is a good system to use if you plan to have your receiving line outside the church. All the guests will be exiting slowly.

For a smaller wedding, guests can exit on their own. After the recessional, the parents and relatives in the first few pews exit. Then all the guests stand and leave using any aisle.

Ushers Passing Out Maps to the Reception

Ushers typically don't stand in the receiving line outside the church, so they can pass out maps or offer directions to guests leaving for the reception. They should also know where the restrooms are for the guests' convenience. After the ceremony site is empty, the ushers should check the pews and restrooms for lost items. If the church allows you to remove flowers, ask the ushers to take the flowers to the reception site. One of the ushers should stay and lock up if necessary, and make sure that the janitor gets in to clean. Explain where facilities are so all ushers are informed. Designate one usher to be in charge of reception maps.

CEREMONY REHEARSAL CHECKLIST

ITEM TO BRING	PACKED
The Working Woman's Wedding Planner	
Checklists for Attendants	
Wedding Ceremony and Reception Time Lines	
Checklists for Parents	
Checklists for Helpers	
Coordinator's Checklist	
Marriage License	
Fake Bouquet (ribbon bouquet)	
Stickers or Tape	
Reception Maps	
Wedding Programs	
Guest Book and Pen	
Toasting Goblets	
Wine Goblets, Wine, and Corkscrew	
Cake Knife	
Fees for Clergymember	
Fees for Musicians	
Fees for Site Rental	
Other Fees	
Gift for Altar Boys	
Camera and Film	

CEREMONY TIME LINE WORKSHEET

EVENT	TIME	YOUR TIME LINE	MUSIC
Guests Arriving			
Processional			
Ceremony			
Recessional			
Assisting Guests			
Receiving Line (If Reception follows at same site)			
Post-Ceremony Responsibilities			

RECEPTION TIME LINE WORKSHEET

LEAVE CEREMONY SITE AT:	TIME	YOUR TIME LINE	MUSIC
First Hour: 　Cocktails 　Receiving Line 　Guests Are Seated 　Announce Bride and 　　Groom and Wedding 　　Party			
Second Hour: 　Lunch/Dinner 　Toasts 　First Dance 　Traditional Dances			
Third Hour: 　Special Presentations 　　by Attendants 　Tables Cleared 　Cake-Cutting Ceremony			
Fourth Hour: 　Bouquet Throwing 　Garter Throwing 　Traditional Grand Exit 　　of Bride and Groom			
Fifth Hour: 　(If bride and groom 　stay to the end of the 　reception, dancing 　continues until the 　band signals closing 　time.)			

16

The Wedding Reception

SELECTING THE LOCATION

Select a reception location to fit the style and size of your wedding. A room that is too large for the number of guests invited can leave guests with an empty feeling. A room that is too small can leave guests feeling claustrophobic. If your reception will take place in the evening, visit the site in the evening before reserving it. You will want to see the facility in the same light in which your reception will be set. This can help you plan your floral decorations and lighting. If you plan to have a band, make sure there is enough room for all their equipment. Select a room with a dance floor large enough to accommodate all your guests. Use the Reception Possibilities Checklist on page 237 to compare facilities before making your selection.

RESTRICTIONS

Make sure that the maximum number of guests permitted will accommodate your guest list. If you want candles at each table, check to see if there are any fire laws prohibiting them. Some facilities don't allow loud rock n' roll. Ask about accessibility for handicapped guests.

QUESTIONS	POSSIBILITY 1	POSSIBILITY 2	POSSIBILITY 3
Reception Site			
Address			
Phone Number			
Manager			
Dates/Times Available			
Length of Time Allowed			
Other Functions at the Same Time			
Minimum/Maximum Number of Guests			
Room for Band			
Dance Floor			
Rock-and-Roll Allowed			
Floral Arrangements			
Candles Allowed			
Bar Facilities			
Independent Caterers Allowed			
Can Independent Caterers Use Kitchen Facilities?			
Tables/Chairs Included in Fees			
Tent/Large Equipment Included in Fees			
Coat/Hat Room			
Audio Equipment Available			
Fees for Audio Equipment			
Parking Services			
Handicap Accessibility			
Site Fees			

CATERING

Find out if the facility allows you to bring your own caterers and whether or not they will allow the caterers to use their kitchen facilities. If they won't allow independent caterers and you must use their catering services, check their menu and equipment. Make sure their dinnerware, silverware, glassware, and linens are suitable. Deal with their catering services in the same way as you would deal with an independent caterer.

EQUIPMENT

Some facilities include all necessary equipment: chairs, tables, stage, microphones, lighting, and so forth. Review your needs and see what they will provide. Reserve any extra equipment from a party rental store. If your reception will be held outdoors on your property, you will need to rent all of your equipment from the tent to the tables and chairs. See the Ceremony and Reception Equipment Checklist on pages 249–250.

Rent all your equipment at the same party rental store. If prices permit, select a store that delivers and picks up its equipment for you. That will save you time and headaches.

TRADITIONAL RECEPTION ACTIVITIES

GUEST BOOK

After the ceremony, the guests drive to the reception and wait for the festivities to begin. The guest book is usually on a table with a pen near the entrance. Your guestbook attendant should encourage guests to sign their names, write their hometowns, and make brief comments. This makes a pleasant memento to look through after the wedding.

RECEIVING LINE

The receiving line is a way for your guests to meet both of your parents and your attendants. You can thank guests for celebrating your wedding with you and, if you remember, you can thank them for their gifts as well. Review the guests' names and gifts received before the wedding. You might want to do this with the groom and both sets of parents. That way parents will feel more comfortable shaking hands and having something to say.

Smile at each person and shake hands or offer a kiss. Say a few words of welcome or thanks and then introduce the guest to the person standing next to you. If you forget someone's name, don't fret; thank the person for attending and introduce him or her to the next person by saying, "This is my second cousin on my mother's side." The person next to you can ask, "and what is your name?"

If your palms perspire when you're nervous or when you shake hands, spray a little antiperspirant into your palms beforehand. Always take gloves off as it is more personal to shake hands skin to skin.

Parents' Role

Traditional

Your father is supposed to act as host and mingle during the receiving line. Your mother heads the line, followed by the groom's father, you, the groom, the groom's mother, the maid of honor, and attendants. The best man, ushers, the flower girl, and the ring bearer do not stand in line.

Contemporary

Your father can enjoy the spotlight of your big day and be part of the receiving line. He can meet all the guests and be congratulated along with the other parents.

To include your father in the receiving line, start with your mother, the groom's father, you, the groom, the groom's mother, your father, the maid of honor, and attendants.

Divorced Parents

Dealing with divorced parents is always a sensitive issue. There are three components to consider when deciding who stands in the receiving line and where they stand: (1) who is paying for the wedding, (2) who raised you or the groom, and (3) how well the ex-spouses and the new spouses get along.

Since your parents and the groom's parents don't stand next to each other in the receiving line, you can use the contemporary lineup: your mother, groom's father, you, the groom, groom's mother, and your father. This lineup is appropriate if the divorce is recent and neither parent has remarried. If one parent has remarried but the stepparent did not actively raise either you or the groom, the stepparent shouldn't stand in line. If the stepparent and the natural parent don't get along, only the parent should stand in line.

The divorced parent's new spouse may stand in line next to him or her if the stepparent was an integral part of raising you or the groom. If new spouses are friendly with the ex-spouses, they may stand in line.

If divorced parents dislike each other and you're afraid they may create a scene during the receiving line, have one parent be the focal parent during the ceremony and the other during the reception. If one parent is hosting or paying for the ceremony and the other is paying for the reception, let that dictate who is the host of each. If your mother pays for the ceremony, she can give you away and sit in the first pew. Your father will be seated in the third pew. She may even escort you down the aisle and her husband may join you if it is appropriate. If your father hosts the reception, he and his wife head the line for the receiving line and your mother doesn't stand in line.

The decision for the lineup in the receiving line is something that you and the groom will have to decide after considering all the variables. There is no "right" way to do it. Try to be fair to all parties.

Toasts

The wedding toast is traditionally given by the best man. It is usually offered after the receiving line when all the guests are seated and served something to toast with.

Offering a toast takes skill and practice. It is often the best man's first toast and he may need some help to prepare it. The best man often rambles on about his relationship with the groom, reminiscing about old times. He may even be a little jealous that you have taken his best buddy away from him. Sometimes the bride's name isn't mentioned until the end of the toast when he wishes you good luck.

The best man should mention how he knows the groom. This should be a small percentage of the toast itself. He should talk about how you both met and how your relationship enhanced your individual lives. He can add funny anecdotes about your courting days. At the end of the toast he raises his glass and toasts you and the groom. The guests all raise their glasses and join in the toast. You and the groom do not toast, just smile and look at the guests and the best man.

The Kiss

During the reception guests may, at any time, start clinking their glasses with their spoons. The resonating sounds will multiply as more guests join in the clinking. They want you to kiss the groom. Kiss him before they start breaking glasses.

THE FIRST DANCE

The traditional first dance usually takes place after the meal is served. The band leader will announce the first dance to clear the floor. It is usually a slow dance or a waltz. Parents and attendants are invited to join about halfway through the first dance.

Select your music for the first dance ahead of time. It should be a song that makes you both comfortable. It could be "your song" or a song that represents the way you feel about each other. Let the musicians know your selection so that they can practice it. You may want to practice your dance with the band to make sure you are comfortable with the tempo and length.

If you're a product of rock-and-roll and the waltz is a foreign dance to you, consider taking a private dance lesson. Your instructor can choreograph your first dance to the music you select. Your first dance will be so polished that you'll look like Cinderella and her handsome prince waltzing on the ballroom floor!

Your father can cut in and be the second to dance with you. The groom's father is usually the third. And then the best man. The groom then dances with his mother, then your mother, and then your maid of honor. Honor attendants dance together and then the bridesmaids and ushers pair off the way they did for the recessional.

Any dance order is acceptable. You can dance the whole first dance with just the groom. Let people cut in spontaneously if they wish. The bandleader should announce the appropriate time for the guests to join in.

THE DOLLAR DANCE

In some societies, the bride and groom dance with the guests during the "dollar dance" ritual. They receive a dollar or check for each dance. The guests line up to dance with the bride or groom. The bride holds the folded dollars in her hand or wears a wrist purse to hold all the money. The guests enjoy dancing with either the bride or groom and the token of their appreciation is just for fun.

SPECIAL EVENT PRESENTED BY ATTENDANTS

Weddings are often enhanced and made more personal when the bridesmaids and ushers put together a special presentation for you and the groom. The guests appreciate the show and everybody becomes more familiar with the whole wedding party.

Typically, the attendants prepare a slide show of you and the groom growing up. The slide show can include your courtship and even the wedding plans.

CHAPTER 16

Some attendants have enlarged baby pictures and other precious photographs displayed on the walls or on easels at the reception site. They can also include wedding photographs of both of your parents and grandparents (only if parents are not divorced).

Attendants can put together a pre-wedding video to share with the guests. This video could show the engagement parties, showers, bachelor parties, shopping for your gown, selecting dinnerware, and so forth. The video could also be selected footage from home movies. These productions are funny and enjoyable for guests. They also make great mementos.

Cake Cutting

The cake-cutting ceremony is one that guests love to watch. You both stand in front of the cake for photographs. Guests take pictures after the bandleader announces the cake cutting. You take the cake knife together and slice the first piece of cake slowly. Then the server places the piece on a plate. You give the groom the first bite, and then he gives you a bite. The guests cheer. Cake is next served to both parents and any other special guests. Then the servers pass out slices of cake to the guests.

Sometimes immature guests encourage you to smash the piece of cake into each other's faces. Don't let their childlike behavior motivate you to deface each other on your wedding day. This creates anxiety and hostility and ruins your attire and make-up.

According to the etiquette experts, guests should stay until the cake-cutting ceremony. They can thank the hosts and bid goodbye to you and the groom and leave once the cake has been cut.

Throwing the Bouquet

After the cake cutting ceremony, the mothers and attendants gather all the single women for the bouquet throwing ceremony. The bandleader stops the music and makes an announcement to that effect. He calls up all single women to the dance floor. You face away from the group, holding your bouquet while the women wait. Toss the bouquet high in the air so it will fall into somebody's arms. Be careful not to throw it directly at any person to avoid accidents. The person who catches your bouquet, according to superstition, will be the next to marry. If you plan to preserve your bouquet, have the florist make up a smaller version of your bouquet for the toss.

THROWING THE GARTER

After the bouquet toss, the groom takes your garter off your leg. This is usually done right on the dance floor as your guests watch. He should bring a chair out so you can sit during this ceremony. This is the only time your hosiery will show so wear nice hosiery to accent your gown.

After he removes your garter, the ushers gather all the single men. The groom faces away from the group and tosses the garter overhead. The lucky bachelor to catch this garter, just as the woman who catches the bouquet, will be the next to marry.

DECORATING THE GETAWAY CAR

The bridal party and close friends traditionally decorate your getaway car. They usually do this during the reception when you and the groom are busy mingling. When you make your grand and final exit, the guests will wave goodbye as you take off in your conspicuous getaway car.

The attendants used to tie old shoes and cans to the bumper of the car. This just added to the noise and excitement of the getaway. This idea proved to be a problem with littering the streets as shoes and cans fell off. Taping signs saying "Nicole and Jason, Just Married!" have become popular. Tying balloons, flowers, and streamers also has a nice effect. Ask the best man to make sure that the "decorating committee" uses materials that won't harm the body of the car (foams and paint) and won't fall off, creating a driving hazard.

TIME TO LEAVE

Traditionally you are supposed to make a grand exit after the bouquet and garter ceremonies. You change into your going away clothes and thank both sets of parents for their support and good wishes. Your attendants pass out rice in little pouches to throw at you and the groom as you make your final getaway. You and your new husband take off into the sunset as your guests wave goodbye.

Many couples feel that the whole wedding celebration goes by so quickly that they want to savor every last moment. Taking off after the bouquet and garter ceremonies is too early for them. They want to mingle with their guests and dance until the wee hours of the night. Guests don't have to wait until you leave; proper etiquette indicates that they can leave after the cake-cutting ceremony. The bandleader might make a statement about your staying to enjoy the reception so guests feel more comfortable leaving when they get tired. So stay and enjoy the best party of your life!

CHAPTER 16

SEATING ARRANGEMENTS

BRIDE'S TABLE

The bride's table is usually centered in the middle of the reception site so that all the guests can see you. You naturally sit next to the groom on his right. The best man sits next to you and the maid of honor sits next to the groom. The ushers and bridesmaids sit in alternating seats to the end of the table.

The bride's table is usually rectangular so guests can see the whole bridal party in one row. If the bridal party is too large, the bride, groom, and honor attendants sit at the bride's table and the bridesmaids and ushers sit at the bridal party table in close proximity.

PARENTS' TABLES

Traditionally your parents and the groom's parents sit together with the officiant and his spouse at one table. Many parents have voiced their opinions though and now often request a parent's table for each set of parents. This allows each set of parents to be seated with their family and close friends. Either choice is acceptable. Ask both sets of parents what they prefer and decide accordingly.

Try to place both parents' tables so they share the center focal point. This has been a sore spot for many parents when they feel they received second billing in placement. If there is only one center, the parents who financed the reception should get top billing.

The officiant and spouse should sit at the host's table. That could be the parents' table, the groom's parents' table, or your parents' table.

Parents who are divorced should each have their own parents' table. They can be seated with their family and close friends. If your parents don't get along, separate their tables by placing the groom's family between them.

ASSIGNED SEATING

For large weddings, assigned seating makes the seating arrangements easier and less stressful for guests. This way guests will be seated with their families and friends. Seat couples with similar interests together to spark new friendships. Single guests can be seated together with the hope that Cupid may strike.

Assigned seating will also be more efficient. Left to their own devices, guests have the bad habit of leaving one chair between them and the unfamiliar couple next to them. That would mean you'd need several more tables to accommodate your guests. Assigning seats prevents guests from leaving such gaps.

CHILDREN'S AND TEENAGERS' TABLES

If you have invited children to the wedding, seat them together unless they are very young (under four). Ask a teenage guest or attendant to entertain the children. Supply coloring books and games that are appropriate for their ages. This will let their parents be free to enjoy themselves.

Teenagers will prefer sitting with their peers instead of with the adults. The adults would probably prefer this as well. Make sure the teenagers' table has only teenagers and not college-aged people. College-aged people should be seated together as an interest group.

RECEPTION FLOOR PLAN LAYOUT

First decide what types of tables you want for the reception. Round tables seat guests in a comfortable fashion so all people at the table can see each other. Round tables usually seat eight to ten people.

Prepare a reception sketch of the bride's table, parents' tables, buffet tables, champagne fountain table, cake table, gift table, place-card table, guest-book table, and dance floor. Then lay out all of the guests' tables so that there is ample room for guests to mingle and walk around. Tables should be situated so that guests will be able to see the bride's table and the dance floor.

Some reception facilities have a diagram of table arrangements for your convenience. Use their diagram if they have listed the same number of tables that you plan to have at your reception. Otherwise, use it as a guideline but lay out your own design so that it is custom-fit for your wedding. Give the facility manager a copy of your layout so she has her employees follow your diagram and not the standard.

SEATING CHART

After laying out the reception diagram, number the tables. Use a logical sequence so guests can find their tables easily. The bride's table can be Table 1 and then go clockwise from there.

Review your guest list and seat guests according to groups: groom's aunts and uncles at one table, groom's cousins at another, groom's college friends, groom's business associates, and so forth. Be careful when preparing seating arrangements. Guests feel more comfortable around people they know or people with similar interest. Put couples together who share similar hobbies or work in the same field. Single women and men will appreciate being seated together. Teenagers and children enjoy the company of their peers rather than sitting with adults.

Use the Seating Chart on pages 247–248 to list the guests at each table. Use a pencil so you can move names around. Do the seating chart after your response date has passed. Allow some extra seating for unexpected guests. You may be surprised how many guests show up without previously responding.

Review the seating arrangements with both your family and the groom's family. Let them know who will be at each table so they can meet special guests whom they haven't yet had the opportunity to meet.

Handwrite the table number cards and the place cards a few days before the wedding. There may be unexpected changes in your seating plans so don't write them too early. Double-check your list to make sure you haven't forgotten anybody or placed too many guests at one table.

Place the seating cards on a table at the entrance to the reception site. Put them in alphabetical order so guests can find their names easily. The card should list the guest's name and table number. Each table should have its number displayed clearly. Ask a helper to stand by the seating-card table to help guests find their cards. He or she should also have a copy of the seating chart in case there is a mistake. This helper can suggest alternate seating in case of an oversight or a surprise appearance by a guest who didn't respond.

EQUIPMENT FOR THE CEREMONY AND RECEPTION

If you're having a church ceremony and a reception at a fine hotel or restaurant, chances are you won't need to rent any equipment. There are advantages to having a traditional wedding celebration. If you're having a unique wedding ceremony in an unusual location with a similarly styled reception, you'll probably need to rent equipment for both sites. Use the Ceremony and Reception Equipment Checklist on pages 249–250.

SEATING CHART

Table 1

_____
_____
_____
_____

Table 2

_____
_____
_____
_____

Table 3

_____
_____
_____
_____

Table 4

_____
_____
_____
_____

Table 5

_____
_____
_____
_____

Table 6

_____
_____
_____

Table 7

_____
_____
_____
_____

Table 8

_____
_____
_____
_____

Table 9

_____
_____
_____
_____

Table 10

_____
_____
_____
_____

Table 11

_____
_____
_____
_____

Table 12

_____
_____
_____
_____

Table 13

_____
_____
_____
_____

Table 14

_____
_____
_____

Table 15

_____
_____
_____
_____

Table 16

_____
_____
_____
_____

Table 17

_____

_____

_____

_____

Table 18

_____

_____

_____

_____

Table 19

_____

_____

_____

_____

Table 20

_____

_____

_____

_____

Table 21

_____

_____

_____

_____

Table 22

_____

_____

_____

_____

Table 23

_____

_____

_____

_____

Table 24

_____

_____

_____

_____

Table 25

_____

_____

_____

_____

Table 26

_____

_____

_____

_____

Table 27

_____

_____

_____

_____

Table 28

_____

_____

_____

_____

Table 29

_____

_____

_____

_____

Table 30

_____

_____

_____

_____

Table 31

_____

_____

_____

_____

Table 32

_____

_____

_____

_____

CEREMONY AND RECEPTION EQUIPMENT CHECKLIST

Rental Store: Manager:

Address:

Phone Number: Hours:

Policies:

CEREMONY: Delivery Time: Tear Down Time:
                Setup Time: Pickup Time:

RECEPTION: Delivery Time: Tear Down Time:
                Setup Time: Pickup Time:

CEREMONY EQUIPMENT

QTY	ITEM	DESCRIPTION	PRICE EACH	TOTAL
	Arch			
	Altar			
	Canopy (Huppah)			
	Backdrops			
	Floor Candelabra			
	Aisle Candelabra			
	Candles			
	Candlelighters			
	Kneeling Bench			
	Aisle Stanchions			
	Aisle Runners			
	Guest Book Stand			
	Gift Table			
	Chairs			
	Dance Floor			
	Stages			
	Lighting			
	Heating/Cooling			
	Umbrellas			
	Tent			
	Electric Bug Eliminator			
	Coat/Hat Rack			
	Garbage Cans			
	TOTAL CEREMONY SITE RENTAL COSTS:			

RECEPTION EQUIPMENT

QTY	ITEM	DESCRIPTION	PRICE EACH	TOTAL
	Tents			
	Flooring			
	Dance Floor			
	Stages			
	Lighting			
	Candelabras			
	Candles			
	Heating/Cooling			
	Umbrellas			
	Canopies			
	Guest Book Table			
	Gift Table			
	Fountain Table			
	Place Card Table			
	Cake Table			
	High Chairs/Booster Chairs			
	Wheelchair Ramps			
	Audio Equipment			
	Visual Equipment			
	Electric Bug Eliminator			
	Coat/Hat Rack			
	Garbage Cans			
	Mirrored Disco Ball			
	TOTAL RECEPTION SITE RENTAL COSTS:			

RECEPTION COORDINATOR

Select a person who is organized and responsible to be the reception organizer. He or she will be in charge of making sure that all the services (bakery, florist, musicians, and so forth) show up on time and get set up without a hitch. List all the names and numbers of the services on the Wedding Coordinator's Checklist on pages 20–21 in case he or she needs to call them. Also give him or her a copy of the Wedding Day Reception Site Worksheet on pages 252–253. This lists the setup time for each service.

Give a copy of the Individual Responsibilities Checklist on page 22 to the organizer. If small tasks (like placing favors at each place setting) are overlooked, the organizer will know who to remind. Also give a copy of the Reception Time Line Worksheet on page 235 to the coordinator so he or she can help remind you of different activities. He or she can also remind the other helpers of their responsibilities, such as gathering single women, passing out rice, and so on.

The person in charge of placing the place cards may forget the seating chart so the organizer should also receive a copy. If guests don't have seats or bring more guests than expected, the organizer will help seat these guests.

WEDDING NIGHT

After your big day has come to a close, you'll be spending your first night together as man and wife. The wedding night traditionally is intended to be the first night to consummate your marriage. Typically, couples stay in a romantic wedding suite in a luxury hotel on the night of their wedding.

Realistically, you and your new husband will be tired from all the excitement and emotions of the day. You may get to your luxury wedding suite only to pass out with exhaustion until the next morning. Don't let this concern you—you'll have plenty of time for romance after a good night's sleep.

If you're having an early afternoon wedding celebration, you will probably have time to rejuvenate and appreciate a romantic wedding night. If you're having a formal evening wedding and you plan to stay and party with your friends and family, you may opt to save money by spending the night at one of your houses or in an inexpensive hotel room rather than a luxury suite. In this case, you can cut corners on your wedding night and then be greatly extravagant on your honeymoon when you'll both appreciate it. Use the Wedding Night Accommodations Possibilities Checklist on page 254 to help you make your decision.

WEDDING DAY RECEPTION SITE WORKSHEET

Location	
Address	
Phone Number	
Manager	
Minimum Guests	
Maximum Guests	
Length of Time	
Date/Time	
Earliest Arrival Time	
Deposit Due/Date	
Fees Due/Date	
Janitorial Fees	
Caterer Setup Time	
Florist Setup Time	
Musician Setup Time	
Bakery Setup Time	
Videographer Setup Time	
Bar Setup Time	
Audio/Visual Setup Time	
Dance Floor Setup Time	
Place Cards, Matches, Accessories Setup Time	
Guest Book Table	
Gift Table	
Place Card Table	

Cake Table	
Fountain Table	
Tables and Chairs Setup Time	
Place Setting Setup Time	
Tent Setup Time	
Person in Charge of Watching Gifts	
Person in Charge of Transporting Gifts/To Where:	
Person in Charge of Moving Reception Flowers to Wedding Suite	
People to Pass Out Flowers or Rice	
Coat/Hat Room Attendant Fees	
Person in Charge of Returning Rental Equipment	
Person to Collect Accessories Left on Tables (Matches, Favors)	

WEDDING NIGHT ACCOMMODATION POSSIBILITIES CHECKLIST

QUESTIONS	POSSIBILITY 1	POSSIBILITY 2	POSSIBILITY 3
Hotel			
Address			
Phone			
Manager			
Date			
Check-in Time			
Check-out Time			
Deposit			
Cancellation Policy			
Room Cost			
Honeymoon Suite			
Hot Tub			
Swimming Pool			
Fitness Center			
Room Service			

NEWLYWEDS' BREAKFAST
(THE MORNING AFTER)

After your big day, you may want to have breakfast or brunch with a few people. It's a nice way to thank those special people for helping with the wedding or thanking guests for traveling a long distance to help celebrate your marriage.

This breakfast can include both sets of parents and siblings, out of town guests, and the wedding party. Try to keep the number of guests to a minimum. You're not trying to create another wedding celebration. Keep it simple and casual.

If you know that you'll be up very late and if you think you'll be drinking more than you should, plan this brunch for the early afternoon. You'll want to sleep peacefully and have a quiet time with your new husband. Consider your lifestyle and then set the time for your breakfast.

On the other hand, if you think your wedding day will be enough celebrating and you would like the next day to be alone together, have a private breakfast in your room. Go with your instincts. Use the Newlyweds' Breakfast Possibilities Checklist on page 256 to review your options and make your decision.

NEWLYWEDS' BREAKFAST POSSIBILITIES CHECKLIST

QUESTIONS	POSSIBILITY 1	POSSIBILITY 2	POSSIBILITY 3
Restaurant			
Address			
Phone			
Manager			
Menu:			
Cost and Tip			
Who Is Hosting			
Date/Time			

GUEST LIST

GUEST	ADDRESS	PHONE	R.S.V.P.

17

Destination Weddings

The destination wedding, sometimes called a honeymoon wedding or travel wedding, is a very contemporary concept. For couples who want a private wedding without the headaches of a large affair in their hometowns or the guilt of eloping, leaving town to get married and honeymoon at the same time can be the perfect solution. There are no secrets or surprises.

The wedding may be strictly private—limited to the bride and groom (in effect an elopement with advance notice)—or may include guests. Usually, guests invited to such a wedding would be limited to close family members and a few very close friends. After all, everyone will be expected to travel to the selected destination; the wedding won't be in any guest's hometown.

A destination wedding takes place adjacent to the honeymoon site. Destination weddings can be either a venue wedding, where a particular wedding site will offer you a variety of wedding services or a travel wedding, where you select the site of your wedding in an exciting and romantic environment while you keep control of making specific wedding arrangements. In either case, there will be a variety of activities already in place for you and your guests which can, in many cases, offset the cost of having the wedding away from your hometown. Venue weddings will have wedding coordinators on hand to accommodate any specific requests you might have for your wedding. For travel weddings, most popular destinations will have wedding consultants or coordinators in the area to help you with any arrangements you will need to make.

WHOM TO CONTACT

Information about wedding destinations can be gotten from a variety of sources. Ask friends and family members for suggestions. You can also consult tourist boards, chambers of commerce, travel agencies, and travel advertisements. For venue weddings, contact the specific sites to find out about what kinds of services and special wedding packages they offer.

VENUE WEDDINGS

Venue Weddings are set in specific locations that offer special wedding packages that include all the arrangements for a wonderful wedding day. If you don't want to worry about the trouble of arranging all the services and details of your wedding then the venue wedding may be your best option. Places that offer venue weddings usually include the site, an officiant, decorations, flowers, music, photography, food, and wedding cake in their wedding packages. Check with specific venues to be sure of what they provide.

TYPES OF VENUES

Bed and Breakfast: Bed and breakfast inns can offer you an intimate, romantic wedding. These inns are often located around historical areas and in some cases are even historical buildings themselves. They are becoming increasingly popular as wedding venues.

Hotels or Resorts: Many hotels and resorts now offer complete wedding packages rather than just hosting ceremonies or receptions. Hotels can be good for a luxurious, formal wedding, while vacation resorts can offer fun and excitement in a unique setting.

Natural Settings: For nature lovers, it is possible to find companies that will arrange a wedding in a beautiful natural setting. Imagine your wedding set among giant redwood trees, a snow-capped mountain, or overlooking the ocean.

Nautical Weddings: Many cruise ships, yachts, and other vessels are now offering wedding packages. The ocean liner Queen Mary, in dry dock at Long Beach, California, is a popular site for an elegant wedding. You could have your nautical wedding without worrying about seasickness.

TRAVEL WEDDINGS

If you prefer to retain control of your particular wedding arrangements, you may choose a travel wedding over the all-inclusive venue wedding. Travel Weddings take place at your honeymoon site. Many couples who don't want to worry about planning their wedding and honeymoon separately prefer the destination wedding to a large, local wedding. Destination weddings can also cut down on the worry of preparing large guest lists and accommodations since not many people are going to be able to travel to a distant wedding site with you. Invite some of your closer friends and family.

Most popular wedding destinations will have wedding consultants and coordinators in the area to help you make specific wedding preparations. Some photographers, videographers, and musicians will travel to wedding destinations if they are adequately compensated.

POPULAR DESTINATIONS

Here are some suggestions of popular wedding destinations. Use the Destination Wedding Possibilities Checklist on page 260 to list your favorite destinations and what wedding packages you find for them.

- Hawaii
- Mexico
- Europe
- The Caribbean
- Nevada/Las Vegas
- Disneyland (Anaheim, California), Walt Disney World (Orlando, Florida)

LEGAL REQUIREMENTS

When marrying outside of the United States, you may need to obtain extra documentation and meet certain legal requirements depending on where you plan to marry. In most cases you will need certified copies of birth certificates, passports, certified copies of divorce papers (if divorced), and certified copies of an ex-spouses death certificate (if widowed). For some destinations there will be waiting periods before a country or territory will issue a marriage license, and there may also be additional residency requirements before you will be able to be married legally. Be sure to consult a travel agent, wedding consultant, the travel board controlling your desired destination, or a venue's wedding coordinator to find out all the requirements you will have to meet for your destination.

DESTINATION WEDDING POSSIBILITIES CHECKLIST

QUESTIONS	POSSIBILITY 1	POSSIBILITY 2	POSSIBILITY 3
Site			
Address			
Phone/FAX Number			
Manager/ Contact Person			
Dates/Times Available			
Length of Time Allowed			
Minimum/Maximum Number of Guests			
Special Package Includes			
Restrictions? (Food, Beverages, Music, Dancing)			
Fees Include? (Food, Beverages, Band, Parking Attendants, Servers, Hotel Room for Bridal Couple)			
Special Rates for Guest Hotel Rooms?			
Total Cost			

18

The Honeymoon

CHOOSING THE BEST TIME OF YEAR

Plan your honeymoon so that you will be at your dream vacation spot at the best time of year. For example, according to honeymoon specialist Tony Yvanovich (owner of Traveltyme in Santa Cruz, California), the vast majority of newlyweds select Hawaii, the Caribbean and Mexico for August honeymoons. Unfortunately, the heat and humidity are unbearable and it's hurricane season at that time in the Caribbean. Consider where you want to go and make sure that the climate will be what you want or your "ideal honeymoon" may end up being a miserable mistake.

If you want a summer wedding because the flowers are blooming in your garden at that time of year, but you want to honeymoon in Jamaica, plan your honeymoon for the fall. You don't need to rush from the dance floor directly to the airport. An ideal wedding deserves an ideal honeymoon.

Some newlyweds wouldn't consider anything but an immediate honeymoon. They may be more romantic and less practical. If you want to take off right after the wedding for the honeymoon of your dreams, plan your wedding and honeymoon dates carefully. Ask about travel days and stopovers. It takes careful planning to have an evening wedding and a flight for your honeymoon the following morning. Your wedding night suite should be close to the wedding reception site so your driver can drive you with ease. You don't want to be driving while being exhausted or intoxicated. A honeymoon behind bars is a terrible way to begin your marriage.

If you're looking for the best value for the money, honeymoon at your dream destination during the off-season. June and July are peak periods for just about anywhere except the Caribbean. The summer months are popular because of school vacations. November and December comprise the peak season for tropical locations like Hawaii and the Caribbean. The demand is higher for warmer climates in the winter for those who want to escape the long, cold winters.

WINTER VALUES

European honeymoons are ideal during the winter. School children are back home and the temperature is milder. Spain, Portugal, and other Mediterranean countries are popular and affordable. The best time to travel is between November and March to get the lowest fares.

SPRING VALUES

After Easter vacation, travel expenses start to rise for the summer vacation traveler. Your best values are found in Canada or the continental United States. If you haven't seen the Grand Canyon, Niagara Falls, or Walt Disney World, this is a great time to honeymoon without the crowds or heat. Walt Disney World is one of the most popular honeymoon locations for American newlyweds.

SUMMER VALUES

Summer tends to be high season everywhere. July and August are typically summer vacation months for all school-aged children. With families taking their summer vacations at that time, the availability for flights and accommodations are limited and air fares are at their highest. The Caribbean offers good values during the summer months but beware of the extremely hot temperatures and the possibility of hurricanes at that time of year.

FALL VALUES

If you're looking for a tropical, romantic honeymoon with the best values, the fall is the best time to go. The Caribbean, Hawaii, and Mexico have all kinds of packages for honeymooners. If your budget allows, Tahiti, Australia, New Zealand, and Europe offer great values between September and November.

CHAPTER 18

PLANNING YOUR DREAM HONEYMOON

TRAVEL AGENTS

Some travel agents are honeymoon specialists who can handle your whole honeymoon. They will help you select the best time of year to travel and offer suggestions for your itinerary. Your costs don't increase by using a travel agent; their commissions are paid by airlines, hotels, and so on. Their expertise on hotels, restaurants, and activities is invaluable. Ask many questions so you can make a good decision. Use the Honeymoon Possibilities Checklist on pages 265–266 to compare options before making your decision.

ITINERARY

Once you select your honeymoon location, call the visitor's bureau or Chamber of Commerce in that area. Ask about special events that may take place when you plan to be there so you can include them in your itinerary. It's a good idea to make tentative plans and reservations ahead of time so you have the option to have a full, busy honeymoon. You can usually cancel reservations twenty-four hours in advance and not lose your deposit.

You may prefer to relax and not be tied to a schedule. After all your wedding preparations and the whirlwind of your big day, you may need a few days to unwind. Lounge in your room and reminisce about your exchange of vows and laugh about stepping on his toes during the first dance.

NEARBY GETAWAYS

Your honeymoon doesn't have to be the typical tropical vacation to Hawaii or the Caribbean. There are a variety of opportunities here in the continental United States, many within a few hours of your town. Check with the Chambers of Commerce in surrounding areas to see what is available. Ask them to send you information about accommodations, entertainment, and dining.

SPORTING ENTHUSIASTS

If you honeymoon in the warmer seasons, tennis buffs can enjoy a week of playing tennis at different resorts and facilities. There are white water river trips for one- to seven-day adventures. Camping in the wilderness with your new husband can be a romantic, back-to-nature experience.

In the winter, skiers can enjoy a honeymoon skiing in deep snow. Cross-country skiers can enjoy trekking through unexplored territory. Ice skate on a frozen pond and then go back to your cabin and curl up together in front of a huge, crackling fire.

Arts and Gourmet Enthusiasts

Those who prefer fine wine and art to active sports can put together an itinerary of museums, historical sites, and gourmet restaurants. Get recommendations from friends or contact the Chamber of Commerce in the area you plan to visit. Napa Valley offers hundreds of wineries for touring and wine tasting. The restaurants are exquisite, naturally, to complement the wines.

Top off the fine wine and food with a night at the theater or opera. Book tickets in advance to get special seating. Plan a week of entertainment to include the theater, museums, wine tasting, and fine food. Schedule an hour massage for both of you to ensure complete relaxation. That would be the ultimate hedonist's honeymoon.

Use the Honeymoon Itinerary form on page 267 to record each activity you plan to include. Remember to leave some time free for just lounging.

HONEYMOON POSSIBILITIES CHECKLIST

QUESTIONS	POSSIBILITY 1	POSSIBILITY 2	POSSIBILITY 3
Location			
Departure Date/Time			
Transportation to Airport/Fees			
Fly or Drive?			
Flight Number:			
Departure Date/Time:			
Transportation Cost:			
Drive — Gasoline Costs:			
Fly — Round-Trip Airfare:			
Luggage Limits:			
Hotel Accommodations			
Hotel Address			
Hotel Phone Number			
Check-in Time			
Check-out Time			
Cost per Night			
Total Number of Nights/Total			
Daily Transportation (Rental Car, Cab)			
Weekly Transportation Costs (Car Rental, Gas, Cab)			
Rental Car: Pickup Time: Return Time:			

HONEYMOON POSSIBILITIES CHECKLIST (continued)

QUESTIONS	POSSIBILITY 1	POSSIBILITY 2	POSSIBILITY 3
Meals (Package price or estimate of meals)			
Activities/Costs Date/Time:			
Return Date/Time			
Airline/Flight Number			
Transportation from Airport to Home			
Total Honeymoon Costs			

HONEYMOON ITINERARY

Event	Day 1	Day 2	Day 3	Day 4	Day 5	Day 6	Day 7
Early Morning							
Late Morning							
Early Afternoon							
Late Afternoon							
Dinner							
Early Evening							
Late Evening							

DOCUMENTS YOU WILL NEED

Review Itinerary and Tickets: Once you've set travel plans for your honeymoon, gather all the tickets and review your itinerary. Make sure all the dates and times are correct. Read cancellation policies for hotels, car rental, airline, and so forth.

List Credit Cards and Other Numbers: List all your credit card numbers, driver's license numbers, traveler's check numbers, and any other important information you plan to take with you on the List of Documents checklist on page 270. In the terrible event that you lose your wallet or it is stolen, you could easily cancel your credit cards and order new traveler's checks without panicking. Imagine being in Paris when you lose your wallet. What did you have in it? Do you know your credit card numbers by memory? Once you return from your honeymoon, put this list in your safe deposit box.

Copy Prescriptions: If your luggage is lost or stolen, you may need to get prescriptions refilled. Bring along copies of your prescriptions for medication and eyeglasses. Keep important medications in your purse, not your luggage while traveling.

Order Traveler's Checks: Carry traveler's checks. If your wallet is lost or stolen you can get your money back. If you carry cash, you're out of luck. Some banks give traveler's checks to their customers free of charge. Others charge a nominal fee.

Carry Singles: You'll need to carry some cash to start with; $10.00 to $15.00 should be enough. If you're flying, you'll need cash to tip bellboys. Once you start using your traveler's checks, you'll have plenty of small change to handle tips and small purchases.

Exchange Foreign Currency in Foreign Countries: If you are honeymooning outside the United States, wait until you get to the foreign country to change currency. Our banks charge a large percentage of the face value of the currency for changing money. Change the money as you need it on your honeymoon. Use the foreign currency in the foreign country. Don't bring it back to exchange currency; it won't be in your best interest.

Take Credit Cards: Take one major credit card such as Visa, MasterCard, or American Express with you. If you run out of money, you can charge meals, hotels, and entertainment to your card. You could also get cash from many banks abroad with your card. It's good insurance.

Apply for Passports in Advance: If you need to get a passport or visa for your travels, you should both get a certified copy of your birth certificates and two passport photos. Check the government offices in your area for dates and times to apply for a passport. Ask about the fees and method of payment. Allow six to eight weeks to receive passports. For an additional charge, a rush order can be made for passports, which are usually processed within ten days.

Use the List of Documents form on page 270 to record all document numbers. Keep a copy with you, separate from your documents, and leave a copy with a family member at home.

WHAT TO PACK

If this is your first extended trip together, you may be tempted to over pack. Review your itinerary and consider the weather. If you are going to a tropical island that is warm and humid and you plan to enjoy many water sports, your packing should consist of bathing suits, shorts, shirts, and cover-ups. Bring along a few summery dresses for evening entertainment and dining.

For colder climates, you'll pack more bulky clothes. You'll have to be prepared for rain and snow. If you're going on a ski honeymoon, your luggage will consist of ski outfits and paraphernalia, ski equipment (skis, boots, and poles), lounging clothes, and dress-up outfits.

Pack an extra collapsible duffel bag in your suitcase to bring back gifts and mementos you purchase. You may want to pack an extra bag for dirty laundry too.

Keep your medications, documents, fine jewelry, cash and traveler's checks, and photography equipment in a carry-on bag which you can keep with you at all times. You wouldn't want your medication missing for twenty-four hours while the airlines hunt down your missing luggage. If you wear contact lenses, you may want to keep your solutions and containers in this carry-on bag too. Trying to find an open drug store after spending hours at the baggage claim department in the middle of the night can be frustrating.

Use the Honeymoon Checklist on page 271 to keep track of everything you need to bring as well as what you need to take care of before you leave home.

LIST OF DOCUMENTS

ITEMS	PACKED
Driver's License (Bride's)	
Driver's License (Groom's)	
Marriage License Number	
Passports or Visa Numbers	
Copies of Prescriptions (Medication, Birth Control Pills, Contact Lenses or Glasses)	
Credit Card numbers and phone numbers	

Checking Account Numbers
 	
His: Bank _____ Account Number: _____
 	
        Address _____ Phone: _____
 	
Yours: Bank _____ Account Number: _____
 	
        Address _____ Phone: _____	

Travelers' Check Numbers
 	
  Bank: _____ Phone: _____
 	
  Check Numbers: _____	

Personal Doctors' Phone Numbers, in Case of Emergency
 	
  His Doctor: _____ Phone: _____
 	
  Your Doctor: _____ Phone: _____	

Airline Tickets	
Itinerary (Hotels, car rental reservation numbers)	

HONEYMOON CHECKLIST

CLOTHING		TOILETRIES		EQUIPMENT	
Underwear		Toothbrush/Paste		Camera/Film	
Socks/Nylons		Lotion/Moisturizer		Games/Books	
T-Shirts		Brush/Comb		Address Book	
Pajamas/Bathrobes		Contact Lens/Glasses		Journal/Diary	
Lingerie		Make-up Purse		Tickets/Itinerary	
Bathing Suit/Trunks		Hair Clips/Pins		Passport/Credit Card	
Shorts		Razor/Aftershave		Insurance Cards	
Comfortable Pants		Perfume/Cologne		Suitcases	
Dress Clothing		Suntan Lotion		Travelers' Checks	
Evening Purse		Tampons/Pads		Cash	
Sweater/Sweatshirts		Birth Control		Swim Gear	
Jacket/Coat and Tie		Soap		Ski Gear	
Dress Shoes		Nail Polish/Remover		Hiking Gear	
Tennis Shoes		Nail File		Tennis Gear	
Sandals		Cotton Balls/Cotton Swabs			
Jewelry		Nail Clipper			
Jogging Suits		Hair Rollers			
Hats/Visors		Hair Spray/Mousse			
Sunglasses		Curling Iron/Dryer			
Sports Clothing		Towels			
		Shampoo/Conditioner			
		Mouthwash			
		Aspirin			
		First Aid Kit (Travel)			
		Dental Floss			

DO		STOP		GET	
Water Plants		Newspaper		Cat Feeder	
Set Light Timers		Mail		Dog Feeder	
Lock House Up!		Housekeeper		Fish Feeder	
Get Time Off at Work		Gardener		Bird Feeder	

GUIDE TO TIPPING

Tipping in the United States is fairly consistent so tip accordingly. If you haven't traveled much or didn't pay attention to tipping, use the following guidelines to help. When traveling abroad, ask your travel agent for tipping guidelines in the countries you will visit.

Taxi Drivers: Add about 15 percent to the cab driver's fare. If he stows your luggage in the trunk, add 25 cents for each piece.

Sky Caps: Tip sky caps $2 for four pieces of luggage. Add 50 cents for each additional piece. The sky cap takes your luggage from the curbside and routes it to the appropriate baggage carts. Be sure to remember to tip your sky cap; they've been known to route ungracious tippers' luggage to the other side of the continent. They are saving you time and energy at the curbside. You won't need to stand in those long lines in the airport lobby to check your baggage.

Bellboys: Hotel bellboys should receive the same tip that you give to the sky cap. They will take your luggage from your rental car or cab and wait for you while you check in. Once you get your room key, they escort or meet you at your room. They unload your luggage and open up your room for you. Most bellboys also tell you where to find vending and ice machines.

Restaurant Waiters: Throughout the United States, waiters receive approximately 15 percent of the meal price (not including the tax). For great service, tip 20 percent, and for mediocre service, 10 percent is appropriate.

Cruise Personnel: Most cruise lines will inform you of the appropriate amounts and when to pay personnel for their services. This is expected above and beyond your fare for the cruise. Your cabin steward and table steward receive about $5 each per day. The dining room captain, deck captain, recreation director, or child-care person can also be tipped. Ask your travel agent or table steward for current guidelines.

Train Porter: Tip your train porter approximately $2 each time he cleans your berth. For your meals, tip according to restaurant guidelines.

Resort Personnel: Guidelines are the same as for cruise personnel, approximately $5 per day for your waiter and $2 per day for your chambermaid. Check with your travel agent or the manager of the resort for guidelines.

Gratuities Included: Many hotels and restaurants include a 15 percent gratuity on the bill. Read through your bills and policies before you ask for services. Room service in most hotels now add 15 to 17 percent gratuities to the bill to assure tips for their waiters. Read the bill carefully or ask the waiter if gratuities have been added to the check.

Who Should Receive Gratuities? There are many guidelines on tipping. Many services are provided by the establishment which should be considered part of the total fee. The customary practice of tipping came about when customers received excellent service and wanted to acknowledge the person giving the service. Tipping is a bonus for good service. If you receive poor service, by all means don't tip. Lodge a complaint with the management to that effect and act accordingly.

THE HONEYMOON'S OVER? WHAT HAPPENS IF . . .

. . . YOU LOSE YOUR TICKETS OR PASSPORT?

If you lose your airline tickets, contact your travel agent or airline. You'll need to know the airline, flight number, and date of travel. You may need to purchase a new ticket and receive a refund after a waiting period. Fill out the necessary forms and hope your flight was not overbooked.

If you lose your passport, contact the nearest U.S. Consulate. They'll give you further instructions. You'll need your passport number and date and place of issuance. This information should be on the List of Documents on page 270.

. . . THE AIRLINE LOSES YOUR LUGGAGE?

If your luggage doesn't come off the baggage carousel, go directly to the airline baggage office. They are usually located right in the baggage claim area. File a claim listing a description of the missing luggage, the contents in each piece, and the content value. You may need to buy some necessities (toiletries and basic clothing) right away. Airlines usually find lost pieces within twenty-four hours. They will deliver the luggage to your hotel.

Airlines occasionally lose your luggage permanently. Give them an itemized list of contents and their value. You'll receive compensation for the necessities you purchase and the replacement of your contents minus depreciation. Most airlines have a limit to liability. Read your policy carefully. If you are carrying more valuables than the airlines will cover, pay a little extra to get the right coverage.

. . . YOUR WALLET GETS STOLEN?

If you filled in the List of Documents on page 270, go down the list and call the credit card company immediately. Give them your account number; they will invalidate your card and send a replacement card (usually within seven days).

Contact the traveler's check company to get more checks as soon as possible. The cash you had is history so don't let it ruin your honeymoon. You'll have to apply for a new driver's license when you return home.

If you don't have a list of your credit card numbers, traveler's checks, or wallet contents, start making a list from memory. Call the 800 information number (1-800-555-1212) for the toll-free number to report lost or stolen cards for each card. The operator will give you three numbers per call. If you are in a foreign country, call your parents or a good friend and ask them to call for you. Calling long distance in a foreign country can be very expensive. You'll need to contact the traveler's check company yourself to get new checks right away. Other contents like library cards and insurance information can be reported when you return home.

... You Miss Your Plane, Train, or Ship?

If you miss your plane and you purchased super-saver flights, you may need to purchase new tickets. Once you book a super-saver flight, you can't change the time or date of your flight. Get to the airport as soon as possible and explain your situation. A sympathetic agent may let you fly on the next flight if seating is available. If you are the type of traveler who arrives at the airport at the eleventh hour, you may want to purchase tickets that allow you the flexibility to change your flight dates and times without penalties. These tickets cost more but if you're paying for the same flight twice, it's a better deal.

If you miss your train, space allowing, they will put you on the next train and charge you a nominal penalty.

If you miss a ship, the cruise line director or port authority may help you catch the ship by launching a boat. They'll do this only if the ship is in eyesight. You may have to catch a flight to meet the ship at its next port. Either way, this will be stressful and expensive.

... Your Hotel Accommodations Get Mixed Up?

When you arrive at the hotel registration desk to find that they don't have a record of your reservation, show them your confirmation number or written confirmation. They may need to make a few phone calls to straighten out the confusion. If they have rooms available, they'll put you in a room and that will be the end of it.

If the hotel is booked, they may upgrade your room to a nice suite or penthouse to accommodate you. Problems like these usually work out to your advantage so try to keep calm. If they are completely booked and don't have any rooms available, they will offer to pay for your stay at a comparable hotel until a room

becomes available in their hotel. As a token of compensation, they may offer complimentary drinks or meals. You may even suggest this if you are held up for hours waiting for accommodations.

If you don't have your confirmation number with you, call your travel agent and let the agent and hotel person handle it between themselves. If you booked these accommodations yourself and it's your word against theirs, you'll need to be convincing for them to offer complimentary services.

... You Become Sick?

If you're in the United States, call the front desk of your hotel. They will either send their house doctor or give you recommendations for doctors. If you are in a foreign country, you'll have to rely on the doctors they have available. Ask your hotel for recommendations for doctors who speak English.

If you have allergies or potential health problems, wear a Medic Alert bracelet. That way, in case you are unable to communicate with the doctors, they can assess your needs better and use the proper medications. They will also know blood type, if necessary.

If you get sick from the food or water of a certain region, local doctors may prescribe medication that can help you recover. If the country you're going to is known to make some travelers sick, talk to your personal physician before you leave. Some doctors recommend taking antibiotics before you leave and through the duration of your stay in a foreign country. This preventive medicine doesn't always work. If you are prone to get "Montezuma's Revenge" while traveling in third-world countries, consider honeymooning in the United States or other countries where sanitation standards are higher, and the water is safer.

... You Lose or Break Your Eyeglasses or Contact Lenses

If you have a copy of the prescription, go to the nearest optometrist to get a replacement. If you don't have your prescription with you, call your optometrist and ask him to call the prescription in to the local optometrist. Doctors usually honor one another's requests for phone prescriptions. If you're in a remote location, contact your optometrist and ask him to send a replacement by overnight carrier to your hotel.

Carry an extra set of contacts and/or eyeglasses as a backup in case of an emergency. That way you won't waste time trying to track down doctors and replacements.

... You Run Out of Money?

Short of losing your wallet, careful planning should eliminate the possibility of this happening. If you don't have credit cards, set aside enough money to pay for your hotel and meals. Also set aside enough money for tips at the airport and parking fees in long-term parking so you can get home. If you lose track of your money and find that you don't have enough to pay for your room, some hotels will bill you at your home address.

If you don't own a credit card, you may want to borrow a credit card to use in an emergency. That way you can pay for your meals, hotel, parking, and so forth and contend with the costs when you get home. The credit card will allow you to make reservations and payments for meals, transportation, and lodging.

If you have a credit card, many hotels will give you cash and charge it to your card. Running out of money isn't as threatening with a credit card.

... You Get Homesick?

This can happen to those moving directly from their parents' homes along with those who have children at home. Make a phone call to find out how things are going back home. You'll feel more comfortable knowing that everyone's fine; and sometimes just hearing familiar voices helps alleviate those homesick feelings.

... You Have the After-Wedding Blues?

Many couples spend every extra minute before their wedding planning and getting ready. All the excitement and attention builds up until their big day. The big day comes and goes so fast that couples often find themselves a little depressed after the wedding. If you feel that way, have comfort in knowing that it is a common emotion felt by many newlyweds. Talk about your feelings so you don't send mixed messages to your husband. He may be feeling the same way.

These after-wedding blues go away in a few days. Some take a few weeks to get adjusted again. Talk about your fondest memories and laugh about all the crazy things you've done to plan the wedding. Then move on and talk about what you plan to do with all the gifts. Discuss whom you'd like to invite over to your house for dinner and plan ahead.

There are many activities you can do to keep busy if you feel the need to be active. Read through the brochures in the hotel lobby for ideas on activities and excursions. See a movie or take in a play.

... YOU HAVE YOUR FIRST FIGHT
AS A MARRIED COUPLE?

Your relationship up until now has been less committed, even if you were living together. Marriage often creates new boundaries and guidelines that you weren't aware of before. Often issues about money and responsibilities create stress for newlyweds. Your first year of marriage will be a year of learning how to communicate together. You may need to establish routines, responsibilities (household and financial), and respect for one another's desires and idiosyncrasies.

As you explore each other's needs and desires, you'll undoubtedly come across aspects that you don't like in each other—things that you may not have known before you married, especially if you didn't live together. Talk openly about your feelings. If you communicate your thoughts without blaming, you may learn more about each other and find a compromise that you could both be happy with.

After your first fight as husband and wife, stop and laugh together. Promise each other that you will listen to one another and talk about disagreements. You'll probably laugh when you stop to think about what was probably just a misunderstanding.

19

At Home

Your big day has come and gone and the honeymoon is over. You're looking forward to living your new life as a married couple. Most couples feel that marriage gives them a closer bond and sense of commitment. They feel more like a family than they did prior to marriage, even if they lived together.

PARENTS' POSTWEDDING BLUES

Just as you may experience postwedding blues, your parents may feel the same way. They worked hard and their emotions ran the gamut with you while you prepared for your wedding. All the excitement and adrenaline ended suddenly after your beautiful wedding, leaving them a little depressed.

Send a postcard or give them a quick call while you're away on your honeymoon. When you return, invite them over for a special dinner at your new home. Let them be involved while you open your gifts. When you receive the proofs from the photographer, look through them together. Put together a special album for each set of parents so they have a memento from your big day. This period of postwedding blues usually doesn't last longer than a few weeks. Be sensitive to parents' feelings and needs at this time.

278

WHAT TO DO WITH YOUR WEDDING GIFTS

Keep the gifts that you will use and gifts that you want to save for future entertaining (china and crystal), even if you have to store it. You'll appreciate it years from now when you bring out your fine china and crystal.

You'll have some gifts that you know you don't like and will never use. Return a gift only if the giver will not know. Get credit at the store where it was purchased and get the something you really want.

YOUR LAST NAME: TO KEEP OR TO CHANGE?

Your name is usually the first impression that a person has of you. Deciding on what name to use after your marriage is important. Most women prefer the traditional choice of taking the husband's surname. Others prefer to keep their maiden name.

TAKING YOUR HUSBAND'S NAME

Taking your husband's name will probably be the least controversial avenue. Most people will assume that you will take his name. Raising children is a little less complicated if the whole family has the same last name.

You'll have to change your name on all legal documents. See the Name and Address Change Worksheet on pages 282–284 for a list of those who need to be notified. You'll find the Name and Address Change Letter Format on page 285 a helpful guide to framing your notification letters.

KEEPING YOUR MAIDEN NAME

More women are now choosing to keep their maiden names. Changing your name in the business world may confuse clients and associates. Women also feel that their names are important; why should they change their names when men keep their own?

This is the easiest avenue to take. You won't need to make any changes except for your marital status on your legal documents like tax forms and insurance policies.

Hyphenating Your Name with Your Husband's

As a compromise, a woman sometimes hyphenates her last name with her husband's. This offers the best of both worlds: (1) You keep your maiden name, and (2) you also take your husband's name. Business associates and clients will still recognize your name and know that you have been recently married. Your children's schools will not be confused with the name difference since you share the same name. The problem with hyphenated names is that your name becomes a very long name to write out and pronounce. Once everyone gets used to the change, it'll become second nature to them.

You'll need to make name changes just as you would if you were taking your husband's name.

Changing Your Name for Second Marriages

There are many variables in second marriages that contribute to your final decision on what name to choose. If you have children from your previous marriage, you'll have to decide if you want to use the same surname that they use. A woman who took her first husband's name and established a career with that name may want to keep the first husband's name and hyphenate it with her second husband's name. Still others who have kept maiden names or hyphenated both choose to take their second husband's name and forget all the names they've used regardless of any children from the previous marriage. Consider your husband, family, business associates, and most importantly your own feelings.

RAMIFICATIONS OF CHANGING YOUR NAME AND MARITAL STATUS

Credit in Banking

According to the Equal Credit Opportunity Act of 1974, all new joint accounts and loans must be recorded in both spouses' names (for credit purposes). Always sign legal documents with your first name, Laura Simpson, not Mrs. John Simpson. This allows you to establish credit in your name.

SOCIAL SECURITY AND THE IRS

If you keep your maiden name, you don't need to do anything, but if you change your name you'll need to contact Social Security. (Your number will not change but you are required to notify the Social Security Administration of a name change). The IRS is cross-referenced with Social Security so you don't need to contact the IRS. They'll pick up your new name and status on your tax returns.

WILLS AND TRUSTS

If you don't take your husband's name, state in both of your wills or trusts that you are spouses so there is no confusion.

"I, Robert Stevens,
leave my estate to my wife,
Susan Nichols."

VOTING

According to the Louisiana Courts in 1959, the wife never loses her maiden name. Only a woman who takes her husband's name must file the change with the registrar of voters. No name change is necessary if you keep your maiden name.

INSURANCE

Notify your insurance company of your marriage plans. Your marital status may reduce your premiums for auto insurance. You may be eligible for maternity benefits. Some companies allow you to change your policy up to thirty days prior to the wedding date.

PROPERTY LAWS

Property Laws vary from state to state. Call your county or city recording office to find out how to change your name on property that you own.

NAME AND ADDRESS CHANGE WORKSHEET

COMPANY	ACCOUNT NUMBER/ OTHER INFORMATION	ADDRESS	DONE
CREDIT CARDS:			
BANK ACCOUNTS:			
SAFE DEPOSIT BOX:			
MORTGAGE CO.:			
LOAN COMPANIES:			
PROPERTY TITLES:			
DRIVER'S LICENSE			
AUTO REGISTRATION:			
AUTO INSURANCE:			

NAME AND ADDRESS CHANGE WORKSHEET (continued)

COMPANY	ACCOUNT NUMBER/ OTHER INFORMATION	ADDRESS	DONE
HOMEOWNER'S INSURANCE:			
PROPERTY INSURANCE:			
RENTER'S INSURANCE:			
MEDICAL INSURANCE:			
DENTAL INSURANCE:			
LIFE INSURANCE:			
DISABILITY INSURANCE:			
OTHER INSURANCE:			
INVESTMENTS: (STOCKS, BONDS, IRAS, ETC.)			
PENSIONS:			
SOCIAL SECURITY:			

NAME AND ADDRESS CHANGE WORKSHEET (continued)

COMPANY	ACCOUNT NUMBER/ OTHER INFORMATION	ADDRESS	DONE
VOTER REGISTRATION:			
PASSPORT/VISAS:			
SCHOOL RECORDS:			
DOCTORS:			
DENTISTS:			
POST OFFICE:			
UTILITIES:			
TELEPHONE CO.:			
GARBAGE CO.:			
NEWSPAPERS:			
MAGAZINES:			
WILL/TRUST:			
OTHER:			

Dear _____ ,

    We would like to inform you of our future marriage and our address change. Our account number

is: _____ .

_____	_____
Husband's Full Name	Your Maiden Name
_____ AND	_____
Husband's Former Address	Your Former Address
_____	_____
City State ZIP Code	City State Zip Code

ARE NOW

_____

Husband's Full Name

_____

Wife's Full Name

_____

New Address

_____

City   State   ZIP Code

DATE OF MARRIAGE

_____

SPECIAL INSTRUCTIONS: _____ We plan to continue service.
(check appropriate
    boxes)

_____ We plan to discontinue service after _____

_____ Please send necessary forms to include my spouse
      on my policy/account.

If you have any questions, please feel free to contact us at (____) _____ .

        Sincerely,

        _____

        Husband's Signature

        _____

        Your Signature

YOUR NEW HOME TOGETHER

Marriage is a new beginning for both of you. This is a good time to make a move to an area in which you've always wanted to live. Chances are, with your combined incomes, you will be able to get a bigger and better place.

Location: If you both work in the same city, select an area that is centrally located between both workplaces. Consider the neighborhoods and the growth of the city. If you plan to stay in the same house or apartment for a while, consider the neighborhoods and their rate of growth. Check to see which school districts are better than others. Call the police department and ask which areas have low crime ratios.

Renting: Look through the local newspapers and call the rental agencies. Landlords generally prefer newlyweds to college students and families. Make appointments to see the houses or apartments of your choice. Ask how much money you'll need to move in to the house. Find out if utilities are included in the rent and if they're not, ask what the average tenant pays for utilities.

STEPCHILDREN

New marriages require considerable patience as you test your relationship. Those who have children from previous marriages can anticipate an adjustment period for the adults as well as the children. First discuss the roles and structure of your new family between you and your future husband. Then discuss the rules, roles, and structure with the children. You can expect anxiety and testing during this transitional period. Children like to know what is expected of them and to understand their boundaries.

If you have an open relationship with your ex-spouse, you can help reduce the amount of stress for all concerned. Work out a schedule that all parties are comfortable with so the children understand their new routine. Discuss where the children will be on weekends, holidays, and birthdays. Then agree to be flexible. Things come up for you as well as your ex-spouse so roll with the changes. If you accept last minute changes, your child will handle it that much better.

Allow for special days for you to be with your natural children alone. This could be a good time for them to tell you how they feel. They may also want to know that they are still special.

Your stepchildren will also need time to spend with their natural mother. They'll need to feel that close bond that has stretched to include you. Take your

stepchildren out without your natural children for a special outing. This will be a good time to start establishing a bond as a stepmother. Give them a chance to tell you what is on their minds.

Most important, let the children and stepchildren know that your marriage was intended to include them. When you both chose to marry each other, you also chose to create a new family with each other's children. Tell them how much you love them and how the new family dynamics will grow to be better than it was before the families merged. Children who feel they are part of the structure of the new family become stable members.

MANAGING YOUR BUDGET

Finances and in-laws tend to be the biggest source of marital disputes. Since you can't choose members of either family, let's look at managing your budget. First you'll need to decide whether or not you will pool your money for all expenditures, for just living expense, or not at all. Divorce attorneys suggest that you keep as many assets and accounts in your individual names as possible to avoid messy court cases deciding who is entitled to what. On the other hand, using separate checking accounts and dividing all the bills can be tedious and stressful.

After you've decided how you will commingle your money, calculate your income. For budgetary reasons, figure out what your combined monthly income is after taxes.

Now for the more complex calculations. Figure out what your monthly fixed expenses are (rent/mortgage, utilities, loan payments, etc.). Then figure out what your fixed annual expenses are (insurance, medical checkups, tuition, etc.). Divide this annual figure by twelve to get the monthly total. Approximate your monthly fluctuating expenses (groceries, gasoline, gifts, entertainment, dining out, etc.).

Add all your monthly expenses, both fixed and fluctuating, and compare them to your monthly income. If you're like the majority of us, your expenditures will be higher than your income. Don't fret; if your expenses aren't double your income you can make some adjustments in your budget to compensate.

Dining out, gifts, and entertainment are usually the categories that put you over your budget. Set your budget so that you have a set amount of money you can spend on each category per month. For instance, if you have $100 for dining out per month, you can have one expensive gourmet dinner or you could dine at three modest restaurants. Do the same for buying gifts. If you want to give lavish gifts and your budget doesn't allow for it, make the gifts yourself. Put away money each month in a Christmas Club fund at your bank to help you save for the biggest

gift-giving season of the year. Another option is to buy Christmas gifts throughout the year. You can take advantage of good sales and avoid the mad holiday rush.

If cutting back on fluctuating expenses still doesn't help your budget, you may need to find a less expensive house/apartment or get a better paying job. Ignoring the budget deficit will not make the problem go away. It will only create stress in your relationship as bills come in along with bounced checks or collection notices. Take the time now to figure out a budget that works for you and then stick to it. Readjust it as your income and expense change. Smart budgeting is part of a responsible relationship.

20

Prenuptial Agreements and Wills

Prenuptial agreements, in theory, have been used in ancient societies for centuries. Marriages were prearranged by families at the birth of each child. Along with the prearranged marriage agreement came future rights to property and other assets. These were known as betrothal contracts. The couple had very little to say about the marriage arrangements. It was a political and financial transaction.

In the United States, romantic courtship precedes marriage. Couples are marrying later in life, establishing careers, and building their assets before tying the knot. Women, as well as men, are working, creating two-income families. Second marriages often involve raising stepchildren or paying alimony and child support to ex-spouses. With all of these variables to consider and to protect, many couple are considering prenuptial agreements to clarify what each person brings into the marriage and how they will separate assets if they should split up.

PRENUPTIAL AGREEMENT

A prenuptial agreement is a legal contract drawn up and/or reviewed by the bride's and groom's attorneys prior to their marriage. The purpose of the prenuptial agreement is to state what each person is bringing into the marriage and how the future assets, earnings, and other responsibilities will be divided in the event of death or divorce.

How Do the Laws Affect a Prenuptial Agreement?

Equitable distribution and community property laws set the proper guidelines but they don't specifically state how to divide community property in individual cases. Each marriage is unique, making it impossible for divorce laws to make fair settlements easily. Prenuptial agreements allow the couple to state how they want their assets divided without the emotions of a divorce getting in the way of a fair settlement. Prenuptial agreements make it easier for the states to decide how assets will be divided. They are becoming very popular and the courts are establishing rules and guidelines for their enforcement. All prenuptial agreements should be drawn up by your attorney and reviewed by your fiancé's attorney. Use the Documents Needed for Preparing a Prenuptial Agreement form on page 292 to gather the necessary information.

Who Needs It?

If you're both living at home with your parents and all you own are your clothes, stereo, and car, a prenuptial agreement may not be necessary for you. You are starting your life together and will build your investment portfolio together.

On the other hand, if you worked hard establishing a career or business and have made some investments on your own, you may want to protect those investments when you marry. Any person who owns real estate, a business, or other investments is a good candidate for a prenuptial agreement. A person with children from a previous marriage may want to protect his or her assets so they get passed along to the children.

Why Couples Don't Want Prenuptial Agreements

Many couples feel that prenuptial agreements destroy the romance in engagements by discussing finances and divisions of assets in the case of divorce. They don't want to ruin the euphoria and excitement as they plan their wedding.

Others feel that asking your fiancé to sign a prenuptial agreement means that you don't trust him or her. They feel that if you have doubts about the person you plan to wed, you must not be committed to marriage.

Some couples don't want to list all of their assets. They prefer to keep them secret. Others just don't know where to begin. The thought of figuring out their assets and discussing it with attorneys and their fiancé is something they put off until it's too late.

How to Approach the Subject of Prenuptial Agreements

Whether you decide to pool your assets when you marry, or keep everything separate down to your checkbooks, requires a discussion. Communication and trust will bond you when you marry. Discussing your relationship and your investments will be an integral part of your marriage. Start discussing your roles, finances, and money. Couples argue about finances more than about any other aspect in their marriage. Those who wait until after they're married to discuss money and investments may be in for a rude awakening.

As you discuss what you each have and what you plan to do in terms of future investments, discuss what you will each keep in your names separately as well as investments that you will make jointly. If you have children from previous marriages or elderly parents who need care, discuss how you want your assets divided in the case of your death. While you are discussing these issues, suggest what you feel would be a fair distribution of your marital assets in the case of divorce. This is a logical, sound approach that is responsible. Suggest that you both list your assets and talk to attorneys to set up a prenuptial agreement along with a will or trust. If you feel comfortable discussing your finances and investments with your fiancé, he will feel comfortable too.

If you have larger assets and your fiancé has little or none, he may be defensive and hurt by the discussion of prenuptial agreements. It will be harder to discuss future investments if he doesn't have the means to participate. Your attorneys will help prepare your prenuptial agreement in a fair fashion so that you both feel comfortable.

Feelings of distrust can surface initially as you bring up the subject of prenuptial agreements, but they will diminish as your fiancé sees that you are being fair and honest about what you have and how it will be divided in the case of death or divorce. On the other hand, if you decide not to use a prenuptial agreement and plan to hide assets, you will always have secrets and paranoia to deal with which will inevitably surface in your relationship. Your husband may suspect an affair or discover a bank statement by accident. A relationship based on deceit or fear of losing assets is bound to be a troubled relationship.

DOCUMENTS OR LISTS	READY
Personal tax returns for the past five years	
Checking account statements for the past five years	
Checkbook registers for the past five years (to remind you of assets you may have forgotten)	
Savings account statements for the past five years	
Money market account statements for the past five years	
All stock certificates/bonds and documents	
Pension or retirement plans and statements	
Profit sharing plans and statements	
IRAs and statements	
Life insurance policies and statements	
Health insurance policies and statements	
Annuities	
List of safe deposit boxes and contents	
Liability insurance policies and statements	
List of real estate and mortgages	
List of debts	
List of liabilities	
List of personal valuables: jewelry, artwork, antiques, coins, precious metals	
List of all partnerships: joint ventures, limited partnerships, general partnerships, corporations	
Employment agreements	
Lists of leases	
List of current and anticipated lawsuits	
List of debts owed to you	
List of wills and trusts of which you are a beneficiary	
Note: Review documents with your attorney	

POSTNUPTIAL AGREEMENT

A postnuptial agreement is the same as a prenuptial agreement except that it is drawn up after the wedding. The purpose is to claim what assets each person had prior to the marriage and to state how the marital assets will be divided in case of divorce. The postnuptial agreement is a relatively new concept.

WHO NEEDS IT?

Those who married in a romantic haze, and then found that discussing finances and money are part of the reality of marriage, often have their attorneys draw up postnuptial agreements once the honeymoon is over.

If one spouse starts a business, he or she may want a postnuptial agreement stating that the business is solely his or hers. Dividing a small business after a divorce can put the company in financial difficulty so couples agree to sign postnuptial agreements if only one partner is involved in the business.

Those who have married for a second or third time may want to state how their assets/estate will be divided in the case of death. This is especially true for couples with children from previous marriages.

WILL THE AGREEMENT HOLD UP IN COURT?

Prenuptial and postnuptial agreements tend to hold up in court when both parties are fair, all assets are disclosed, and attorneys are used. Both the husband and wife should seek counsel when reviewing and writing marital agreements. They should never be signed under duress. If one party gives up his or her rights to assets, he or she should be compensated in an equitable fashion for the courts to consider the agreement valid. In short, premarital and postmarital agreements will modify the divorce laws and make your settlement easier if they are written properly.

WILLS AND PRENUPTIAL AGREEMENTS

Once you write your prenuptial agreement, rewrite your will or trust to reiterate the same agreement. If your prenuptial agreement states one thing and the will states another, you may be setting up years of court battles among all beneficiaries trying to determine your intent. Have your attorney write both your prenuptial agreement and will or trust to insure their validity.

CHILDREN FROM PREVIOUS MARRIAGES

Children from previous marriages tend to look at their parents' new spouses as a threat to their inheritance. Prenuptial agreements refine what the new spouse is entitled to in the event of divorce. With this agreement, your children won't have underlying feelings of distrust and paranoia. This can facilitate better relations between stepchildren and stepparents.

COUPLES WHO MARRY AFTER RETIREMENT

Those who marry after retirement have been around the block a few times. Your marriage plans may be romantic but this marriage may also be considered a business relationship. You probably have assets and children. You'll need to discuss what you both have in assets before your marriage, along with who will be paying the bills afterwards. If you have promised to put your grandchildren through college, your fiancé should know about it. These decisions and finances need to be addressed and stated in both your prenuptial agreement and will.

If you are over fifty-five and own your own home, you may want to take advantage of the one-time tax exemption for selling your home before you get married. Once you get married, you are both eligible for only one tax exemption, not two. Consult your tax advisor for details.

SELECTING AN ATTORNEY

Selecting an attorney is very important. Don't use your fiancé's attorney or anybody closely affiliated with him. There could be a conflict of interest. Choose an attorney who specializes in divorce (family law), estate planning, and contract drafting. The attorney should be familiar with your state's divorce laws and how prenuptial agreements need to be drafted to be valid.

Get recommendations from friends who have had prenuptial agreements drawn up. Check the yellow pages under "attorney" to read the advertisements. Law firms will state their specialties. Call to speak to an attorney before you set up an appointment. You should feel at ease talking to your attorney.

21

Insurance

Among the many issues to consider while planning for your wedding is making sure you have adequate insurance coverage. Insurance can help enhance your quality of life and protect the ones you love.

You may want to consider taking your current insurance policies along with the following pages in this planner to your agent's office. This will allow the agent the opportunity to review your coverages and evaluate your needs.

Use the following checklist to prepare for questions your insurance agent may ask. Your answers can help your agent provide proper coverages to fit your lifestyle and budget.

AUTO INSURANCE

How many cars will be in your household?
_____

How far will the cars be driven to work/used for business?
_____

What's the average annual mileage on your vehicles?
_____

Will there be other drivers in your household?
Yes _____   No _____   Who? _____

Will you have other vehicles such as a motorcycle, boat, or motor home?
Yes _____   No _____   What other vehicles? _____

Do you plan to purchase or lease any new vehicle?
Yes _____   No _____

Does your car have an installed cellular phone, compact disc player, cassette radio?
Yes _____   No _____   List: _____

FIRE INSURANCE

Have you insured your engagement/wedding rings?
Yes _____   No _____

Do you own a home or are you renting?
Own a home _____   Renting _____

Have you made any improvements to your home since it was insured?
List improvements: _____

Do you have an office in your home?
Yes _____   No _____

Have you taken a home inventory and have photos of your possessions?
Yes _____   No _____

Do you own: Camera _____   Stamp Collection_____

Other Collections_____   Oriental Rugs_____

Computer_____   Jewelry_____

Furs_____   Fine Art_____

Coins_____   Gold_____

Silver_____   Other Valuables_____

FIRE INSURANCE (continued)

Have you installed smoke alarms in your home?

Yes _____   No _____

Do you have dead bolt locks?

Yes _____   No _____

Do you have a security system?

Yes _____   No _____

Are you located in an earthquake-prone area?

Yes _____   No _____

Are you located in a flood-prone area?

Yes _____   No _____

Do you own rental property, other homes, or a farm?

Yes _____   No _____   List: _____

_____

LIFE INSURANCE

Have you thought about updating the names of beneficiaries on your life policies?

Yes _____   No _____   Do you have any life policies? _____

Have you considered making a will?

Yes _____   No _____

Page numbers in italics refer to checklists and worksheets.